From Willis

BEING BLACK
Aboriginal cultures in 'settled' Australia

Front cover
    Painting by Willie Gudubi
    Alawa
    South West Arnhemland, NT, born c 1917
    Alawa sacred sites at Llangabun. 1987
    Synthetic polymer paint on canvas
    840mm x 320mm
    Collection Australian National Gallery, Canberra

Reproduced with the permission of the Australian National
    Gallery, Willie Gudubi and Mimi Arts and Crafts,
    Katherine.

Edited by IAN KEEN

BEING BLACK

Aboriginal cultures in 'settled' Australia

Aboriginal Studies Press, Canberra 1991

First published in 1988 by
Aboriginal Studies Press
for the Australian Institute of Aboriginal and
Torres Strait Islander Studies
GPO Box 553 Canberra ACT 2601.

Reprinted 1991.

The views expressed in this publication are those of the authors and not necessarily those of the Australian Institute of Aboriginal and Torres Strait Islander Studies.

© Ian Keen 1988.

Apart from any fair dealing for the purpose of private study, research, criticism or review, as permitted under the Copyright Act, no part of this publication may be reproduced by any process whatsoever without the written permission of the publisher.

National Library of Australia
Cataloguing in Publication data:

Being black: Aboriginal cultures in 'settled' Australia.

Bibliography.
Includes index.
ISBN 0 85575 185 1.

[1]. Aborigines, Australian — Social conditions. [2]. Aborigines, Australian — Economic conditions. [3]. Aborigines, Australian — Social life and customs. I. Keen, Ian. II. Australian Institute of Aboriginal Studies.

305.8'9915

Designed by Maureen MacKenzie, Aboriginal Studies Press.

Typeset in Compugraphic Avant Garde by Aboriginal Studies Press.

Printed in Australia by Griffin Press Limited, Netley, South Australia.

2000 05 91

Contents

	Acknowledgements	vii
	Foreword by Marie Reay	ix
	Contributors	xiii
1.	**Ian Keen** Introduction	1
2.	**Diane Barwick** Aborigines of Victoria	27
3.	**Barry Morris** Dhan-gadi resistance to assimilation	33
4.	**Julie Carter** 'Am I too black to go with you?'	65
5.	**Jerry Schwab** Ambiguity, style and kinship in Adelaide Aboriginal identity	77
6.	**Diana Eades** They don't speak an Aboriginal language, or do they?	97
7.	**Jeremy R Beckett** Kinship, mobility and community in rural New South Wales	117
8.	**Chris Birdsall** All one family	137
9.	**Basil Sansom** A grammar of exchange	159
10.	**Gaynor Macdonald** A Wiradjuri fight story	179
11.	**Marcia Langton** Medicine Square	201
12.	**Patricia Baines** A litany for land	227
13.	**Peter Sutton** Myth as history, history as myth	251
	Index	269

Acknowledgements

'Kinship, mobility and community among Aborigines in the far west of New South Wales' by Jeremy Beckett is reprinted with kind permission from the *International Journal of Comparative Sociology*.

'What it means to be an Aborigine' is reprinted from *The Aborigine Today* edited by Barbara Leach, published by Paul Hamlyn, 1971. I thank Dr Richard Barwick for permission to include Diane Barwick's paper.

I am grateful to Libby Keen for her editorial assistance, and Judy Bieg for her patience in typing the manuscript. Also, thanks to Heather MacDonald who prepared the index.

Foreword

Looking back on my own research among Aborigines of mixed descent in settled eastern Australia, I envy those who have come after me with their tape recorders, bibliographies, and other modern aids; the companionship of colleagues working in the same field; and, importantly, their experience of working among people with a higher morale and a greater knowledge of the world than the people I knew. The Aborigines of forty years ago were a depressed segment of Australian society. There were always exceptions, but most of them lived in appalling conditions. Remnants of several different tribes had been forced to cluster together and each group was suspicious that at least one other might 'steal your kidney fat' or 'slip something in your tea'. The men worked as shearers, station hands, or railway workers, and only saw their families periodically. The women, left at home, filled in their time with gambling and gossiping. Many used to express concern lest the children should be rounded up and taken away to an institution just because they were Aboriginal. Occasionally children were indeed taken away. Relatively few appreciated that by the 1940s the children who were institutionalised were those who were judged to be neglected, whether they were black or white.

Youngsters were the sentimental concern of their mothers and the practical concern of their maternal grandmothers. It was the granny who bathed the children and combed their hair and saw that they had clean clothes to wear and plenty to eat. She saw them off to school and also watched that they did not go too close to the river. At weekends she would take them into the scrub to find bush tucker. The children who were taken away were those who had no grannies, were skinny and unkept, wagged school, and subsisted on whatever they could scrounge from their various aunties.

That was forty years ago. Now Dr Ian Keen, a distinguished scholar of Aboriginal society and culture, has collected a set of essays on cultural continuity among Aborigines in settled Australia. A common theme is its importance for cultural identity. It is refreshing to find two classic pieces included. Jeremy Beckett's seminal discussion of the 'beats' traversed by Aborigines in the far west of New South Wales is valid elsewhere, as Chris Birdsall shows, and it would be worthwhile to discover whether there is any part of the continent that is not made up of overlapping and intertwined beats. Diane Barwick, to whose memory the book is very fittingly dedicated, analyses the influences affecting Aborigines of mixed descent, not neglecting the supportive warmth of belonging in the Aboriginal community itself. She reminds us that white Australian culture is a varied and loosely interlocking congeries of many different subcultures.

In discovering continuity with the past we need to be wary of attributing facets of contemporary Aboriginal culture to tribal antecedents. Our knowledge of the pre-colonial past in the long settled areas is not fine-grained enough for us to be certain of much we need to know. And in the absence of anthropological studies of the white communities in towns with a significant proportion of Aborigines our knowledge of the many relevant white subcultures is incomplete, impressionistic and slanted by our own experience. A next step should be to relate Aboriginal culture in settled Australia to the various non-Aboriginal subcultures there. It may sometimes be difficult to determine whether a shared trait originated in pre-colonial Aboriginal society, colonial white society, or the shared experience and situation of itinerant rural workers.

The essays stress the realisation of Aboriginal identity on the bases of links with the tribal and colonial past. They contribute greatly to an understanding of contemporary Aboriginal behaviour and the assertion of Aboriginal identity in conflicts with the norms of the dominant white society. Aboriginal identity has several positive features. Its greatest strength is the continuing importance of kinship at a time when, in urban subcultures at least, the white family is disintegrating and further kin ties are severed. The close association between the alternate generations of grandparents and grandchildren, which ensures cultural transmission in many societies and finds expression in some Aboriginal societies in a terminological equating of the two, contrasts with the white society's separation and effective alienation of youth and age generally. Aborigines have thus a better chance of keeping alive their family traditions.

By and large, the essays are concerned with behavioural continuity with the past. But this is not so important for a feeling of identity as for a consciousness of ethnic and family tradition. A fifth-generation-born person of Irish descent may believe in independence for Ireland and feel a special affinity for Ned Kelly without either aiding the IRA or going around shooting constables. Similarly, a public servant can be proud to be descended from the original inhabitants of this country without having a tooth knocked out or inciting his people to avenge past wrongs.

In the 1940s the old and middle-aged people I knew cared deeply about 'keeping the line straight and clean' and they were frustrated by their inability to prevent 'wrong' marriages—wrong according to the rules of the section system and totemic clan organisation. This was comparable to the disapproval of marrying close kin in some, though not all, white Australian subcultures, since the disapproval was based in both cases on a belief in the deleterious effects of inbreeding. But the Aboriginal prohibitions, expressed in terms of distinctively Aboriginial institutions, formed an important aspect of the ethnic identity of people of mixed descent at that time. Forty years later these prohibitions have been diluted to a general avoidance of marriage between close cousins and many Aborigines in settled Australia have grown up with no knowledge of them. The traditional marriage rules and the unsuccessful struggle to preserve them after white settlement in eastern Australia are embedded in the memory culture of a few old people. They are an essential part of Aboriginal history in the region. Also, a knowledge of sections and clans can help to establish relationships through long-dead people to particular tracts of land. (This point arose in discussion with Owen Dennison who is currently writing up research on his people—the Gamilaroi.) I am not, of course, arguing for a revival of the traditional marriage laws, even if this were feasible. It is a mystery how they evolved into a set of complex arrangements and they deserve to be remembered among the treasures of the tribal past.

Marie Reay
Research School of Pacific Studies
Australian National University

Contributors

Patricia Baines, based at the University of Western Australia, has recently completed her PhD research with Nyungar people of the Perth area. She is currently engaged in research in an Aboriginal community in Darwin.

Diane Barwick began her long term studies of Aboriginal people of Victoria in 1960, as a research scholar at the Australian National University. She lived and worked in Canberra, where she was employed by the Australian National University and the Australian Institute of Aboriginal Studies. Diane was a founder and editor of *Aboriginal History*. She died prematurely and unexpectedly in April 1986.

Jeremy Beckett, senior lecturer in the Anthropology Department of the University of Sydney, has conducted research in western New South Wales in the late 1950s, and more recently among Torres Strait Islanders, whose culture and history are the topics of his most recent book.

Chris Birdsall lives in Canberra where she is employed as a bibliographer and works on the Regionalisation Program at the Australian Institute of Aboriginal Studies. She carried out studies of Nyungar social life in the southwest of Western Australia while affiliated with the Anthropology Department of the University of Western Australia.

Julie Carter completed her MA in Anthropology at the Australian National University. During this period she lived with Aboriginal people of a New South Wales coastal town. She is currently writing about a Queensland Aboriginal community.

Diana Eades is a lecturer in Communication Studies at the Darling Downs Institute of Advanced Education. Her research has included the grammar of a northern New South Wales Aboriginal language as well as the sociolinguistics of Aboriginal English in southeast Queensland.

Ian Keen has carried out anthropological research in northeast Arnhem Land, the Alligator Rivers region and at Tennant Creek in the Northern Territory. He is senior lecturer in the Department of Prehistory and Anthropology at the Australian National University.

Marcia Langton studied Anthropology at the Australian National University, and is now head of the research section of the Central Land Council in Alice Springs.

Gaynor Macdonald is a lecturer at the MacArthur Institute of Higher Education. Her research, based at the University of Sydney, has been with Wiradjuri people of New South Wales.

Barry Morris has carried out historical and anthropological research in the Macleay Valley (New South Wales), through the University of South Australia. He lectures at the Mitchell College of Advanced Education in Bathurst.

Basil Sansom is Professor of Anthropology at the University of Western Australia. His fieldwork areas include southern Africa, the Fezzanese Sahara, Lebanon, and most recently Darwin in the Northern Territory of Australia.

Jerry Schwab carried out fieldwork in Adelaide while a research scholar at the Australian National University. Since returning to the United States he has been investigating the social impact of computers on behalf of a computer company in Portland, Oregon.

Peter Sutton has extensive experience in linguistic, sociolinguistic and anthropological research in many regions of Australia including Cape York Peninsula, the Northern Territory and the southeast. He is now head of the Anthropology Division of the South Australian Museum in Adelaide.

This volume is dedicated to the memory of Diane Barwick.

1. Ian Keen   Introduction

According to the perceptions of many people including anthropologists and other researchers, Aboriginal people of mixed descent, classified in earlier decades as 'part-Aborigines', have no distinctive culture (eg Bell 1964, 64; Barwick 1964; Beckett 1964; Rowley 1971; Hausfield 1977, 267; RM Berndt 1979, 87; and see Read 1980, 112). Fink (1957, 110), for example, has judged that the Aborigines of a New South Wales town simply possessed a common group identity as 'black' and an opposition to white people. In Eckermann's view (1977), the Aboriginal people of a southeast Queensland town have been assimilated and integrated, having a mode of life typical of working class culture (see also Smith and Biddle 1972, xi). To the Berndts (1951, 275–76; Berndt 1962, 88), the Europeanisation of so small a minority has seemed inevitable.

In contrast, others (and sometimes the same authors writing at different times) have detected a distinctive, even unique, culture or way of life, with its own folkways, mores and beliefs (Calley 1956; Bell 1961, 436–37; Smith and Biddle 1972, 124; Howard 1979, 98; Crick 1981). Langton (1982, 18) has remarked that 'loss of culture' should not be a matter of faith, but of investigation. Indeed, much of the substance of the publications cited above, as well as the results of current research, show that many features of the social life of these people are distinctive, and also display marked similarities to aspects of the cultures of Aboriginal peoples whose social lives have been changed to a lesser degree by the process of colonisation. Calley (1956, 213) wrote that the people of mixed Aboriginal descent possessed a society 'leaning heavily on the logic and outlook on life of the indigenous traditions', yet quite well adapted to the white community that surrounds it.

It was my familiarity with some ongoing anthropological research into the social life of Aboriginal people of southeast Queensland, New South Wales and the southwest of Western Australia, that led me to invite contributions to a volume on continuities in the culture of Aboriginal people living in what Rowley (1971, vii) called 'settled' Australia. The closely settled regions, by contrast with what Rowley termed 'colonial' Australia, dominated by pastoral production, are those which have been most radically transformed by people of European origin. They lie mainly in the southeastern and southwestern parts of the continent, extending on the east coast north to Cairns, and north to Carnarvon on the west coast. The category should also include Darwin, the major European and Asian settlement of the north.

This volume (*Being Black*), brings together some of the results of a continuing interest among anthropologists in the social life of people who used to be labelled 'part-Aborigines' or 'urban Aborigines'. Studies burgeoned during the post-war decades when 'acculturation' was a major anthropological interest, although research dwindled somewhat through the 1970s. Meanwhile research by geographers and economists has greatly extended our knowledge of the social and economic conditions of Aborigines of these regions, and the new Aboriginal history has revolutionised our perceptions of Australian history. Aborigines themselves are increasingly writing (and making films and videos) about their own lives (eg Bropho 1980; Clare 1978; Davis and Hodge 1985; McLeod 1982; Miller 1985; Mum Shirl 1981; Pepper 1980; Perkins 1975; Rosser 1978; Simon 1978).

My purpose here is to set the themes of each chapter in this book within the broader context of studies of Aboriginal social life in 'settled' Australia. The chapters describe many dimensions of the social life and culture of Aboriginal people living in southeast Queensland, New South Wales, Victoria, South Australia, the southwest of Western Australia, and the Darwin fringe. The majority present the results of recent research; however Diane Barwick and Jeremy Beckett kindly agreed to the reprinting of two of their early articles here, and I thank Marie Reay for contributing the Foreword. I am especially grateful to Richard Barwick for consenting to the inclusion of Diane Barwick's article. This book is dedicated to her memory.

Cultural continuity

Many of the papers in this volume speak of continuities among elements of the culture of Aboriginal people of 'settled' Australia and of people more remote from the area of dense European settlement, implying the reproduction of some cultural forms from the pre-colonial era. Diane Barwick (Chapter 2) believes the Koori subculture to be compounded of indigenous and introduced traits, and points to the prohibition of close cousin marriage as well as certain beliefs as continuities from the past. On the other hand, practices such as modes of dress, certain patterns of speech and drinking habits were gained from European rural workers. Other features are typical of itinerant workers generally. Barry Morris (Chapter 3) takes a different view. With the increasing loss of conspicuous cultural forms such as ceremonies, Dhan-gadi culture in the assimilationist era was a culture of resistance in the context of manager-supervised institution, which attempted to inculcate the values of the dominant society. Forms of resistance included the control of information, illegal drinking and gambling, and the establishment of fringe camps free from institutional control. The emergence of idioms of stigma in a New South Wales town (Julie Carter, Chapter 4) is, of course, a response to relations with non-Aborigines in Aboriginal identity formation. In Jerry

Schwab's opinion (Chapter 5), such identity among Adelaide Aboriginal boys is more ambiguous than in pre-colonial Australia.

Other continuities are documented (or posited) by contributors here: between the forms and use of Aboriginal English on the one hand and indigenous languages on the other; in the extent and form of kin networks; in the structure of the exchange economy, into which money is assimilated; in the forms and contexts of swearing and fighting; in beliefs; and in attitudes to the past. However, our purpose is not simply to tally culture traits, but to describe the way of life of a particular category of people—what 'being black' is.

Aboriginal identity

Aborigines in 'settled' Australia form part of a distinct, though heterogeneous and loosely bounded ethnic category. In this volume Diane Barwick (Chapter 2) addresses the question of identity within a broad sketch of the social life of Aboriginal people in Victoria. The chapters by Barry Morris, Julie Carter and Jerry Schwab (Chapters 3, 4 and 5) outline social processes through which a distinct Aboriginal identity has been formed and reproduced.

The categories 'Aborigine' and 'Aboriginal' arose, of course, through interaction with colonising peoples mainly from Europe (Crick 1981). In pre-colonial Australia, as now in areas more remote from European settlement, manifold ethnic categories divided the Aboriginal population according to criteria of language, locality and descent (Berndt 1961; Merlan 1981). People of mixed descent who are a part of 'settled' Australia identify themselves variously as 'Aborigines', 'dark people', 'coloured' or 'blacks', and employ labels with regional application such as Murri, Koori, and Nyungar, which mark internal divisions, and contrast with terms such as 'Gubba' (white person). Markers like Wiradjuri or Gooreng Gooreng ('tribe' or language names) are more specific still.

In spite of the ambiguities of imposed categories (Jordan 1985), identification as Aboriginal is no post-Whitlam phenomenon. During the late 1950s people of mixed descent in Adelaide and La Perouse (Sydney) identified themselves as Aborigines or dark people regardless of skin colour (Berndt and Berndt 1951, 262; Inglis 1961, 201; Bell 1961, 432; Barwick 1963, 28). In the late 1960s only 4.4 per cent of a sample of the population of Aboriginal descent around a coastal New South Wales town did not identify as Aboriginal (Hausfield 1977, 266). The erosion of the numbers of 'half-castes' in the census data from the period before the World War II is due to people re-identifying as Aboriginal as much as non-Aboriginal in Smith's opinion (1980, 264). Jordan (1985, 31) also reminds us of the uncertainties of identity. A person could be classified in official transactions as 'white' and 'half-caste' on the same day.

Whereas many have denied Aboriginal people of mixed descent the status of Aboriginal, some have denied their own identity as Aboriginal, and affirmed half-caste status (Gilbert 1977, 143). Restrictive protectionist legislation motivated people to adopt a European style and identity in order to gain exemption from the terms of legislation, and to 'be treated like a human being' (Jordan 1985, 33). However, working in the 1950s and 1960s, when the prevailing government policy was one of assimilation and subsequently integration, several anthropologists have stressed that far from desiring assimilation, many Aboriginal people feared the threat of group extinction, and did not see assimilation as realisable (Barwick 1962, 18, 22; 1964, 28; Beckett 1964, 46). Fearing extinction, Melbourne Aboriginal people pursued self-consciously Aboriginal activities (Barwick 1964, 21–24). Freedoms from restrictions associated with the 1967 Referendum and the self-determination policies of the Labor government have led some who previously did not identify as Aboriginal to identify or re-identify.

Prejudice and disapproval on the part of non-Aborigines, together with discrimination in employment and social exclusion, have in part engendered the cohesion of the Aboriginal category (Calley 1957, 209; Fink 1957, 102), an example of a more general phenomenon (Spicer 1971, 797). However, the degree to which Aboriginal people have experienced prejudice varies (Inglis 1961, 206). What has been referred to as the 'caste barrier' (Calley 1957) was maintained in northern New South Wales during the 1950s: Aboriginal employees ate separately from non-Aborigines, and were excluded from local dances and pubs (Calley 1957, 196). Only in sport were individuals treated as equals (1957, 197). Segregation had the effect, in Calley's opinion (1957, 202; see also Berndt and Berndt 1951, 174; Howard 1979, 94), of turning Aborigines' attention inward toward the potentialities of their own group.

Internally, group conformity has been enforced through gossip and the fear of being 'shamed'. In Chapter 2 of this volume, Barwick describes how the levelling process among Victorian Aborigines has inhibited some individuals from 'getting ahead' and from neglecting their obligations to kin. Those who have separated themselves off from the group identifying as Aboriginal have been the objects of mockery, and few Melbourne people have tried to leave the Aboriginal community (see also Barwick 1964, 27). Several other studies have described similar processes. Aboriginal people of Robinvale in northwestern Victoria, for instance, have expressed antagonism toward those who have moved out of town and cut off ties, or who have succeeded in activities seen as typical of white Australia—such as buying a block of land for fruit growing. These people are said to live like a 'gub' or 'white fella' (Bryant 1982, 77; see also Fink 1957; Beckett 1964, 35). People of Yarrabah in Queensland accuse one another of 'talking like a white' if they use inappropriately 'big words' (Hume nd).

Paradoxically people have also been prevented by shame from continuing with conspicuously Aboriginal practices in the face of managerial hostility, or the indifference and mockery of the young. Morris (in Chapter 3) argues that the pervasive levelling mechanism of shame prevented some individuals and families from succeeding in European terms, but people have also been 'too shamed' to continue with obviously Aboriginal practices because of European hostility. As a result of indoctrination on missions and government settlements, or of the dormitory system, or for other reasons, expressions of embarrassment about performances of traditional songs and ceremonies by older people, or about the telling of stories to do with the pre-colonial past, have frequently been recorded. Younger people have said they were 'shamed' to hear them because they were 'like white folks now' (Calley 1957, 206; Fink 1957, 109; Beckett 1958, 32), while older people have been afraid of mockery by the young or by white people (Koepping 1977, 173). Cherbourg people had internalised mission values of cleanliness, orderliness, strong punishment, belief in authority, and a negative attitude to their 'uncivilised' past (Koepping 1977, 173).

Some Aboriginal people have adopted the stereotypes about themselves held by European Australians (eg Calley 1957, 209). Fink (1957, 103) interprets this adoption as 'an aggressive assertion of low status' (see also Gilbert 1977, 267); whereas Jordan (1985, 32) interprets it as a refuge from ambiguous identity. Bell (1961, 438) on the other hand implies that La Perouse people have had a more positive attitude to their own knowledge of totemic ancestors and sites, use of indigenous language and lifestyle, all of which marked them off from the non-Aboriginal population.

Criticisms of perceived aspects of Euro-Australian social life have also been recorded, for example the lack of family care of the aged, individualism and lack of concern for relatives, meanness and insincerity. These criticisms have not been so strongly subscribed to among city dwellers (Inglis 1961, 205), and perhaps this is not surprising given the high incidence of intermarriage between Aborigines and non-Aborigines in the cities (discussed later).

Ambivalent attitudes to identity are apparent in patterns of socialisation. The children of a southeast Queensland town were made aware from the earliest years of their identity through the use of terms such as 'black', 'boong', 'blackfella', 'dirty black' and so on, which prepared them for later experience of racism. (Robert Bropho [1980, 6] and Jimmie Barker [see Mathews 1977] have documented their own experience of hostility.) But children are also taught that Aborigines are people of a superior kind—more trustworthy, kind, warm and ready to share than non-Aborigines (Eckermann 1977, 300). This theme is developed by Julie Carter in her essay in this volume (Chapter 4). Identity development presents Aboriginal children of a coastal New South Wales community with a problem, for when they enter high school they usually form a minority and their social identity is challenged. The socialisation of stigma, Carter argues, prepares them for this experience. Idioms in the language of teasing, jokes and stories strengthen corporate identity through the use of epithets incorporating the word 'black'. In this way parents invest the idioms with positive values and associations. Carter suggests that this process is found in other cultures of pariah status.

Among Aboriginal boys in an Adelaide hostel, identity is reflected in a distinctive style including the use of elements of indigenous language (Lingo), mode of dress, music, body language and etiquette, as well as support for key issues and a degree of local knowledge. In Jerry Schwab's account (Chapter 5), the identity of some boys in the hostel is ambiguous, unconnected as they are to the others by kinship or common experience. Skin colour is important in such cases, but it is important also not to try to force the pace: a person has to wait for recognition. Outsiders, however, are unlikely ever to be fully accepted.

Aboriginal identity has been maintained despite the high incidence of marriage between Aborigines and non-Aborigines in the cities. Gale (1972, 171–72) posited three broad stages in the history of biological interaction between Aborigines and other ethnic categories: first, matings between Aboriginal women and non-Aboriginal men on the frontier; second, relatively closed communities under protectionist policies that restricted contacts and encouraged endogamy; and third, renewal of contacts following migration into the cities. The older reserves such as Point McLeay near Adelaide tended, in the 1960s, to be endogamous, and the majority of mixed marriages were between Aboriginal women and non-Aboriginal men (Gale 1972, 168). In Brisbane and Adelaide in the mid 1960s about forty per cent of Aboriginal marriages were to non-Aboriginal partners, and by 1980 more than half (53.7 per cent) of female Aboriginal marriages in Adelaide, and forty per cent of men's, were to non-Aboriginal partners (Gale and Wundersitz 1982, 37), a level of out-marriage similar to that recorded in a southeast Queensland town in the period 1969–71

(Eckermann 1977, 295). The incidence in Victoria as a whole in the early 1960s was lower, with eleven per cent of women's and thirty-seven per cent of men's marriages being to non-Aboriginal partners (Barwick 1974, 202). Barwick pointed out that intermarriage had been highest in the towns and cities, where prejudice was less strong (1974, 202). Eckermann explained this high rate of out-marriage as due to a long period of interaction between non-Aborigines and a stable Aboriginal population, in conjunction with rising living standards. This degree of intermarriage does not seem to imply assimilation in any simple way, for members of a southeast Queensland Aboriginal community have identified non-Aboriginal spouses as members of the 'clans' into which they marry (Eckermann 1977, 294); however, Diana Eades (Chapter 6) shows that southeast Queensland people who marry non-Aborigines tend to drop the extended use of kin terms.

A heterogeneous category

Neither the social and economic conditions nor the culture of Aboriginal people of 'settled' Australia is homogeneous. We can distinguish a variety of Aboriginal styles of life (Bell 1965).

For the most part Aborigines have been a rural population in these regions but the focus has changed. Between 1947 and 1976 the proportion of Aboriginal people living in towns and cities in New South Wales rose from twenty-eight per cent to eighty per cent, and has reached ninety per cent in Victoria (Young 1982, 1). (In 1981 over Australia as a whole forty-one per cent of Aborigines were residing in cities, and thirty-four per cent in towns.) Now, throughout Australia, people live in communities of various kinds: on reserves, missions and government settlements, many of which are now Aboriginal townships; in temporary dwellings on the fringes of country towns; and in European style housing in towns and cities. The degree of long term association of local Aboriginal populations with the area in which they live varies greatly. Some populations are the descendants of groups with traditional ties to a region (Donaldson 1984); some come from settlements of long standing such as Point Mcleay near Adelaide, and have formed attachments with these localities. In settlements such as Cherbourg, the first residents were drawn from all over the State. Others, such as Robinvale in northern New South Wales (Bryant 1982, 41) and the populations of major cities, consist mainly of people who have moved to the community from far and wide within the last few decades, although networks with different origins tend to remain discrete.

People of the older reserves have developed a rather settled and isolated existence. New South Wales people have identified with the community and have a strong sense of belonging to it. Their attitudes have been ethnocentric, combining continuing tribal identification and hostility toward other Aboriginal communities as well as Europeans (Bell 1964a). Extensive kin ties have bound members of a community together. European and Aboriginal spheres have been kept separate and marked by hostility (see Fink 1955, 35–39; cf Trigger 1986). The kin network at Cherbourg in southeast Queensland, an isolated and somewhat endogamous community, led to strong community feeling as well as shared values and attitudes (Koepping 1977, 171).

People have migrated into the cities from communities such as these, as well as from country towns and reserves, in increasing numbers up until the 1970s, maintaining contacts with the home community through mutual visiting. City populations have provided the staging houses for migration (Gale 1972; Gale and Wundersitz 1982; Lickiss 1971, 218; Inglis 1961, 202; Smith and Biddle 1972). A route of migration is referred to by Nyungar people as a 'line' (Chris Birdsall, Chapter 8). Despite dispersal, migration to towns and cities, and patterns of visiting between towns and between town and country, people remain attached to a general locality of origin (see Young 1982, 9).

Some Aboriginal communities living in isolated country towns appear to be divided by what have been described as class attitudes, forming upper and lower categories, either within the same town or separated as town dwellers and fringe camp or settlement residents (Reay and Sitlington 1948; Fink 1955, 1957; Bell 1965, 409). These categories are better described as status categories rather than in class terms (Gerth and Wright-Mills 1970), for they are based on evaluations according to criteria of lifestyle, values and prestige, and are not associated with radically different economic roles. Nor are these categories very clearly defined.

The upper category in one New South Wales country town (Reay and Sitlington 1948) aspired to live in European style houses, and discouraged reserve people from settling in the same area of town. Their standard of living was similar to that of working class Europeans. Upper category people preferred to marry among themselves where possible, and espoused values of sexual morality, thrift, romantic love, and 'good family', and disapproved of habitual drunkenness. They regarded the lower category people as dirty and polluting, to the extent of forbidding their children to drink out of the same vessels. Although they did visit the reserve to gamble, they would ignore reserve people in public places and dubbed them 'uncivilised'.

Similar attitudes divided the Aboriginal community in another country town in New South Wales (Fink 1955; 1957). The upper category consisted of generally light skinned people who disowned their mission relatives, even in some cases repudiating sibling links (1955, 30). They identified themselves with European values and lifestyle 'even to the point of adopting its colour prejudice and stereotypes of the aborigine' (Fink 1955, 5). Marriage to Europeans was common in the upper category, but absent in the lower. Here, the upper category held its own parties, card games and dances (Fink 1957, 106). In Chapter 8 Chris Birdsall relates a case in which an Aboriginal girl's family put pressure on her not to marry a young man because his skin was too dark, suggesting divisions of a similar order in the southwest.

The style of the lower category in these cases (Bell 1965, 411–12) has included living in humpies, shacks and derelict houses with minimum domestic equipment. Employment has been casual, intermittent and often seasonal in nature, supplemented by welfare payments and borrowing. Many have considered the government to be obliged to support those unemployed on the grounds that white people took their land (Fink 1955, 4). Marriages have tended to be short-lived, and drinking has been heavy. People have symbolised their style by eating damper and tea and cooking in ashes (Fink 1955, 53). They have said they differ from white people in not acting 'flash', not being interested in saving or becoming rich. The upper category has been critised for being 'flash' and 'stuck up', or 'black whitefellas', and for failing to uphold kin and group obligations. (Robert Bropho's 1980 personal testament of the fringe dweller's life illuminates the experience of severe economic hardship as well as subjection to the power of authorities.)

Some families in towns such as those mentioned in the above studies, known by the Aboriginal community to be of Aboriginal descent, have married into the European community, broken their ties with Aborigines completely, and do not identify as Aborigines (Reay and Sitlington 1948, 180; Bryant 1982, 29). Eckermann (1977, 300) found no evidence of 'passing' in the region of a southeast Queensland city, but a greater degree of interaction between Aborigines and Europeans than reported elsewhere among fringe dwellers on the outskirts of towns.

Some ex-residents of reserves living in Adelaide have deliberately cut themselves off from other Aborigines of the city in order to pass as white (Inglis 1961, 204–05). The community was heterogeneous in origin and style in the 1940s and 1950s, divided into rather distinct kin networks who used rather different terms to refer to themselves: 'Narrinyeri' for Point McLeay people, 'Nunga' for Point Pearce people and 'Murrall' for northerners (Inglis 1961, 202–03; see Berndt and Berndt 1951, 236). People from the north of the state, brought as children to be raised in children's homes, had few ties with other Adelaide Aborigines or with their own families, and moved into skilled and semi-skilled occupations (Berndt and Berndt 1951, 239; Inglis 1961, 204). These general divisions have remained (Gale 1972, 249; Gale and Wundersitz 1982, 75).

Some Aboriginal people of the southwest have also restricted their ties to the rest of the Aboriginal community (Howard 1979, 94). Barwick (1962, 18) found that in Melbourne, however, there was no upper class of outsiders who were the product of hostels or mission training schools. Residents were migrants from mission stations in search of improved living situations, and divided themselves on the basis of regional associations. Most people married within the regional group, and saw strangers as different or inferior (Barwick 1964; see also Schwab, Chapter 5).

Differences in relations between Aborigines and non-Aborigines are striking in Lyons' comparison (1983) of two country town communities and a Melbourne suburban Aboriginal community. Unemployment was high in one town as well as the Melbourne suburb. In the other town the Aboriginal population had been resident for much longer, relations between Aborigines and non-Aborigines were more amicable, and Aboriginal unemployment was lower. Another important dimension of heterogeneity lies in the differences between generations (Read 1980, 113). The views and attitudes of older men of Erambi in New South Wales has differed from those of younger men as a result of changes in European attitudes toward Aborigines, as well as changes in economic and social conditions. The older men have adopted the European work ethic and respect for authority (Read 1980 101, 108), and have shown little interest in the pre-colonial past. Younger men, with experience of greater hostility, have looked back to the pre-colonial culture for a model of a stable past (Read 1980, 111).

The above studies reveal a great variety in Aboriginal styles of life, but the gulf between these and the social life of other Australians is even greater.

The Aboriginal domain

Trigger (1986) uses the term 'domain' to capture the very distinct networks of interaction, with spatial correlates, which divided Aborigines and non-Aborigines on a remote Queensland settlement. Aboriginal communities in 'settled' Australia also occupy a distinct domain. The main loci of intensive interaction with non-Aborigines are education, employment, social service and legal agencies, and community associations. Extensive contact with social service agencies is ensured by high unemployment, and consequent reliance on social security payments. Outside such spheres of interaction Aborigines maintain, and are constrained to maintain, a rather separate life. As Barwick expresses it (1962, 21), 'The Aboriginal social world consists of the voluntary activities undertaken after work is finished.'

In the far west of New South Wales in the 1950s people entertained themselves with hillbilly songs, and drinking sprees provided excitement for men in an otherwise dull life, at a time when Aboriginal liquor consumption was prohibited (Beckett 1958). People of Melbourne and Adelaide organised social occasions such as dances, weddings, twenty-first birthday parties and barbecues, restricting participation largely to Aborigines (Fink 1957, 102; Barwick 1962, 22, 1964, 29). Lower Murray River and Adelaide Aboriginal people in the late 1940s enjoyed dances, football, movies and race meetings (Berndt and Berndt 1951, 232, 259). During the mid 1950s Aboriginal people of the north coast of New South Wales were excluded from participation in many aspects of community life. The Pentecostal movement provided Aborigines with a distinct and exclusive institution through which they believed they were receiving spiritual gifts unavailable to whites (Calley 1957, 205–06).

Language and style

Interaction within the Aboriginal domain has its own style, which includes (in many communities) the use of parts of indigenous languages as well as characteristic forms of English.

Notwithstanding the common view that indigenous languages have completely died out in 'settled' Australia, older people of at least one language group in New South Wales were speakers of their language in the late 1970s (Donaldson 1984). Many people still use words and phrases in restricted contexts, for example La Perouse Aboriginal people employed phrases of their original tongues as a secret language (Bell 1961, 436; see Kennedy and Donaldson 1982, 8; Schwab, Chapter 5). Diana Eades (Chapter 6) also records the use of indigenous language in restricted contexts among people of southeast Queensland whose first language is English. However the forms of English spoken by Aboriginal people are also distinctive.

Whereas many non-Aboriginal people regard Aboriginal English as an inferior variety of that tongue, Eades shows that it is a language in its own right, with similarities to indigenous languages (and differences from Standard Australian English) in syntax, semantics and pragmatics. Eades relates features of language use in which restrictions are placed on people's ability to elicit information from one another, to the very public nature of Aboriginal social life (see also Eades 1981).

The degree to which the English of other Aboriginal communities of 'settled' Australia is similar to that of southeast Queensland Aboriginal people is unclear, although the English of Yarrabah people in Queensland has at least some grammatical features in common with southeast Queensland Aboriginal English, as well as pragmatic rules (Hume nd; and see Eades, Chapter 6). Aboriginal people of Yarrabah switch from Yarrabah English to Standard Australian English depending on the context (Hume nd). To clarify similarities and differences of language within the Aboriginal community, as well as between Aboriginal English and the English of non-Aboriginal country people, more comparative research is needed. The structures of the household and kin network have been widely studied, however, and display broad similarities across 'settled' Australia.

Kin and household

The prevalence of what Sansom (1982) has called the 'concertina household' is reflected in data on household composition in Brisbane, Sydney and Adelaide, in which relatively large, extended households, including a variety of relations and tending to change rapidly in composition, have formed a large proportion of the total (Barwick 1974, 198–200; Smith and Biddle 1972, 69–70; Lickiss 1971, 208, 224; Gale and Wundersitz 1982, 69–70; Young 1982, 6). In Melbourne at the time of Barwick's studies (1962, 21, 1974, 196; see also Calley 1956, 213; Lickiss 1971, 218), households were rather mobile, and as cause or consequence, people did not have a strong attachment to house as home, but rather to a general locality and community of origin. Gale and Wundersitz (1982, 87, 95–97) however, have shown that it is the new migrants to Adelaide who are mobile, in order to establish residence close to their kin. Longer term residents have more stable residence, albeit usually in rented homes (Smith and Biddle 1972, 69; Gale 1972, 119; Gale and Wundersitz 1982, 50).

The matrifocal structure of households is widely though not universally reported: in southeast Queensland (Koepping 1977, 171), Adelaide (Gale and Wundersitz 1982, 69), and New South Wales as a whole (Young 1982, 6), although Hausfield (1977, 267) found no marked matrifocality among the Aboriginal population in the vicinity of a coastal New South Wales town. Women have also tended to dominate larger kin groups (see below). Langton (1982, 18) sees the matrifocal family as a preferred form in which mothers, grandmothers and other female relatives provide a 'cultural core', passing on knowledge which is the basis of identity in a crowded urban environment.

Care of children by people other than the parents, variously termed 'adoption' or 'fostering' in the literature, appears commonplace. A grandmother, mother's sister or other relative will take the child temporarily or permanently into her care, perhaps on the occasion of the mother's remarriage (Calley 1956, 203-04; Smith and Biddle 1972, 37; Lickiss 1971, 212; Birdsall, Chapter 8). At a time when illegitimacy was stigmatised in the general community, Victorian Aboriginal people were more tolerant (Barwick 1974, 204). Childcare has tended to be shared by members of a household (Barwick 1974, 207). Patterns of Aboriginal socialisation practices remain quite distinctive. In common with northcentral Arnhem Land Aboriginal people (Hamilton 1981), Aboriginal children of 'settled' Australia are indulged and given considerable freedom in the early years, developing self-reliance and independence. Physical punishment is rare (Lickiss 1971, 212; Barwick 1974, 206-57; Eckermann 1977, 299). Ridicule is employed as a levelling device to teach a child not 'to think too much of himself' (Eckermann 1977, 299). According to Barwick (1974, 208), Victorian Aboriginal children learn from people rather than objects, and are trained to be gregarious, cooperative and passive rather than competitive and aggressive—a pattern similar to the one found in a northeast Arnhem Land community (Harris 1984).

If the matrifocal household owes more to the impact of capitalism on Aboriginal social life than to traditional institutions, the same cannot be said of the importance and extent of the kinship network. In spite of earlier attempts by authorities to break up the Aboriginal family, and weaken kin networks and obligations (Gale 1972, 260), Aborigines of 'settled' Australia place high value on maintaining ties among kin (Barwick, Chapter 2, 1964, 27; Gale and Wundersitz 1982, 75), although some households have cut themselves off from their kin as we have seen (see also Barwick 1962, 22). The family provided a great degree of emotional and economic support, important for an indigenous minority (Barwick 1974, 197).

In this volume Barwick stresses that basic Koori social ties and allegiances are based on family and locality. People enjoy the complete acceptance of belonging by birth and of right. Obligation to relatives is 'an over-riding duty'. Western New South Wales Aboriginal people preferred, at the time of Jeremy Beckett's study (Chapter 7) to live near some of their kinsfolk, especially parents, siblings and affines. The prohibition against marriage between close kin, a continuity from the past, resulted in intermarriage between localised groups which were formerly more or less endogamous. A similar pattern of residence has prevailed in Adelaide (Gale and Wundersitz 1982, 77, 81).

Not only are Aboriginal populations divided into networks with distinct regional ties, but these may be internally divided into cognatic kin groups. The Aboriginal population of one southeast Queensland town refers to its cognatic kin groups as 'clans', headed by or at least oriented toward women members (Eckermann 1977, 289). The clans have been interlinked by ties of marriage, visiting, foster-parenting and a common history (Eckermann 1977, 290). Nyungar people of the southwest of Western Australia refer to their kin groups as 'all one family' (Birdsall, Chapter 8), and the people of a coastal New South Wales town are organised in a similar way (Carter, Chapter 4), although the Wiradjuri are not (Macdonald, Chapter 10). As Chris Birdsall shows, without membership of a kin group the Nyungar individual is unable fully to participate in social life, and lacks the bases of social identity.

Traditional marriage rules have largely disappeared. However in the southeast, marriage with close kin is frowned on, although Melbourne people have preferred to marry those of the same regional affiliation (Barwick, Chapter 2, 1962, 21, 1974, 197; Beckett, Chapter 7). Following pre-colonial patterns, residence in northern New South Wales in the 1950s was matrilocal in the early years of marriage (Calley 1956). In many Aboriginal communities marriage has tended to be established by stable cohabitation rather than by a legal ceremony, and civil divorce has been rare (Calley 1956, 202; Smith and Biddle 1972, 27; Gale and Wundersitz 1982, 30). In Victoria in the early 1960s, church marriage was the norm (Barwick 1974, 204). In Adelaide in the mid 1960s a very high proportion of males remained single (forty-one per cent of adults; Gale 1972, 150), while more than a third of Aboriginal women's marriages were to non-Aboriginal men; moreover Aboriginal males outnumbered females in Adelaide, an imbalance that continued to a lesser degree in 1980 (Gale 1972, 146; Gale and Wundersitz 1982, 26).

But is kinship simply ascribed? Chris Birdsall (Chapter 8) and Basil Sansom (Chapter 9) both emphasise that kin links are fully operative only where a person has been reared-up by the relative concerned. Sansom adopts Goody's (1982) expression of 'operative kinship'—paternity may be denied and maternity devalued where a person has contributed little or nothing to the rearing-up. Conversely, rearing-up for a period can be the basis of multiple relations of parenthood.

To maintain links between dispersed kin, people travel on a 'beat' or 'run'. Jeremy Beckett shows that the beat in western New South Wales (Chapter 7) has formed a community larger than the local residence group, consisting of localities where a person can find kin who will provide hospitality. Thus each individual has his or her own personal community, although the beats of close kin tend to overlap. In Western Australia, each Nyungar family, part of a larger cognatic kin group referred to as 'all one family', is scattered among towns on a run around which members travel (Birdsall, Chapter 8; see also Carter, Chapter 4).

Economic processes

Most studies of Aboriginal economy have been in terms of formal economics, examining levels and types of employment, and poverty. The Aboriginal population of the cities and country towns is young compared with the general population (Gale and Wundersitz 1982, 19; Lyons 1983, 46). The economic corollary of this has been a high dependency ratio, with its consequence of impoverishment. Employment has been predominantly unskilled, and unemployment levels have been high (Altman and Niewenhuysen 1979), reaching about fifty per cent in New South Wales in 1980 (Young 1982, 18). In the rural areas people have been engaged for the most part in pastoral and farm work, often seasonal and requiring a high degree of mobility, such as crop-picking (eg Bryant 1982, 53; Lyons 1983; see also Bropho 1980, 20). Research about city life in the 1960s showed that Aboriginal people had higher incomes and lived in better conditions in the cities than in rural areas—a primary motive for migration (Smith and Biddle 1972, xi; Gale 1972). More recent studies have shown this no longer to be the case (Gale and Wundersitz 1982, 106), and migration into the cities has consequently slowed down. The effect of increased unemployment benefits and other social security payments has been offset by widening unemployment (Young and Fisk 1982, xiv). In Adelaide employment levels have been very low, with a consequent reliance on social security (Gale and Wundersitz 1982, 107, 109). Nevertheless Adelaide people were somewhat better off in money terms in 1980 than they were in 1973 (Gale and Wundersitz 1982, 179).

The economic goals as well as economic processes and values within the Aboriginal domain are distinctive, however. Earlier writers described a category of people who pursued target employment—people who would remain in short term employment for limited short term economic goals, and for whom accumulation was not a value (Calley 1956, 207; Bell 1965). This category has been distinguished from the category of those who adopted European values of property accumulation, thrift and regular employment and, significantly, tended to be accused by others of lacking generosity, and of cutting themselves off from their kin.

It would be an over-simplification to say that economic relations among kin is simply a matter of sharing. Kin do have the right to make demands on each other for hospitality, food, financial help and other services (Barwick 1974, 198), although these can be one-sided (Fink 1957, 107), and a person is responsible only for those who are known (see Beckett, Chapter 7). Calley found in northern New South Wales communities, that a person's siblings were expected to feed his or her children, and to lend money. A person with a surplus was subject to demands for money, and people with cars were subject to constant requests for transport from kin (Calley 1956, 202–11). The obligation to share with kin who demand support has been a disincentive to accumulation of goods or money (Fink 1957, 107; Bell 1956, 197). Conversely, the support offered by extensive kin networks has sometimes been attributed to poverty.

Recent research has interpreted gambling, a major pastime in many Aboriginal communities, though generally with small stakes, as a means of distributing unequal income, allowing individuals the possibility of chance windfalls (Bell 1965, 187; Calley 1957, 193; Fink 1957, 109; Altman 1982).

Apart from these general statements about demands, sharing and economic goals, little has been written about the internal economy of the Aboriginal domain. This is the topic of Basil Sansom's contribution to this book (Chapter 9). In an earlier work Sansom (1982) described Aboriginal economy as a 'service' economy. The owner of a ceremony, of trouble, or of a problem owns 'a slice of action', and offers service. Each category of ownership has a capacity to generate and regenerate debt in an exchange economy (Sansom 1982, 132–35). In this volume Sansom examines economic processes within a Darwin fringe camp in more detail, describing orders of service within a 'grammar' of services. Although he uses some economic terms, Sansom has not found economics useful to his analysis, for the premises in which the internal economy of the fringe camp is grounded are not those of capitalist economics. Rather, a voluntaristic philosophy of action counterposes the Western philosophy of money. A person with a surplus is subject to continued demands for 'help'. One who helps others is making a long term investment, but with a generalised potential to collect a return rather than a specific one. There are no going rates: the amount in a reclaimed debt is a function of the liquidity of the debtor, which depends on circumstances, balanced against the creditor's powers of extraction, which depend on the relationship. People can resist the claims of others by 'vectoring' cash allocated to some morally unchallengeable purpose.

Government

Barwick (1964, 27) attributed the only formal effective control of behaviour, within the Aboriginal domain in 'settled' Australia, to the family. Beckett (1964) found that few groups in western New South Wales larger than the family operated on a regular basis, a lack he attributed to habitual drunkenness. Football teams were organised and dances were held only on special occasions. Even then, pretensions to leadership were ridiculed. Old men enjoyed little respect from younger people, whereas the status of women increased with the years, and they became more demanding and outspoken (Beckett 1964, 42–44). Inglis (1961, 207) also reported difficulties in organising group activities such as a club in one city, and commented on the incidence of heated arguments, backbiting, sexual jealousy and violence between families. Robinvale men were similarly reluctant to perform organisational roles (Bryant 1982, 57).

Despite these negative reports Aborigines have long been involved in voluntary associations such as the Temperance Union and Aborigines Advancement League in Adelaide during the 1940s (Berndt and Berndt 1951, 258), the Aborigines Progress Association and Council for Aboriginal Women in the 1960s (Gale 1972, 259; Pierson 1977), and more recently the Aboriginal Legal Rights Movement, the Aboriginal Child Care Agency and the Aboriginal Health Unit (Gale and Wundersitz 1982, 109). The last decade has seen a proliferation of Aboriginal-run organisations in cities and towns including Aboriginal legal services, independent Aboriginal medical services, independent schools and preschools, cooperatives funded by Department of Aboriginal Affairs or the Aboriginal Development Commission, independent land councils, and radio stations. Crick (1981) argues that the Victorian Aboriginal Education Consultative Group was not the modification of an indigenous structure, but the deliberate creation of a new organisation to cater to new needs which were the result of changed circumstances, although like other organisations it was drawing on traditional values (Crick 1981, 53). Careful studies of the functioning of such organisations would be enlightening.

In this volume Chris Birdsall (Chapter 8) reveals something of authority relations within the Nyungar family, focussing on the authority of older Nyungar women who travel to ensure that their daughters are rearing-up their children properly, to oversee marriages, and to protect their children from in-laws. Women of the upper generation, who have devoted themselves single-mindedly to child-rearing, are the undisputed heads of families. They avoid conflict among themselves by maintaining separate networks of authority. Constant travel around the run ensures the unity of the family. Eckermann (1977, 290) found kin group structure in southeast Queensland to be female oriented, and attributed the matrifocal emphasis to the culture of poverty (Eckermann 1977, 298). 'Matriarchs' were important also in Moree (Reay and Sitlington 1948). In Melbourne, too, the heads of families were older women (Barwick 1964, 27). That fathers do not exercise authority within the household, and often have little to do with child-rearing is the other side of the matrifocal coin (Lickiss 1971, 213).

Are there no other structures of social control in Aboriginal social life in 'settled' Australia? Pre-colonial Aboriginal societies did not include over-arching governmental and legal bodies with powers to control disputes. It was up to the aggrieved and their close kin to settle matters for themselves on a self-help basis (see Berndt 1965). However where grievances were aired, punishments inflicted and disputes settled by violence, they were in general ritualised, rule-governed and controlled procedures, carried out in public, in the course of which people placed limitations on the level of violence.

The constitution of formal social groups as well as religious beliefs in pre-colonial Aboriginal social life was land based. These beliefs depended for their reproduction on a continuing context of religious practice. Religious beliefs and practices were the foundation of law and governance, for the laws were believed to have been laid down by ancestral spirit beings, and therefore legitimate, and authority was based in the control of esoteric religious knowledge and performance. The suppression of these practices, and the erosion of conditions for their continuation (through population decline, population movement, lack of privacy, etc), amounted to the removal of public governance, to be replaced by the authority of the settlement, station and state.

It is the more implicit, general and informal beliefs, rules and practices that have continued (see Spicer 1971). And it is the structures of the domestic domain that have endured, albeit transformed to a greater or lesser degree. Public modes of government based in religious practice have been undermined; more informal public modes of social control have continued to some degree. The role of men and women in religion and public government based in religion has been undermined; women's authority in the domestic domain has shown greater resilience.

Among informal modes of control, levelling and shaming have already been discussed. 'Witnessing' is another important aspect mentioned in Sansom's and Baines's analyses (Chapters 9 and 12). Another mode of social control that remains in the Aboriginal public domain is fighting. According to Gaynor Macdonald's analysis of Wiradjuri fighting (Chapter 10), fighting is not to be attributed simply to alcohol, low socio-economic status, or to the ravages of colonisation; rather it is a rule-governed activity with social control functions. In the absence of over-riding controls, social order has continually to be renegotiated. Fights inform the community about the current state of certain relationships, as well as providing an outlet for tensions and conflicts.

Marcia Langton argues that swearing as well as fighting are aspects of Aboriginal customary law (Chapter 11). They are 'ritualised codes' which constitute means for processing disputes and ordering social life. Swearing has a somewhat different set of functions in Aboriginal social life than in the lives of European Australians. Swearing is on the one hand an expression of amity between close kin and friends, and part of a linguistic arsenal for inciting disputes on the other. It can also be an instrument of sedition. The requirement that fighting take place in public, where controls can be imposed on the protagonists, brings Aborigines in conflict with the police to whom the ordered nature of the activity is not apparent. Thus cross-cultural miscommunication in general (a theme also of Eades's chapter), and differences in social rules about dispute processing in particular, contribute to the over-representation of Aborigines in prisons. Langton ends with a plea for law reform giving recognition to Aboriginal modes of processing disputes.

These ordered procedures contrast with the pathological individual and private violence which has been associated with excessive alcohol intake and the constraints of life on settlements, for example in Queensland (Wilson 1982). Alcohol consumption is a dominant and much discussed aspect of Aboriginal social life. In the far west of New South Wales drinking provided one of the few diversions during the 1950s (Beckett 1964, 46). In the period of prohibition consumption was interpreted as a symbol of defiance (Fink 1957, 207; Morris, Chapter 3). Drinking has been a source of conflict between husband and wife, both for budgetary reasons and because of alcohol-induced violence (Beckett 1964, 45; Lickiss 1971, 215). One strategy used by women has been to call on police or other authorities to assist them against violent husbands (Calley 1957, 193). Norms and values about alcohol consumption vary among Aboriginal status categories, however, as we have seen. High alcohol consumption affects health as well as social relationships—half of Aboriginal male deaths and one fifth of female deaths in New South Wales are said to be alcohol-related (Health Commission of New South Wales 1979, 4, cited in Young 1982, 15). The experience of living in alcohol-dominated communities has been vividly described by Bropho (1980).

Beliefs
Religious beliefs were indissolubly linked to government. Although traditional organised religious practices have been largely discontinued throughout 'settled' Australia, many aspects of belief show strong continuities with the pre-colonial past. Among these have been beliefs in the power of magic, sorcery and bone-pointing, in the efficacy of curses, in ghosts, and in some traditional healing practices (Berndt 1947; Berndt and Berndt 1951, 230; Lickiss 1971, 220–21; Fink 1957, 109; Bell 1961, 437). Victorian Aborigines maintained beliefs in herbal curing and in harbingers of death

(Barwick, Chapter 2). At the time of Eckermann's research, some southeast Queensland people believed that their contact with the old ways gave them special insight. Among some older people cases of sorcery and the powers of 'clever men' were remembered, and people believed in the power of human hair for good luck, as well as in harbingers of death. But beliefs varied with the personal history of kin group members (Eckermann 1977, 290, 304–05). Despite their heterogeneous origins, members of the Robinvale Aboriginal community in northern New South Wales have subscribed to many beliefs and practices of traditional origin: people would often move out of a house after a death, or purify the house with smoke, and people believe in the presence and activities of spirits of the dead (Bryant 1982, 75).

Where a community or social network has consisted of people who have recently moved to the region, or who are the descendants of such people, such as the Robinvale community, then attachment to land has not had the religious basis characteristic of Aboriginal populations with a long term connection with an area (Bryant 1982, 56). Where a community has remained on or near the land of their ancestors, or has migrated from a discrete region, beliefs about the spiritual significance of the land and waters have continued (Beckett 1958, 97; Bell 1961, 437). Hausfield (1977, 271) found that authority was focussed among the men in a hinterland New South Wales community. Here the people were all of one 'tribe' and living on their own country. Knowledge of country and land tenure was strong among older people, although these were said not to be transmitting that knowledge to younger people. We should note, however, that this is not a failing in the old or the young, because knowledge is transmitted through engaging in the performance of ceremonies, or travelling over the country, rather than in formal teaching (Harris 1984). The removal of these contexts leads inevitably into the loss of knowledge.

In this volume Baines (Chapter 12) illustrates the salience of beliefs about country, in an account of the struggle by a group of Nyungar people in Perth to protect a sacred place at the heart of their attachment to land, threatened by a proposed pipeline. The scenes from Nyungar social events which she paints also reveal much about the quality of social relationships, as well as the attachment of individuals to a personalised landscape. Baines illustrates too the telling of myths as commentaries on present events, to embed them in wider significances, and to enfold them in humour.

History as myth

Sansom (1982) has drawn our attention to the similarity in function between Nyungar legends of familial heroes and traditional land-related myths. Groups of Nyungar people of the southwest possess legends about the travels of (exclusively male) human ancestors that convey ownership of the territory the ancestors covered and made over. Possessing a story for the ownership of country is traditional, but the stories are about familial heroes rather than Dreamtime ancestors. Gaynor Macdonald (Chapter 10) treats the fight story as a myth; the Wiradjuri use 'history-stories' to symbolise relationships once encapsulated in myths. It is this theme that Peter Sutton elaborates (Chapter 13).

Since the 1970s Aborigines have become incorporated into sectors of the Australian economy and administrative structures to an unprecedented degree, especially in the welfare sector. People in these occupations have to possess or learn many of the basic requirements of being a public servant, yet they must identify as different. At the same time Aboriginal people of 'settled' Australia are seeking bases of identity in various ways. Economic and political changes have begun a process of constructing a continent-wide Aboriginal consciousness. The interest of urban Aborigines in Aboriginal history has to do with the constitution of that identity. But where differences between Aborigines and non-Aborigines are somewhat indefinite this history creates identity as much as explains it, so it is very similar in function to the Dreaming: the past is also the present and underpins present reality. This role of history, in Sutton's view, explains the clashes between Aborigines and non-Aboriginal historians, and Aborigines' attempts to control the writing of their own history.

We could, perhaps, take this point a little further. Many Aborigines of 'settled' Australia have a distinctive attitude to historical knowledge, and indeed to knowledge more generally. It is not regarded as a free good, but is owned by groups. This is as true of gossip, the everyday construction of ongoing affairs and 'history-stories', as it is of myths and religious knowledge (Eades 1981; Sansom 1980). The possession of knowledge and adherence to beliefs expresses affiliation and loyalty to a group or network. There are two important corollaries: one is that the academic and journalistic ideal of the dissemination of 'objective' knowledge is not an Aboriginal ideal; a second is the strong view, discussed by Sutton, that Aboriginal history should be written by and be under the control of Aboriginal people.

Barwick (Chapter 2) writes of an increasing consciousness at the end of the 1960s which stimulated a search by Aboriginal people for their own history and for their traditional culture. Nyungar people seek knowledge of their past in their search for identity (Berndt 1979). Some individuals in New South Wales, as elsewhere, have attempted to re-establish traditional languages, to protect sites of significance, and in at least one case to re-establish control of 'tribal' boundaries (Thomas 1980; Creamer 1984, 10.5). These moves have been referred to as cultural 'revival' or 'revitalisation' (see Sutton, Chapter 13). For example the National Aborigines' Day Observance Committee (NADOC) week in 1978 had as its theme 'Cultural revival is survival' (Crick 1981, 55).

Conclusion

The chapters in this volume contribute to a body of ethnographic, sociological and economic studies of Aboriginal social life in 'settled' Australia. They describe and analyse various dimensions of culture, from various standpoints. Thiele (1984) has recently expressed concern over the absence of coherent theory in the related area of race relations in Australia. Should we expect or seek a theory of the social life of Aborigines in 'settled' Australia, and their relations with the wider society? I think it is no more realistic to do so than to seek a theory of grass, butterflies or iron. Different aspects of these phenomena can be studied from many points of view.

Many theoretical perspectives inform the contributions to this book. They include a post-structuralist Foucaultian approach to power (Morris); concepts drawn from the existentialist writings of Jean Genet (Carter); interactional sociolinguistics (Eades); network concepts of structural functional anthropology (Beckett); a Manchester emphasis on transactions (Sansom); and a Geertzian concern with meaning (Macdonald and Baines). We should view this diversity as a strength. Nevertheless we can look forward to the production of syntheses, built on the accumulating body of Aboriginal history and ethnography, setting the developing indigenous and colonising cultures within the social, political and economic history of their inter-relatedness.

References

Altman, J.C.
1982 Hunter-gatherers and the State: The Economic Anthropology of the Gunwinggu of North Australia, PhD thesis, Australian National University.

Altman, J.C. and J. Niewenhuysen
1979 *The Economic Status of Australian Aborigines*, Cambridge University Press, Cambridge.

Barwick, D.
1962 Economic Absorption Without Assimilation? The Case of Some Melbourne Part-Aboriginal Families, *Oceania* 33(1), 18–23.
1963 A Little More than Kin: Regional Affiliation and Group Identity among Aboriginal Migrants in Melbourne, PhD thesis, Australian National University.
1964 The Self-Conscious People of Melbourne. In M. Reay (ed), *Aborigines Now: New Perspectives in the Study of Aboriginal Communities*, Angus and Robertson, Sydney.
1974 The Aboriginal Family in South-Eastern Australia. In J. Krupinski and A. Stoller (eds), *The Family in Australia: Social, Demographic and Psychological Aspects*, Pergamon Press, Sydney.

Beckett, J.
1958 Aborigines Make Music, *Quadrant* Spring, 42.
1964 Aborigines, Alcohol and Assimilation. In M. Reay (ed), *Aborigines Now: New Perspectives in the Study of Aboriginal Communities*, Angus and Robertson, Sydney.

Bell, J.H.
1961 Some Demographic and Cultural Characteristics of the La Perouse Aborigines, *Mankind* 5(10), 425–38.
1964 Assimilation in New South Wales. In M. Reay (ed), *Aborigines Now: New Perspectives in the Study of Aboriginal Communities*, Angus and Robertson, Sydney.
1965 The Part-Aborigines of New South Wales: Three Contemporary Social Situations. In R.M. and C.H. Berndt (eds), *Aboriginal Man in Australia*, Angus and Robertson, Sydney.

Berndt, C.H.
1961 The Quest for Identity: the Case of the Australian Aborigines, *Oceania* 32, 16–33.
1962 Mateship or Success: An Assimilation Dilemma, *Oceania* 33(2), 71–89.

Berndt, R.M.
1947 Wuradjeri Magic and 'Clever Men', *Oceania* 17(4), 327–65; 18(1), 60–94.
1965 Law and Order in Aboriginal Australia. In R.M. and C.H. Berndt (eds), *Aboriginal Man in Australia*, Angus and Robertson, Sydney.
1979 Aborigines of the South-West. In R.M. Berndt (ed), *Aborigines of the West: Their Past and Present*, University of Western Australia Press, Nedlands.

Berndt, R.M. and C.H. Berndt
1951 *From Black to White in South Australia*, F.W. Cheshire, Melbourne.

Bropho, R.
1980 *Fringedweller*, Alternative Publishing Cooperative, Sydney.

Bryant, J.
1982 The Robinvale Community. In E.A. Young and E.K. Fisk (eds), *Town Populations*, The Aboriginal Component in the Australian Economy 2, Development Studies Centre, Australian National University, Canberra.

Calley, M.
1956 Economic Life of Mixed-Blood Communities in Northern New South Wales, *Oceania* 26(3), 200–30.
1957 Race Relations on the North Coast of

New South Wales, *Oceania* 27(3), 190–209.
1964 Pentecostalism among the Bandjalang. In M. Reay (ed), *Aborigines Now: New Perspectives in the Study of Aboriginal Communities*, Angus and Robertson, Sydney.

Clare, M.
1978 *Karobran: The Story of an Aboriginal Girl*, Alternative Publishing Cooperative, Sydney.

Creamer, H.
1984 A Cult and a Dreaming: The New South Wales Survey of Aboriginal Sacred and Significant Sites, 1973–1983, unpublished report, National Parks and Wildlife Service.

Crick, M.
1981 Aboriginal Self-management Organizations, Cultural Identity and the Modification of Exchange, *Canberra Anthropology* 4(1), 52–81.

Davis, J. and B. Hodge (eds)
1985 *Aboriginal Writing Today*, Australian Institute of Aboriginal Studies, Canberra.

Donaldson, T.
1984 What's in a Name? An Etymological View of Land, Language and Social Identification from Central New South Wales, *Aboriginal History* 8, 21–44.

Eades, D.
1981 'That's Our Way of Talking': Aborigines in South-East Queensland, *Social Alternatives* 2(2), 11–14.

Eckermann, A.K.
1977 Group Organisation and Identity Within an Urban Aboriginal Community. In R.M. Berndt (ed), *Aborigines and Change: Australia in the '70s*, Australian Institute of Aboriginal Studies, Canberra.

Elkin, A.P.
1962 Australian Aboriginal and White Relations: A Personal Record, *Journal of the Royal Australian Historical Society* 48(3), 230.

Fink, R.
1955 Social Stratification—A Sequel to the Assimilation Process in a Part-Aboriginal Community in New South Wales, MA thesis, University of Sydney.
1957 The Caste Barrier—An Obstacle to the Assimilation of Part-Aborigines in North-West New South Wales, *Oceania* 28(2), 100–10.

Gale, F.
1972 *Urban Aborigines*, Australian National University Press, Canberra.

Gale, F. and J. Wundersitz
1982 *Adelaide Aborigines: Case Study of Urban Life*, The Aboriginal Component in the Australian Economy 4, Development Studies Centre, Australian National University, Canberra.

Gerth, H.H. and C. Wright-Mills (eds)
1970 *From Max Weber: Essays in Sociology*, Routledge and Kegan Paul, London.

Gilbert, K.
1977 *Living Black: Blacks Talk to Kevin Gilbert*, Allen Lane, London.

Goody, E.
1982 *Parenthood and Social Reproduction*, Cambridge University Press, Cambridge.

Hamilton, A.
1981 *Nature and Nurture: Aboriginal Child Rearing in North-Central Arnhem Land*, Australian Institute of Aboriginal Studies, Canberra.

Harris, S.
1984 *Culture and Learning: Tradition and Education in North-East Arnhem Land*, Australian Institute of Aboriginal Studies, Canberra.

Hausfield, R.G.
1977 Basic Value Orientations, Change and Stress in Two Aboriginal Communities. In R.M. Berndt (ed), *Aborigines and Change: Australia in the '70s*, Australian Institute of Aboriginal Studies, Canberra.

Howard, M.
1979 Aboriginal Society in South-Western Australia. In R.M. Berndt (ed), *Aborigines of the West: Their Past and Present*, University of Western Australia Press, Nedlands.

Hume, L.
nd Big Words—White Talk: Code-Switching on a North Queensland Aboriginal Reserve, typescript.

Inglis, J.
1961 Aborigines in Adelaide, *Journal of the Polynesian Society* 70(2), 200–18.

Jordan, D.F.
1985 Census Categories—Enumeration of Aboriginal People, or Construction of Identity, *Australian Aboriginal Studies* 1985(1), 28–36.

Kennedy, E. and T. Donaldson
1982 Coming up out of the Nhaalya: Reminiscences of the Life of Eliza Kennedy, *Aboriginal History* 6(1), 5–27.

Koepping, P.
1977 Cultural Patterns in an Aboriginal Settlement in Queensland. In R.M. Berndt (ed), *Aborigines and Change: Australia in the '70s*, Australian Institute of Aboriginal Studies, Canberra.

Langton, M.
1982 Urbanizing Aborigines: The Social Scientists' Great Deception, *Social Alternatives* 2(2), 16–22.

Lickiss, J.N.
1971 Aboriginal Children in Sydney: The Socio-Economic Environment, *Oceania* 41(3), 201–28.

Lyons, G.
1983 Aboriginal Perceptions of Courts and Police: A Victorian Study, *Australian Aboriginal Studies* 1983(2), 45–61.

Mathews, J.
1977 *The Two Worlds of Jimmie Barker: The Life of an Australian Aboriginal 1970–1972, As Told to Janet Mathews,* Australian Institute of Aboriginal Studies, Canberra.

McLeod, I.
1982 *Shade and Shelter: The Story of Aboriginal Family Resettlement,* Jacaranda Press, Brisbane.

Merlan, F.
1981 Land, Language and Social Identity in Aboriginal Australia, *Mankind* 13(2), 133–48.

Miller, J.
1985 *Koorie: A Will to Win*, Angus and Robertson, London.

Mum Shirl
1981 *Mum Shirl: An Autobiography* (assisted by Bobbi Sykes), Heinemann, Richmond, Victoria.

Pepper, P.
1980 *You Are What You Make Yourself To Be: The Story of a Victorian Family 1842–1980,* Hyland House, Melbourne.

Perkins, C.
1975 *A Bastard Like Me*, Ure Smith, Sydney.

Pierson, J.C.
1977 Voluntary organisations and Australian Aboriginal Urban Adaptations in Adelaide, *Oceania* 48(1), 46–58.

Read, P.
1980 Fathers and Sons: A Study of Five Men of 1900, *Aboriginal History* 4(1), 97–116.

Reay, M. and G. Sitlington
1948 Class and Status in a Mixed-Blood Community (Moree, New South Wales), *Oceania* 18(3), 179–207.

Rosser, B.
1978 *This is Palm Island*, Australian Institute of Aboriginal Studies, Canberra.

Rowley, C.D.
1971 *Outcasts in White Australia*, Australian National University Press, Canberra.

Sansom, B.
1980 *The Camp at Wallaby Cross*, Australian Institute of Aboriginal Studies, Canberra.
1982 The Aboriginal Commonality. In R.M. Berndt (ed), *Aboriginal Sites, Rights and Resource Development*, University of Western Australia Press, Nedlands.

Simon, E.
1978 *Through my Eyes*, Rigby, Adelaide.

Smith, H.M. and E.H. Biddle
1972 *Look Forward, Not Back: Aborigines in Metropolitan Brisbane, 1965–1966*, Australian National University Press, Canberra.

Smith, L.R.
1980 *The Aboriginal Population of Australia*, Australian National University Press, Canberra.

Spicer, E.H.
1971 Persistent Cultural Systems, *Science* 174(4011), 793–800.

Thiele, S.
1984 Anti-intellectualism and the 'Aboriginal Problem', Colin Tatz and the 'Self-determination Approach', *Mankind* 14(3), 165–78.

Thomas, G.T.
1980 *Mumbulla Spiritual Contact*, Department of Prehistory, Research School of Pacific Studies, Australian National University, Canberra.

Trigger, D.
1986 Blackfellas and Whitefellas: The Concepts of Domain and Social Closure in the Analysis of Race-Relations, *Mankind* 16(2), 99–117.

Wilson, P.R.
1982 *Black Death, White Hands*, George Allen and Unwin, Sydney.

Young, E.A.
1982 Aboriginal Town Dwellers in New South Wales. In E.A. Young and E.K. Fisk (eds), *Town Populations*, The Aboriginal Component in the Australian Economy, Development Studies Centre, Australian National University, Canberra.

Young, E.A. and E.K. Fisk
1982 Introduction. In E.A. Young and E.K. Fisk (eds), *Town Populations*, The Aboriginal Component in the Australian Economy 2, Development Studies Centre, Australian National University, Canberra.

2. Diane Barwick — Aborigines of Victoria[1]

The word Aborigine is best used the way the dark people of southeastern Australia themselves use it: to include any person of Aboriginal ancestry. To be Aboriginal, in their own view, is to belong to, to be loyal to, the small closed communities of kin and friends who are fellow Kooris, scattered enclaves in a world of whites.

Their own full cultural tradition has gone but in its place is a subculture compounded of traits both indigenous and introduced, blended by historical circumstances. The modern Aboriginal subculture is one of many in southeastern Australia. Although journalists, politicians and preachers are prone to talk of 'the Australian way of life' there is of course a commonsense popular recognition that bankers and barbers, squatters and shearers are likely to live in very different styles. The accepted content of the nation-wide cultural pattern is modified by various groups: particular habits and attitudes differ according to region, social class, occupation, and religious or ethnic background. Certain groups with a distinctive history may have cultural peculiarities which are not part of the nation-wide pattern, although more or less tolerated by other segments of society.

For Aborigines the basic subcultural ties are those of locality and family. They identify or place one another not by asking 'What work do you do?' but rather 'Which place do you come from?', 'Which family is yours?' This subculture emphasises allegiance. Its members share a strong attachment to the land, to the 'home place' or region surrounding the Aboriginal reserves where their forebears lived, worked and lie buried. Members of each regional population are knit together by reciprocal obligations of hospitality and help, by lifelong bonds of affection, duty and loyalty to the relatives and friends who alone provide complete acceptance and security in a seemingly hostile world. To publicly identify oneself as an Aborigine is a matter of defiant pride for many who could readily 'pass' and be lost as anonymous citizens. Their refusal 'to be ashamed of our blood and our people' is an explicit demonstration of allegiance to a small community bonded by shared experience, common memories and inherited legends of oppression as a despised indigenous minority.

For its members this subculture has many attractions. Tolerance, compassion, humour, and the emotional warmth of personal relationships together make up an ethos comparable to the notion of 'soul' for the American Negro. Members relish the cosiness of knowing and being at ease with all others who belong. They enjoy and need the complete acceptance of belonging by birth and by right, whatever their follies or failings, their status or successes. To outsiders the visible characteristics of this subculture may seem negative: poverty and perhaps squalor, poor health, some alcoholism, recurrent unemployment and housing problems. Many welfare workers and would-be reformers hear the hard luck stories but do not participate in the community's life sufficiently to understand its compensations. They note the fact of unemployment, but do not notice that an unemployed father is likely to spend his day teaching his children songs and stories of the past, and devising games and puzzles for their entertainment; they deplore shared households but ignore the value of assistance and companionship for the burdened and lonely young mother.

Each person's circle of kin, known throughout life, is his or her main source of security, companionship, and economic and emotional support. Inevitably kinship solidarity has a heightened value for members of an ethnic minority: denial of ancestry or neglect of obligations can threaten the survival of a small racial group. Partly of necessity (because of poverty and the prejudice of landlords), and partly by preference (because they enjoy companionship and wish to repay past obligations) many dark people continue to live in large households shared with needy relatives. This continued sharing and the foster-rearing of children maintain close ties among a large number of relatives and encourage adherence to common norms and values, while the adoption of new cultural forms is consequently inhibited because young parents are not isolated in separate dwellings with sole responsibility for child-rearing. The resulting economic interdependence is an important source of group solidarity. It has perhaps prevented ambitious families from greatly bettering their individual living standards, but reciprocal sharing has insured the majority against want when few other sources of assistance are available. Because most expect to remain battlers, depending on relatives during recurrent financial crises, they are more interested in keeping these ties in good repair than in 'getting ahead' by turning kin away to keep the terms of a tenancy which is likely to be ephemeral anyhow.

Few dark people today are so completely absorbed in the larger society that their earlier identification and association with their natal membership groups is no longer meaningful to them. Most still marry within their own local groups, and prefer to live in the known territory of the home region, since 'you know where you are with your own people and you've got your own relatives around you so you don't get lonely'. The regional population to which each adult belongs is usually the 'reference group' whose opinions and expectations shape individual conduct. Strong emotions enforce allegiance to the group's ways and beliefs, and to the people from whom the person learns these. Gossip and public reproach provide shaming and hurtful punishment for the disloyal or deviant. An individual may strive to identify with some other reference group—many, for example, wish to share the style of life of white acquaintances. But especially in rural areas prejudice may create insurmountable barriers for those visibly

Aboriginal. No matter what their habits and their self-identification, local whites are not likely to let them forget their origins.

In the modern Aboriginal subculture some elements of traditional culture survive: 'the old law' still operates to forbid first and second cousin marriages, and vestiges of the section system define marriage choices even more narrowly in remoter districts; beliefs in certain spirits and harbingers of death are still passed on; some of the lore of herbal curing is still found useful; and some of the older mourning practices are still considered proper. Other features of the present-day subculture are common to Australian rural workers generally, for Aborigines have worked for a century as itinerant farm labourers in the southeastern States. Their patterns of speech and dress, their sporting interests, their preferences in music and entertainment are similar to those of their white workmates and neighbours. Some European elements in the subculture were originally introduced last century by mentors who were themselves members of aberrant subgroups in Australian society. Work habits and drinking patterns were initially acquired from the shearers, stockmen and swagmen they worked beside. Religious beliefs and community organisation were shaped by the institutional atmosphere of the Aboriginal stations, where the early managers were typically puritanical and authoritarian missionaries, representatives of fundamentalist sects who tried to inculcate their own subcultural values. Since intermarriage was rare, there were few resident models of European family life and those men who did form households were itinerant workers unlikely to practise the domestic graces of the urban middle class.

The Aboriginal subculture, developed in a rural setting, maintains certain features which are both adaptive extensions of traditional norms and typical characteristics of migratory workers. These include job opportunities and preferences; their necessary nomadism; their generosity in sharing what they have; and their disinterest in possessions and achievements which are status symbols to settled white collar workers. Migratory workers everywhere have a distinctive style of life and create a world for themselves. Their lively scandalous gossip and distinctive, slangy, vivid language serve to demonstrate the separateness of such groups from the larger society. Their world is demarcated, closed to outsiders who do not share their wanderings and their interests and their jokes, who cannot join in their prideful recounting of their own history and their legends of the wonderful and funny exploits of their own heroes. All such worker groups have closed communities, but the basis of recruitment, of belonging, is different here, for Aborigines are recruited by birth.

Aborigines are not merely a category of migratory workers. They are members of an indigenous minority long subject to special legislation and government control. Official statements about the national policy of assimilation often imply that Aborigines form a group defined both by visible physical differences and by a style of living unacceptable to other Australians. Governments, press and public still speak of 'The Aboriginal Problem' and demand 'the wholehearted adoption by the Aborigines of the so-called Australian way of life' (Aborigines Welfare Board 1960, 4).[2] In fact the majority of Aborigines in southeastern Australia have been more or less absorbed in the economy and urbanised. Their lives and their problems are similar to those of their working class neighbours who must also support large families on small incomes. A major aim of State administrations in recent decades has been the dispersal (more or less forcibly) of rural Aboriginal communities to further the policy of assimilation. Having little understanding of the reasons for the variant forms of family structure and household composition usual among the dark people, the policymakers have assumed that scattering families in town houses among white neighbours and preventing the visits of 'blow-ins' will quickly transform Aborigines into ordinary citizens. The authorities have ignored the security value and strength of kinship, community and regional bonds. Existing community ties and powers of social control have not been utilised to encourage better standards, but instead family loyalties are deplored as a hindrance to dispersal and absorption. A typical government report says, 'Some of the people now regarded as Aborigines could "pass" and become assimilated if they broke away from their old mode of living, associates, surroundings and behaviour' (Aborigines Welfare Board 1959, 5). The effect of such official pressures has been tellingly summarised by an experienced social worker: 'Authority represents a constant threat to the very small area of personal security which they do have: to be able to live in a known place among known people' (Boas 1964).

The authoritarian implementation of policy, without consultation, has been resented by Aboriginal communities for a century. The long tradition of Aboriginal protest, so great a part of the folk history passed on within these communities, is virtually unknown to the larger society, for the letters and petitions and records of deputations which go back to the 1850s are sealed in State archives. These protests and strikes and rebellions, unheeded by contemporary officials but remembered with bitterness by participants and their descendants, have had two continuing themes: the alienation of land, and the threat of physical and cultural extinction. The land rights issue has been the subject of continuing petition and protest since 1859, for the reserves have a symbolic as well as an actual value for a landless minority whose original title was never recognised nor extinguished by compensation. The imposition of policies which threatened the cohesion and persistence of this ethnic group merely strengthened distrust of officials and made more vehement the continuing demand for greater self-determination. The curious paternalism of Australian administrators, stemming from the old belief that this was a 'childlike' race in need of authoritarian management, has always included an inability to recognise (or at least a refusal to acknowledge) that protest action could be self-inspired and capably organised by Aboriginal communities. 'Outside interference' was the euphemism of the 1870s; 'stirrers' or 'Communist agitators' are blamed today. Sympathetic whites have indeed often helped by penning letters, arranging interviews, and soliciting press attention for existing grievances, but any 'incitement' by outsiders must always have been both unnecessary and ineffectual.

The difference in income and possessions which has visibly demarcated this subgroup in Australian society is shrinking, for equality of opportunity has become more real in the last decade, special aid is encouraging educational achievement, and discrimination is being discouraged. But pressures from within the group, as well as the whites' periodic displays of prejudice, still encourage individuals to maintain their identification as Aborigines. The dark people have been conditioned, by their own experience and by the tales of their elders, to believe that government policy decisions are both arbitrary and unpredictable, and that their only lasting security lies in a continuing allegiance to their own community.

The many older adults who have for decades spoken out against government neglect and fought for the repeal of restrictive legislation, who have spent much money and time in organising activities to ensure the perpetuation of their distinct community, are being joined now by a majority of the better-educated urban young. These young spokesmen, many of whom could readily 'pass', have explicitly chosen to demonstrate their pride in belonging to this minority. They value both allegiance and self-improvement. More and more activities, organised by and for dark people only, have the specific aim of 'keeping our people together' and improving self-image and status by 'showing those Gubbas (whites) what dark people can do'. The more thoughtful white sympathisers are consciously tempering their well meaning paternalism and encouraging Aborigines to assume real executive powers in the many leagues and welfare groups. There is no cohesive nation-wide organisation of Aborigines yet: it could not be expected because the small territorial clusters have been so long isolated by distance, illiteracy and regional factionalism. But sentiments of pan-Aboriginal solidarity strengthen yearly, as members of remote communities meet at conferences convened by voluntary associations, universities and churches. For a decade more, young people especially have been reading novels, news reports and serious writings on race relations, and contacting 'coloured' visitors in attempts to learn about and make sense of their own position as an ethnic minority.

Their self-consciousness has also stimulated a search for their own history. They seek knowledge of the traditional culture, and of the remote ancestors who conquered a continent with digging stick and spear. They realise their own role as carriers of a folk history composed of memories and legends of a century of European contact, and listen with respect and attention to their elders' recollections of the forebears who pioneered and farmed the Aboriginal reserves.

For officials (and much of the public) the very existence of this separate subgroup in Australian society has constituted 'The Aboriginal Problem'. Their distinctive language, religion and cultural traditions have been long suppressed by official fiat. Yet an Aboriginal subculture persists in southeastern Australia despite a century of official pressure. A self-conscious interest in their history and a new pride in their separateness is clearly improving morale in many Aboriginal communities. This pride in themselves and in their inheritance seems to be encouraging an emotional security and self-respect which in turn can aid the achievement of real social equality.

Notes

1. Reprinted with kind permission from 'What it Means to Be an Aborigine'. In B. Leach (ed), *The Aborigines Today*, Paul Hamlyn, Melbourne, 1971.
2. Diane Barwick wrote here of policies and attitudes of the 1960s, but they are no doubt still widely current, if not officially (editor).

References

Aborigines Welfare Board
1959 *Annual Report*, Aborigines Welfare Board, Government Printer, Melbourne.
1960 *Annual Report*, Aborigines Welfare Board, Government Printer, Melbourne.

Boas, P.
1964 Report on Framlingham Reserve, unpublished, Aborigines Welfare Board, Melbourne.

3. Barry Morris   Dhan-gadi resistance to assimilation

For the Dhan-gadi people of the Macleay Valley, European domination has been a constant feature of their lives since occupation of the valley in the mid nineteenth century. The historical specificities of this colonial domination—the kinds of Aboriginal-European interaction and the mechanisms of cultural, political and economic subordination—have changed continually through time. The aim of this chapter[1] is to examine one of these moments of domination. It explores the way a changing configuration of power has in part structured Dhan-gadi responses, while itself being subject to subversion by continuous attempts by the Dhan-gadi to resist incorporation into an encompassing state system. In the period I am considering, namely the era 1936–68, during which the Aborigines were subject to institutionalisation, one sees the emergence of subtle, non-violent forms of resistance.

In the first part of this chapter, I outline the transformation of power relations between Aborigines and the state. It is these changes in the modalities of domination which, in effect, brought about changes in the modes of resistance. The reformulation of power relations was initiated by an administrative inquisition in 1937 into policies toward Aborigines in 1937. The recommendations redirected policy toward assimilation and altered the forms of control to which Aborigines were subject. In dealing with 'the Aboriginal problem', policy moved toward increasing institutionalisation for retraining. What was required was the total control of the social environment through a manager-supervised institution, which was to organise the inculcation of Aborigines with what were regarded as the superior values of the dominant society. In terms of Aboriginal administration, the total institution functioned as a cultural apparatus to implement an educational programme of homogenisation in which the eradication of 'otherness' was to be achieved.

The second part of this chapter considers the forms of collective identity which sustained the continuity of the Dhan-gadi in this period. In this, I am not so much concerned with identifying and isolating a set of essentialist categories identified with 'traditional' culture. Indeed, I reject the cultural essentialism that this entails. Such a singular search for 'authentic' cultural forms often produces a reified view of culture as something which exists outside of time and place. Following Sider (1980, 20), I argue for a processual and relational view of culture, that is to say, 'the historical specificity of culture'. The point I would stress is that identity was constituted in part by resistances to the segregating policies of institutionalisation as well as by the policies themselves. In short, my concern is with the processes of becoming in a context where the Dhan-gadi did not have the social and political autonomy to sustain and develop relatively unchanged cultural forms.

My principal concern here is with the cultural forms of resistance to institutional domination. Such resistances are not constituted in direct and violent confrontations, but rather indirect and discrete forms of resistance which are inscribed at the level of culture. Such indirect resistances seek to impose limitations on a system of power in which those in authority appear to exercise unlimited control. In the following, I will attempt to consider these responses to the implementation of institutional forms of control placed upon the Dhan-gadi in the Macleay Valley.

The establishment of the Aborigines' Welfare Board

Assimilation of the aborigines into the general community is the keynote of the Board's policy. When it is considered that 95 per cent of the so-called Aborigines of New South Wales are half and lighter castes, whose social fabric has been torn asunder by the onrush of western civilisation, and who if left alone would have neither the traditional background of the aboriginal way of life nor the culture of the white man to stabilise or guide them, the need for this policy should be abundantly clear. *The policy has a positive aim, to make the aborigines responsible, active, intelligent citizens*. The Aborigines Welfare Board realises the difficulties arising from a different mode of thinking, content of knowledge and emphasis on different values and ideals. It realises that the aborigines inherit a different view of life, and that the value of our culture must be proved to them before it will be accepted (New South Wales Aborigines' Welfare Board 1948, 3, emphasis added).

Such statements signified innovative shifts in the administrative policy toward Aborigines. During this period the policies and political practices were characterised by the emergence of liberalism as the dominant ideology in Aboriginal administration. State control of Aborigines was regarded as a means of erasing the discrimination associated with their treatment as a distinctive social group. This was the ultimate aim of liberal political strategy. Such 'solutions' however simply continued racism in a different mode, insofar as the Aborigines continued to be made to surrender cultural, social and political autonomy. The underlying pre-supposition on which this policy was based was an historicist racism, reflecting the view that through the systematic training of Aborigines at the local level they could be 'uplifted' to take their place in a superior culture and society. The aim of such totalising strategies was to break down any lingering cultural residues and to eradicate environmental sources of 'inferiority' or 'disabilities' through intervention at the local level. If earlier policies and ideologies had stressed what Aborigines could not be, the new policy of assimilation stressed what they should be and would be.

Such perspectives, in effect, embodied the liberal critique of discrimination and segregation. By focussing on what were regarded as past errors, the new policy in effect legitimated itself as a positive and progressive policy. Thus, the immediate past (the wrongs) helped to obscure the dark side of the present and future of government policy.

The disciplinary and surveillance policies of monitoring and correcting of the 'redeemable plague victim' gained ascendancy during this new era of state control.[2] The stress on environment as the source of 'the Aboriginal problem' underpinned the escalation of pedagogic or sociological intervention of state power. The biologism which denied the possibility of such intervention was rejected in the new policies: racial inferiority which had been seen to be congenital was now seen to be environmentally determined.

The control by the Aborigines' Welfare Board, which superceded the Aborigines' Protection Board, closely approximated what Goffman (1961) has called the 'total institution' and, more recently, Foucault (1982) has labelled the 'carceral'. Supervised stations, which became the major armature of administrative policy, centralised within one institution the functions of various institutions found dispersed at different sites in the wider society, for example education, health, accommodation, and so on. The process of decision making was invested in the authority of the resident manager, and deference to and dependence on his authority became regular aspects of the institutionalised life of the inhabitants of these newly created reserves. By the late 1930s, the majority of Aborigines in the Macleay region lived on government stations. Prior to this, they had lived on unsupervised reserves and fringe camps. The Welfare Board introduced a more comprehensive regime of control within the bounded Aboriginal communities at Bellbrook and Burnt Bridge. For these Aboriginal communities, the change in policy involved a significant break in the political and social relations of their existence.

The abolition of the Protection Board in 1940 came as a result of growing public criticism from both Aboriginal and European groups. Organised public protests by Aboriginal organisations throughout the 1920s and 1930s had drawn attention to Aboriginal dissatisfaction with the Board's control of their affairs (see Morris 1985). In 1937, the Legislative Assembly established a Select Committee to inquire into the administration of the Protection Board. The inclusion of an Aboriginal member of the Aborigines' Progressive Association on the Select Committee may be seen as an index of the effectiveness of Aboriginal agitation against the Board. For two decades, the

Progressive Association had been seeking the abolition of the Board as a fundamental pre-condition to full citizenship rights for Aborigines.

Contrary to one of the primary concerns of the Progressive Association, the proceedings of the Select Committee were concerned with the nature rather than the continuing existence of Aboriginal administration. The criticisms of the Protection Board's past performance were countered by the establishment of uniform and centralised bureaucratic intervention. The proceedings reduced themselves to what Duncan (1969) has called a 'witch hunt' concerned with the personal misconduct and mismanagement of some of the Board's managers and the inefficiency of the general administration. Such criticisms of managers amounted to a critique of personal, arbitrary power. The recommendations were a demand that managers should be subject to centralised surveillance mechanisms and to rational, bureaucratic rules. The rejection of arbitrary, personal power rested on the bureaucratisation of power—the assertion of the rule of impersonal law rather than absolute power. In effect, the proceedings were concerned with establishing a more comprehensive custodianship of Aborigines by instituting more effective bureaucratic procedures.

This bureaucratic critique of the previous regime provided the means by which state policies toward Aborigines pursued lines of centralised control and, at the same time, increased the incorporation of Aborigines into the power mechanisms of the state. The misconduct of managers also provided the basis of concern for the representative of the Progressive Association, Mr W Ferguson. As he stated in evidence before the 1937 Select Committee on Administration of Aborigines' Protection Board (53–54, emphasis added):

> This meeting gives me the opportunity of placing before the public the conditions under which our people are living, and also to let you know the hardships and many injustices handed out to them by the so-called Protection Board. In presenting our case I will endeavour to put all my points as clear and concise as possible. I realise that we have all the best learned men and women in the world opposing our claim to freedom, for we have learned by past experience that the scholars and students will recommend that the race be preserved for scientific purposes. What a fallacy! What is there left to experiment with...*To begin with, we are asking for the abolition of the Aborigines' Protection Board*. You ask why should it be abolished? I say that it is not functioning in the best interests of the Aboriginal people. The Board appoints managers and protectors to help the people and look after their interests. But *the managers have so much power, their power is greater than any other public servant in Australia. I say that no public officer, no magistrate, or no other man, I do not believe*

the King of England, has power under British law to try a man or a number of men or women, find them guilty and sentence them without giving them a fair and open trial and without producing any evidence to convict except in countries where there is no handy law to convict such as Papua New Guinea.

As we have seen from Ferguson's evidence, the Progressive Association sought the abolition of the Aboriginal administration and not its bureaucratic reform. The state responded, however, by bureaucratising its policies. The response took this direction with the aim of liberating the Aborigines from personal arbitrary power, of defending them from oppression. Those who formed this policy, therefore, were able to construct their interventions as positive and progressive reforms.

The final recommendations in the report sought an elaboration and intensification of institutional control. According to the findings of the Public Service Board report (1940, 12), the necessity for close supervision of all Aborigines was an essential aspect of policy. This reorganisation was to make Board members more available for inspections of stations and reserves, and to provide more and better-qualified staff as a more effective means of controlling and monitoring Aborigines on stations. The policy would ensure more success for the Welfare Board (1940, 27–31) than had been achieved by its predecessor. If Aborigines were to be regarded as equal, it would be through pedagogic intervention, in which they would be progressively constituted as free, autonomous subjects.

Following the bureaucratic logic of the report, the establishment of a more efficient and effective chain of command was seen as an initial but inevitable step in the transformation of existing station residents into more disciplined and useful communities. The extension of state control and the use of what was called 'detailed administration' constituted major changes in the world of Aborigines. The changes in control did not simply represent an amplification in control for its own sake but a change in the aims of Aboriginal administration. The principal recommendation of the Public Service Board report (1940, 12) had been 'to mould the administration so as to ensure, as early as possible, the assimilation of these people into the social and economic life of the general community'. Both the emphasis on closer surveillance of Aborigines and more developed techniques for obtaining biographical knowledge of the 'inmate' were in keeping with practices of bureaucratic custodianship found throughout the wider society. Here, for the first time, one finds their systematic application to the Aboriginal population in the state.[3]

These new techniques of power sought to train individuals, and to socialise or resocialise those classified as deviant, rather than to punish. The patterns of social control were organised around systems of disciplines rather than systems of punishment. Thus the intention of institutional control should not be seen as a negative, repressive power which depersonalises and humiliates individuals. The application of these new pedagogic techniques of power must be seen as positive in as much as they do not merely seek to confine but to remodel individuals.[4] The new policy of the Welfare Board, then, marked a major change in the forms of state power applied to Aborigines.

In this we are not dealing with a benevolent pedagogic apparatus of state power, nor simply with repressive power, but with the gradual extension of power through mechanisms of discipline which produce trained individuals. As Foucault (1982, 138) so aptly puts it, such 'disciplines' constitute,

> a policy of coercions that act upon the body, a calculated manipulation of its elements, its gestures, its behaviour. The human body was entering a machinery of power that explores it, breaks it down and rearranges it.

As he has stressed, important to such control were comprehensive techniques of surveillance, of obtaining and retaining knowledge, and of ordering and partitioning the target of control. The accumulation of knowledge and the use of power reinforced each other. Individuals are the objects of pedagogic strategies and normalisation is the aim of the exercise of control, to internalise self-regulation within each individual.

The administrative guidelines for the assimilation of Aborigines stipulated such practices and procedures. The Public Service Board (1940, 17) could suggest,

> no better policy than the present, viz., the aggregation on stations, under close supervision, of those aborigines who are not yet fitted to be assimilated into the general community, with the provision of suitable training schools.

It was also recommended that a more detailed administration was required, since according to the report it had not been adequate in the past. It was thought that with better methods and an increase in the staff then 'better results must follow' (Public Service Board 1940, 29). To ensure a consistent application of these new measures an up-to-date code of instructions was to be issued to managers and other staff to 'ensure uniformity of action' (Public Service Board 1940, 24).

Perhaps the most significant intrusion of rational bureaucratic procedures associated with these new forms of power was the expansion in the accumulation and use of knowledge about station Aborigines. Monthly reports from managers were considered to provide a limited form of knowledge of the stations' inhabitants and the monitoring of these Aborigines was to take a more sustained form in a weekly diary. As the Public Service Board report (1940, 24) concluded,

> It is the Public Service Board's view that at this stage, in order to deal adequately with the problem, there should be a complete record of all aborigines coming within the purview of the Act. The Public Service Board cannot see how the problem can be dealt with otherwise than by close personal study of the individual and his problems and this is impossible without a comprehensive record of the individual. This record does not exist in respect of adults and is not sufficiently comprehensive even in the case of children admitted to the institutions.

Such individualised monitoring and surveillance serves to extend and reinforce the positive power to transform individuals. Each individual is subjected to a 'normalising judgement' set by an administrative hierarchy. The performance of each individual is differentiated, and ranked according to their ability to conform to the set normative standards. The carrot, so to speak, for station Aborigines was to be the granting of an Exemption Certificate whereby they would no longer be subject to the discriminatory legislation that applied to other Aborigines in the State. What was created here was the means whereby the rate at which each Aborigine proceeded could be individually assessed.

The application of such policies in relation to the Aborigines of New South Wales was set out in amendments in 1940 and 1943 to the Aborigines' Protection Act. For the Aborigines on government stations in the Macleay Valley the legislation formalised the authority of the managers who had been appointed to Bellbrook (1932) and Burnt Bridge (1937). The most immediate consequence for the Aborigines on these government stations was the invasion of personal and familial space. The administrative control of Aboriginal stations was codified in the *Manual of Instructions to Managers and Matrons of Aboriginal Stations and Other Field Officers* (1941) which was issued to all Welfare Board staff as part of a policy of bureaucratic standardisation. One of the main duties of the manager was to strictly control access to the station. In practice, this meant that every person who entered the station had first and foremost to report to the manager and explain why they were there, who they were staying with and for how long. It was the manager who determined if and under what conditions they could stay. In effect, the manager was able to regulate and scrutinise relations between residents, their relatives and friends. In addition, the manager and matron had the right to enter Aboriginal houses on the station at any time. These policies were in keeping with maintaining total control over the Aboriginal environment.

The managers and matrons were expected not simply to exercise control, but to create new forms of social identity among Aborigines through institutional practices. This can be seen in the regulation which required the matron to inspect houses. The inspections were to be carried out in the following manner (see *Manual of Instruction* 1941, 3):

> The women folk, with the knowledge that the inspection is to be made, can prepare their homes and have them bright and clean on that particular day. The inspection of homes should, therefore, be irregular, particularly in those cases where it is suspected that the occupants of any home are inclined to 'polish up' for the occasion. Residents should be given to understand...that when any visit is made by the matron it will be expected that the house will be clean and tidy.

Such techniques of control created a one-way relationship of visibility, where the random nature of the surveillance in such a confined area renders it continuous. In addition, the calculated use of such techniques ensured that the 'inmates' had limited scope to maintain some degree of autonomy as even the most personal aspects of social life were open to the scrutiny and judgement of those in authority. As one woman stated:

> She was the matron. She'd go around want this done, want that done. Well I mean most of the womens knows, they knew how to clean their own...[If you] lived in a house with no water you can't keep it as much as you keep this [present house]. You think they'd know that. No, they want it spotless.

On Aboriginal stations the domestic sphere was not a private space but was continually accessible to those in authority who might wish to pass judgement. Such invasions of domestic life provided knowledge which was recorded and made available to those in authority. The appropriation of such knowledge is intended to increase the power of the staff to intervene and to correct and control the behaviours of the 'inmates', that is, it involved the government of the private sphere. The abolition of private space through its accessibility by a specialised hierarchy was an essential feature of the total control of the institutional environment felt necessary to change Aborigines.

The rationale for pedagogic intervention was not simply domination and control by authority. The reason for institutional separation was to concentrate a more effective regime of reform on the individual—the use of monitoring and surveillance which act upon the individual to break down existing patterns of behaviour and to construct new ones. This is clearly seen in the simulated surveillance and monitoring of the individual houses of Aboriginal women which required them to attend continuously to housework as a daily routine. It was precisely this, the acquisition of a permanent and disciplined economy of habits for each individual, that the application of such forms of power sought to achieve. In this respect, the aim was to internalise individual self-government rather than continually maintain external forms of control.

The most explicit application of such disciplinary techniques was found in those institutions set up specifically for Aboriginal girls. For these girls, according to a former inmate, the daily routine began at 5.00am. For the older girls, the day began with the regular scrubbing of the dormitory floors. It was each child's responsibility to clean six floorboards for the length of the dormitory. By the ordering of time and space into specific activities and actions through timetabled routines, individual movements were regulated, controlled and disciplined. If on inspection the boards were found to be wet, the girl responsible would have to do the whole section again. This meant missing breakfast, as institutional life was strictly regulated by a time schedule. Furthermore, each piece of equipment—hessian apron, scrubbing brush and bucket—was marked with the girl's initials so that punishment could be dealt out to those who misplaced, neglected or lost them. Punishment expressed the negative aspect of power, it was not the ultimate end. The pedagogic or positive aspect of power was to inculcate habits of work and the notion of responsibility for personal possessions. To avoid such punitive interventions, the girls had to police themselves.

The stress on self-regulation was an attempt to inculcate a regime of rational and calculating individual behaviour which is closely associated with cultural notions of possessive individualism within the wider society. In official policy, work was never simply instrumental but associated with the acquisition of a regime of ordered conduct. For example, Aboriginal men who could not get work outside the stations were forced to work for the manager for three days, in order to learn the value of work, before they could be given the ration. Such compulsory labour had a pedagogic function: the individual was conditioned toward regularity and order rather than the product of labour itself. An extension of this can be seen in the practice, widespread among managers, of withholding child endowment from mothers. This was held in trust until a sufficient amount accumulated. The mother or parents were then given the money and directed to buy something substantial, for example, the materials to build a new house or durable consumer items such as furniture. Here, then, the managers attempted to 'educate' Aborigines in the rational and calculating use of money for saving and consumption. In effect, the use of such pedagogic practices on stations was an audacious attempt to restructure both the personal and domestic sphere of Aboriginal existence.

The perpetuation of external constraints and physical segregation of Aborigines in the state was no longer an end in itself but an indispensable part of this new pedagogic regime. Closer surveillance and control required segregation. It is in this way that one can understand the conclusion of the Public Service Board (1940, 20) that 'the restrictions imposed by the present law of the state are in the interests of Aborigines'. Similarly, rather than a liberalisation of the repressive laws associated with the Aborigines' Protection Act, for example laws giving wide-ranging powers to the managers, control of the movements of Aboriginal adults and children, and so on, the Public Service Board (1940, 28) recommended that 'greater use is possible of these powers'. The same situation remained in terms of the discriminatory legislation, State and Commonwealth, that existed for Aborigines, for example, exclusion from obtaining liquor, unemployment relief, pensions, maternity allowances or direct cash payments of child endowment (Public Service Board 1940, 20). Exemption from such discriminatory and repressive legislation could only be achieved by individuals through their ability to conform to the normative pre-requisites of the state.[5]

Nevertheless, we are dealing with a transformation in official policy. Aborigines were regarded as 'redeemable' and hence assimilable through the systematic intervention of the state. Racist ideology was now embedded in notions of environmental deprivation and the policy of 'civilising' Aborigines into a superior culture and society. As the Public Service Board report (1940, 20) asserted, 'their education had not yet reached the stage where the restrictions can be lifted as a general policy, without harmful effects on the majority'. The ideology of biological racism, of Aborigines frozen in time, was gradually replaced with an ideology which stressed the transformative potentials of knowledge and education. Preparation for citizenship was considered in the following manner:

> It is obvious that in order to lead the aboriginal people to a proper understanding and appreciation of the mental processes involved in Australian civilisation and life an education system in its various forms and degrees must be established. This education must extend beyond the more formal primary school education and should involve technical, industrial, agricultural, secondary, and perhaps ultimately, professional education (New South Wales Aborigines' Welfare Board Report 1944, 3).

In this way an ideology of the development of potentials through knowledge replaced an ideology which stressed the limited potentials of the race, as the *raison d'etre* for government control of Aborigines.

What is submerged and mystified within the rhetoric of the progressive potentials of pedagogic intervention is that this form of control is seen as divorced from power relations. The application of such techniques of power are so commonplace within the wider society that they are regarded as neutral rather than as political/cultural forms of power. Such disciplinary regimes have established themselves throughout such a broad range of institutions, for example schools, workplaces, hospitals, and prisons, that they have become dehistoricised or 'naturalised'—naturalised as eternal or necessary forms of social existence. As Foucault (1982, 170) puts it,

> Discipline 'makes' individuals; it is the specific technique of power that regards individuals both as objects and instruments of its exercise. It is not a triumphant power, which because of its own excess can pride itself on its own omnipotence; it is a modest suspicious power which functions as a calculated, but permanent economy. These are humble modalities, minor procedures, as compared with the majestic rituals or great apparatuses of the state. And it is precisely they that were gradually to invade the major forms, altering their mechanisms and imposing their procedures.

The Public Service Board report had provided the blueprint for the extension of such mechanisms of discipline to Aborigines.

This intervention in Aboriginal administration had its political underpinnings in a liberal critique of previous policy. The contemporary commentators perceived assimilation as a progressive policy. Pedagogic intervention was seen as representing a responsible and compassionate concern for the Aborigines of New South Wales. This positive policy of assimilation, as I have illustrated, was continually contrasted with earlier negative policies (Elkin 1944, 1973; Bell 1959, 1964; Bleakley 1961). As Bleakley (1961, 218) stated,

> The policy is to assist in the uplift of Aborigines, pure and mixed blood, to fit them for assimilation in the general community; by encouraging and helping these people to uplift themselves, and by winning the tolerance and forbearance of the white people. This laudable work is done by the superintendent of Aboriginal Welfare with a staff of welfare officers to inspect, instruct, guide and encourage their proteges: a female inspector of women and children; a trained nurse for mothers, babies and adolescent girls; and managers and teachers for the stations.

Within this rhetoric of progressive development, however, what we have is a multiplication of surveillance and monitoring mechanisms and their increasing specialisation.

Such an apparently unproblematic understanding of the progressive potentials of 'knowledge' is sustained by a particularly narrow definition of power. Bell (1964,

61–62) makes this clear when he lauds the positive benefits of assimilation: 'encouragement, rather than force, is the keynote of assimilation', and again, 'force had not been employed...at any time in connection with assimilation policy'. Here one finds a view of power only in terms of its negative instance, in policies which repress and forbid. Domination is located only in those repressive state apparatuses, the judiciary, the police and the military.

It is not intellectual laziness or bad faith that renders those pedagogic forms of power that underpin assimilation policy transparent, but the commonsense, taken-for-granted nature of the educative process. The apparent naturalness of such forms of power rendered them invisible and ensured that the premises and presuppositions upon which they were founded escaped attention. This major methodological and conceptual flaw shared the same uncritical and unquestioned assumptions underlying liberal support for assimilation; regardless of the historical origins of the social and political relations of the dominant society, they were perceived as progressive and as universal.

The emergence of a culture of resistance

The change from reserves to supervised stations in the 1930s was not the only factor affecting change for the Dhan-gadi. On the one hand, there was an increase in the power and control exercised over these Aborigines through state policy. On the other hand, independent factors also conditioned the Dhan-gadi response. Principally, these concerned the serious decline of those institutional and other cultural practices which had neatly defined their cultural/political boundaries vis-a-vis the European community. There was a radical discontinuity in the social development of the Dhan-gadi at this point, which was not simply causally determined but over-determined by the conjuncture of two seemingly separate yet parallel developments, that is, the decline of conspicuous cultural practices and the imposition of managerial control. The adaptive strategies which had provided the Dhan-gadi with a relatively stable, distinctive and autonomous existence in relation to the European community in an earlier period were no longer sufficient. In the period of Welfare Board control new directions and different adaptive strategies were required and developed.

This conjuncture of events engendered quite a profound change in the life of the Dhan-gadi, and for most of my older informants, it was a period identified with change. The era of manager control provided a clear point of demarcation from earlier patterns of social existence. A number of expressions characterise people's understanding of this change, for example 'everythin goin out, nothin comin in', or alternatively, 'whitefella's way comin in'. Correspondingly, and in contrast with information from earlier periods, there was an emphasis on the distinction between 'blackfella's way' and 'whitefella's way'.

This demarcation was most apparent in those spheres where cultural boundaries are most explicitly expressed. That is, it was the end of the initiation ceremonies, and of the dancing and singing associated with such ceremonies and corroborees, and the use of the Dhan-gadi language declined. It is these aspects of social life that are referred to in the expression 'everythin goin out.' This was most significantly the case with the initiation ceremonies, which constituted a major aspect of Aboriginal life. As one man put it,

> Everybody what's on the station would have to be there. You can't go and say I'm not going and I'm gonna be here or there. You got to obey the Law see. [They'd say] 'Come out and get over here.'

Initiation ceremonies had been held regularly throughout the early period of this century. The young men of Bellbrook had been expected, as a matter of course, to go through at least one ceremony. It is still a sign of knowledge to recall which men were put through the rule, at what ceremony, with whom and at what level they were initiated. Despite a rapidly changing and hostile world, the ceremonies retained the status as a way of life encoded in the words, 'you got to obey the Law see'.

For the Dhan-gadi men the decline of the ceremonies produced quite a distinctive break between themselves and the following generation. The period of the Welfare Board marked a clear break in continuity as it coincided with the first generation of young men who remained uninitiated. This rupture marked the end of a central cultural practice by which the Dhan-gadi maintained themselves as an entity vis-a-vis their European neighbours. The decline of these ceremonies removed from these Aborigines one of those obvious cultural/political differences which was on explicit criterion of membership of the group. It is in this context that the seeming all-pervasiveness and inevitable dominance of Europeans can be read in such expressions as 'all goin white fella's way'.

Such distinctions between blackfella's way and whitefella's way were not simply confined to ceremonial life, but were also apparent in the conspicuous area of Aboriginal music and dancing. Here, the distinction was between the various forms of European dance and singing and those associated with the ceremonies and corroborees. As one woman recalled,

> They really knew what they were singing about and if they had that boomerang or two sticks and hit it like that, you know, they'd keep time with that and they'd sing. Oh, they had *real music* them people and I don't think that there is anybody [left] that I can think of. Might have been over there [Bowraville] but none here on this Macleay.

The same applied to corroborees held at Bellbrook which were regarded as dancing in the Koori way.[6] The most vivid memory concerning these dances was that of the dancer who performed the *gurginj gurginj* (praying mantis) dance. Complete with a big mask and accompanied by other dancers this man would dance his particular story. Such corroborees were regarded as very different to those that had been performed at shows for Europeans. As one person described this latter day version, 'Oh, I don't know what you'd call it, it wasn't really the old timers' song, I think it was only made up one, song, but it was there with the beat.'

The major distinction between blackfella's way and whitefella's way was made in relation to European dancing and singing and that of the Dhan-gadi people. It is not as if we are considering a rejection of European dancing and singing—the Dhan-gadi had been holding European dances for many years. Men had learned to play the violin and the accordion, concertina, the gum leaf and the bones or spoons; these musicians accompanied the dances which were held on the river flat by the light of a big fire, and a number of men would be called to sing their set pieces during the evening. Rather, what conspicuously makes the 1930s a watershed is the end of purely Aboriginal singing and dancing, those significant cultural practices which were distinctively Aboriginal.

When these people allude to these discontinuities, they are attempting to present an image of themselves as they were in the past, and also attempting to redefine who they are in the present. While this is an ordering of the past from the present, it is not merely some imaginary projection into the past of the Dhan-gadi. I take issue here with Reay's (1949, 101) understanding of the Aboriginal historical vision, 'Without hope for a different future they look backwards to a Golden Age which is believed to have existed in living memory'. This approach represents a deprivation theory, one that is further sustained by an ahistorical, psychological reductionism. It would suggest that the content of such recollections is illusory. To dismiss such recollections as historically irrelevant, however, effectively denies the facticity of the people's own experience. If such an historical ordering is illusory, it is not so in its content but because of what has been left out.

In the segregation of an earlier period the Dhan-gadi had been able to maintain a significant degree of cultural autonomy. This had been primarily because of the rudimentary forms of control that had been exercised through the local police and Protection Board officers in the form of sporadic interventions on the reserves (see Morris 1985). Such forms of control differed significantly from the totalising control exercised through managers and matrons in residence on the stations. In this new era the culture of the Dhan-gadi no longer produced doctrine, cultural practices, artefacts, and so on, which were handed down to each succeeding generation through formal institutions. The over-arching institutional forms into which the Dhan-gadi were subsumed were those of the dominant culture. They could not continue to develop their own independently determined form of culture and consciousness. Instead, the cultural forms, practices, values and the structures of attitudes and feelings generated in this period developed largely as concrete forms of resistance to the attempts by the wider society to impose a coercive structure. We are dealing with a 'profane' culture (see Willis 1978) developed through concrete forms of struggle. Such cultural forms are, in part, a response to the specific context of cultural/institutional subordination; they are an attempt to subvert the most immediate and oppressive aspects of that domination. These conditions of existence profoundly shaped Dhan-gadi culture, rather than determined it, by providing the agenda with which that culture had to deal.[7]

What is equally important here, however, is that this culture of resistance involved the remaking of the cultural distance from European society that had been lost in the increasing absence of the more conspicuous boundary markers which had constituted a distinctive social identity. Opposition to European domination was grounded for them in attempts to subvert total subordination by creating free space, where some degree of autonomy could be exercised within the stations.

The development of the particular meanings, knowledge and experiences of these Dhan-gadi people was forged in two major ways: first, in the accompanying struggle against the most immediate forms of their oppression in institutions; and second, as a rejection of the racial and cultural secondariness associated with the institutionalisation. The period of the Welfare Board was characterised in the following way by one informant:

> Just like buying bullocks up at Bellbrook and bringing them down to Burnt Bridge, packing them into one paddock. After a few weeks there is no grass. That's the way it was!

This statement unites the two major aspects of institutionalisation: in the first place, the feelings and emotions associated with a sudden loss of personal autonomy and control that accompanied the change from a reserve to a supervised station; secondly, the interpretation of institutionalisation as an expression of collective racial and cultural secondariness, cattle being something less than human. (This latter aspect will be discussed more fully later.)

The development of cultural forms of resistance was, at one level, located in the struggle against the most immediate forms of oppression—the physical and social limitations and liabilities. It was not the Welfare Board members themselves who were the focus of attention, but their representatives on the stations, namely the managers and matrons who carried the responsibility for the implementation of Welfare Board policy and exercised extensive control over Aborigines on stations. The role of the manager and matron was to uplift and to encourage Aborigines through instruction and guidance, but among the Aborigines their presence was continually referred to as an obstacle to such possibilities. As one man stated, 'Stead of the Board thinkin if anyone want to get on in life, let him go, no, they want to put him down a step instead of letting him go up a step!'

The manager was in complete control of the running of the stations. It was he who had the authority to refuse or allow residence on the station, and he made all decisions about the running of the station. He also controlled the distribution of rations, could recommend people for exemption passes or, at the other end of the privileges and punishment, expel people from the station. As one woman put it, 'You couldn't do much in them days...you just had to grin and bear it sort of thing.' In effect, the manager's word was law. Station Aborigines were given no opportunity to make decisions or control matters that affected them directly.

On the station, Aborigines were expected to be submissive and suppliant to the manager's and the matron's authority. This hierarchical structure of command was concretised by a number of gestures and actions. Verbal deference was expected. The manager and matron always had to be addressed formally, and some managers insisted that they be called 'master'. Similarly, all decisions made by the managers had to be obeyed no matter how trivial and menial. This provided a great deal of scope to make what were seen as humiliating demands on the Aboriginal 'inmates'. On many occasions adult men were used as 'messenger boys' by the manager or the matron. As one man recalled indignantly, one matron expected the men who cut wood for her to clean up all the wood chips as well. Such petty tyrannies could be legitimated by staff on the pedagogic grounds of inculcating Aboriginal men with values of discipline and orderliness. In an earlier period, the men had the option of simply withdrawing their labour from employers as a face-saving device, but such self-protective measures were no longer an option if one wished to remain on the station.

It is not surprising, then, that the character and capacity of the managers and matrons received close scrutiny from the Aborigines. As one person stated, 'You only got to do one wrong, see, the whitefella, and it's goin round the mission straight away. Broadcast what sort of fella he is.' In this regard, such staff–inmate interaction could be seen as conforming to the general features of institutional relationships. Intelligence about those in authority and covert communication networks are essential if some measure of prediction and anticipation of possible responses or likely actions of those in authority are to be mediated or avoided. Rather than compliance with institutional authority, what was produced was covert, collective information that was used to place limits on the manager's control. This also generated an oppositional sense of identity.

Similarly, Aborigines deliberately limited the information, about themselves and their social relationships, available to those in authority.[8] This is especially significant given the Welfare Board's emphasis on detailed administration through the gathering of biographical information. The frustrations of the managers were significant in this regard. As one woman stated, 'I can remember a manager sayin to me that you can go to any of them and you know they know about it, but they'd say they don't know.'

The denial of knowledge was two-pronged as it safeguarded information which could be used against Aborigines, and, in an immediate sense, it was also an act of tacit defiance or insolence to authority. Such resistance sought to limit the power of state officials who exercised seemingly unlimited control over social relations and personal lives.

In many ways we are dealing with a more complex phenomenon than the exercise of power relations associated with institutionalisation. The Dhan-gadi gathered reconnaissance information not only about those Europeans in charge of the station, but also about the Europeans with whom they were liable to interact in the wider society. For the Dhan-gadi knowledge of the dominant society was a necessity if they were to limit their own vulnerability to European control. The most important index of this function of information was the level of knowledge held by members of the Aboriginal and European communities about each other. Aborigines consistently possessed more information about and understanding of the European community than the reverse. European information about Aborigines was seldom more than rudimentary, and pejorative stereotypes often passed as information. By contrast, Aborigines could often provide detailed information about the personal proclivities, social and economic status and careers of the Europeans with whom they interacted. For these Aborigines the possession of knowledge about Europeans, and conversely the limiting of knowledge about themselves, served a strategic, and hence political, function. Limiting information was synonymous with limiting the capacity of Europeans to control and dominate their lives.

Similarly, such reconnaissance activity became highly functional in the event that other acts of opposition to the manager's control of the station were successful. This can be interpreted by us as the creation of 'free space' wherein people construct for themselves the scope to engage in a specifically unauthorised activity or range of activities. Goffman's concept of 'secondary adaptations' in analysing staff–inmate interactions is useful in this respect. Goffman (1961, 189) defines such adaptations as,

> any habitual arrangement by which a member of an organisation employs unauthorised means, or obtains unauthorised ends, or both, thus getting around the organisation's assumptions as to what he should do and hence what he should be.

The two major areas of such secondary adjustments that have been widely recorded in the literature are the illegal drinking and gambling of Aborigines (eg in New South Wales: Reay 1949; Fink 1956; Calley 1957; Beckett 1964). Despite the strenuous efforts of the police and the local officers of the Board such 'vices' remained a prevalent part of Aboriginal existence (see Aborigines' Welfare Board Reports 1944–45). The creation of free space on the stations for such activities was at one level a subversion of the manager's authority, and at another level a denial of what Aborigines should be, given the explicit charter of assimilation that local authorities of the Board were expected to carry out.

Although Goffman's notion of secondary adjustments may cover the range of attitudes and responses to institutional control, it nevertheless tends to obscure crucial differences that occur in the wider social context (eg Rowley 1973). Yet what is clear in the case of station Aborigines is that both their institutional existence and their existence in the wider society was subject to the same restrictions and likewise constituted a similar set of 'secondary adjustments'. The legislative authority of the Aborigines' Protection Act (1943) extended both to the stations and to the wider society. The establishment of fringe camps and their persistence is an example of the creation of free space, outside institutional control and in defiance of local authorities, for the legislation decreed that Aborigines could be forced back to stations and their houses knocked down without any need to proceed through the courts (Rowley 1973,

272). Similarly, the employment of Aborigines in the local economy was essentially an institutionalised form of secondary adjustment. By securing irregular contract work, Aborigines could be their own bosses and thus minimise European control outside as well as inside the total institution.

If we consider the total context of Aboriginal drinking the notion of secondary adjustments is particularly relevant. Since it was illegal, drinking alcohol was a complicated and essentially clandestine process. One informant recalled that, to obtain grog, it was necessary for someone who could pass for a whitefella to get it or, more frequently, to illicitly secure sly grog, at the back door of some local hotel. Once someone had procured the sly grog while everybody else involved waited out of sight, it was necessary to proceed back to the Aboriginal station in the most inconspicuous manner to avoid detection. Their journey was considerably aided by the local railway line which was built through high ground and provided cover until they reached the free space on the station.

The meaning of such practices therefore goes far beyond a response to the domination of institutional authorities. This point has been made by a number of studies (Reay 1945, 300–01; Fink 1956, 103; Beckett 1964, 40). In the case of Fink and Reay, however, such activities are interpreted as pathological adaptations to European domination rather than, as Beckett argues, measures which secured a degree of Aboriginal autonomy. In many respects drinking and gambling did represent direct acts of defiance to the Board's policy of assimilation as they were a clear inversion of bourgeois notions of social respectability, including sobriety, industry and self-discipline. The Welfare Board's position reflected such sentiments (New South Wales Aborigines' Welfare Board Report 1945, 11):

> Alcohol:–The vice of drinking still persists to a degree amongst a certain section of the Aborigines, and money, which at present time is able to be earned in large amounts, is often misapplied, causing misery to the families and trouble to the administration. ...
> Gambling:–Gambling amongst Aborigines is prevalent throughout the whole state. While it must be regarded as a vice that should be discouraged, it must be remembered that gambling amongst Aborigines lacks the economic and social consequences which it frequently has amongst white people. It does, however, tend to become an obsession and an obstacle to the development of more useful forms of activity. It is a retreat for the Aborigine from the hard facts of the white man's world, a means of putting in time, and doing something emotionally exciting in a purposeless life.

Excess, indulgence and wastefulness acted as effective statements of opposition to those European values which the Welfare Board sought to cultivate.

The significant emphasis on the suppression of gambling and drinking, however, is linked to a more fundamental aspect of the culture of the dominant society. The collective activities of gambling and drinking act as a counterpoint to individual rights and property. The essential aims of assimilation sought social development based on the individualisation of the collective. That is, that people consume as isolated individuals and nuclear families, and accumulate goods (things) as personal property. The individual asserts a separate entity by affirming the right to personal possessions over and above the rights of the group. The perception of 'bad' values (drinking) and 'good' values (saving, work, discipline) was informed by a focus on the individual.

By contrast, Aboriginal drinking and gambling remained collective group activities based on the exigencies of establishing 'free space'. Such collective activities, in a sense, reproduced a cultural emphasis on sharing. In the context of assimilation policy where the dispersal of sites which might produce a sense of collective identity was an essential part of policy, their persistence became a political act, and remained so through to the 1960s.

In a more immediate sense, however, illegal drinking was a rejection of one of the main discriminatory laws applied to Aborigines. As Reay (1949, 103) puts it, 'being drunk expresses the aborigines' contempt for a law which they consider unnecessary and ineffective'. As she points out, drinking and imprisonment were a matter of boasting and social prestige, signifying the capacity to secure what is illegal. Similarly, Beckett (1964, 40) states that drunken Aborigines often made no effort to keep out of the way of police, and certainly they were not deterred by fines, prison sentences, and beatings allegedly inflicted on them. Such activity he considers 'a continued cycle of defiance, arrest and renewed defiance' against a discriminatory law which was bitterly resented (Beckett 1964, 40). The easy access by Europeans to alcohol provided a continual reminder to Aborigines of their inferior status. It is perhaps cruelly paradoxical that defiance through drunkenness was an assertion of equality with Europeans—a political assertion of their humanness.

Nevertheless, there can be little doubt that such resistance took a heavy toll of Aborigines, both socially and physically. The most extreme instance is found in those Aborigines who became addicted to methylated spirits. One woman recalled the consequences of methylated spirits for her close family and relatives:

> I don't know whether I should say it, but ah, they [local property owners] were only paying them 5/- a week and methylated spirits. A couple of bottles of methylated spirits they were paying them. A lot of them died. A____'s three brothers died because of that, my brother died. We had an adopted brother and when he was fifteen he died…Metho killed a lot of our people. My brothers and cousins, some of them were younger than me.

Such acts of personal annihilation represented the dark underside of Aboriginal drinking. This extreme and dramatic example shows the 'brittle dichotomy', to use Genovese's (1974, 78) term, between resistance and accommodation. Such ambiguity underlines a dialectical process whereby resistance cannot be readily divorced from accommodation but is organically connected to it (Genovese 1974, 78). To focus on such activities only in terms of resistance and defiance is to avoid the problem of hegemonic domination.

The ambiguity embodied in such collective, spontaneous, and immediate acts of opposition, summarised by Fink (1956, 103) as 'gambling, drinking to excess, wasting money, and neglecting homes and personal appearance', is that it also permits an accommodation to those very structures of domination. The apparently anti-social behaviour involved in such inversions of bourgeois values ensured that Aborigines were confined by such values. In effect, such acts of resistance were incapable of transforming the most immediate effects of their oppression, yet they were a clear refusal to submit to European domination, and did provide the basis for a distinctive group identity—as Fink (1956, 118) has stated, a 'self-conscious sub-society' or alternatively, as Reay (1949, 117) has suggested, 'the strongest integrative force is common membership in a rejected minority'.

The struggle for social meaning

The effects of government policy were not experienced only as physical and social liabilities and limitations—they were also a pervasive factor effecting consciousness of social/cultural identity. What is perhaps most clear is the radical disjuncture between the meanings and values envisaged in policy and those of the Aborigines. The range of meanings and values for the Dhan-gadi were constituted in their own forms of knowledge and derived from their own different sets of experiences with the dominant society. Nevertheless, the knowledge and meaning of experience was not simply constituted within a particular cultural logic, but also as subversive 'readings' and symbolic violations of the social order imposed upon them. As Sider (1980, 26) has argued,

> Counter-hegemonic cultural forms often use an arsenal of symbols which are borrowed from the existing hegemony (and inverted, mocked, etc) in order to express experiences and claims different from the elite's; the use of these symbols implies limits and constraints to the thoroughness of the opposition. These constraints can, however, be partly breached: first, by the fact that counter-hegemonic strategies can expose the contradictions within the existing hegemony, and second, by creating an experience of opposition. Counter-hegemonic strategies, like other forms of culture, do not just emerge out of people's thoughts and individual experiences, but out of their mutual understanding of their social relations.

The mutuality of experience that occurred through the intensification of institutionalisation in effect provided the raw materials for the ordering of a domain of meanings which continually reinforced their group distinctiveness. Yet expressions of subordinate group identity are ambiguous as an oppositional culture. In this instance, group distinctiveness was generated in response to the agenda set down by the dominant society. The central tenet of hegemonic domination was the denial of the integrity of a separate Aboriginal identity, as a precondition for their acceptance of the superiority of the norms and values of the dominant society.

The stations established in the Macleay Valley, in many respects, institutionalised in a more intense and systematic way those features of low status and disrespect accorded Aborigines in the wider society. Many common practices within these institutions were regarded as racial slights. Thus, the subordinating practice of assembling for the receipt of rations was assessed as a sign of collective disrepute. As one woman stated,

> Different stores would put in for it [supply the ration]. The cheapest thing he could find. I can remember that K_____ had the shop in Bellbrook. I can see them measuring the tea out and the sugar, brown sugar, all that sort of thing. They'd have white sugar, but this was the ration supply.

The items supplied were interpreted as symbols of disrespect: the 'black' tea which was 'like dust' and seen as 'the sweepings off the floor'; inferior brown (raw) sugar instead of white sugar which the Europeans would buy; and inferior meat that was 'mostly bones'.

What is equally significant is that such assertions also contain a moral critique of the dominant society. That is, they expose a contradiction residing within the dominant society's claim to a superior set of human values, customs and laws and, thereby, they challenge the legitimacy of such a claim. Such inattentiveness to equality in the critical sphere of food exchanges, especially in a community where the reciprocal sharing of food has been (and remains) a cultural norm, led to a particularly negative evaluation of the 'superior' values of the dominant society.

Similarly, the manager's conduct and relations with the people on the station were seen as an important index of the perceptions of Aborigines held by the wider society. The control by the manager over all aspects of station life was symbolic of the notions of inferiority and incompetence which sustained European paternalism. If racial inferiority was implicit in such paternalistic control, it was often made quite explicit in the treatment dealt by some managers. As Fink has pointed out, the recruitment policies of the Welfare Board (1955, 27) did allow, unintentionally, a number of 'maladjusted individuals, drunkards or people who hated blacks' to be employed. The number of these people in the ranks of the Welfare Board and their constant rotation ensured that station Aborigines would never know when they would get a 'bad boss' who would make life intolerable for them. At Bellbrook, for example, one manager patrolled the station dressed in a white suit and a pith helmet. As described to me, 'They was real bullies they was [to] mens, womens and kids. When they found out they were bosses over the people, they treated them like dogs.' Such managers and matrons exemplified through their actions what was felt to be appropriate for dealing with Aborigines as secondary and subordinate people. Although an extreme example, the attitudes embodied in such treatment were fundamental aspects of Dhan-gadi interactions with Europeans. Yet what is also indicated by, and inscribed into, such comments is an understanding of the contradiction between the values of the managers and matrons and their pedagogic role of uplifting and educating Aborigines. In effect, their role as representatives and dispensers of superior cultural values was being questioned: that men and women who treated people 'like dogs' should be put in charge of the lives of the Dhan-gadi was also a statement about the values of the dominant society.

The manager's credentials and competence in running the station were also subject to scrutiny. This is made quite clear in the following remark:

> They [Welfare Board] don't care who he is, if he's from overseas and never seen a blackfella before, he get the job and yet he come to run the true Australian. Well, look at Mr L_____, he come from overseas. He didn't know anything. He was down at Laper [La Perouse Aboriginal station] there, well what did they do in Laper? Then he came up to try and rule us in Burnt Bridge.

Such scrutiny carries with it a double meaning. In the first place, the appointment of such men reflected the inferior status, the lack of care, accorded them by the wider society. Secondly, the rejection of the manager's credentials and capacity denied him the legitimate authority in the eyes of the community, to govern their affairs.[9]

The subversion of the manager's authority in this manner was exacerbated in an institutional context, where it was in the interests of the manager to limit and discredit the initiative of the 'inmates' as a means of sustaining his own authority (see Goffman 1961, 154). As one man put it, 'You couldn't tell em anything. If you knew too much they'd send you.' This staff–inmate conflict effectively meant that if assimilation policy sought to 'remake' Aborigines then it was in the interests of each manager, in establishing his credentials and authority, to impose his own particular vision as to how to bring about such assimilation. Let me provide an illustrative recollection:

> Whatever work we did for this manager to make [things] up to date—get another one and he'd change it all around and do it his way. In that way I reckon they was no good. Instead of building it up to follow on the right way, they'd pull it down. See Bellbrook we had our fences in front of the house and had a garden right around. The next fella come and pull it down.

Or again,

> We had a banking account. We called it Bellbrook Progressive Association. We had to get people to sign to get any money out. That's alright. We had so much money in the bank. Well, when some other manager come, he wouldn't go on with that...One fella do, the other fella come and change it.[10]

The people on stations could expect constant changes where the practices and policies of one manager bore no resemblance to the next. Such changes were an integral part of the concretisation of the manager's authority and control of institutional life. Yet, paradoxically, in rejecting the work projects of the previous manager, each successive manager relativised and subverted his own authority. During the period of Welfare Board control, Bellbrook was said to have had twenty managers.

The understanding of the secondariness and subordination experienced by the Dhan-gadi was firmly grounded in the constant changes to the social world of the station over which they had no formal control. The uncertainty generated by such acts of authority, the demoralisation and debilitation of Aboriginal initiative and the relations of dependency also expose a fundamental contradiction in such policy. As one man said, 'They wouldn't let you tell em anything. If I did anything and went and told em, I'd be wrong. As we saying, "takin notice of a blackfella".' The maintenance of the manager's authority and control through the denial of any expertise by Aborigines effectively sustained Aboriginal dependence at an individual and collective level. As characterised earlier, such practices were seen not to 'let him go' but rather to 'put him down a step instead of letting him go up a step!'

What was equally paradoxical in a structural sense was that such discrediting was not internalised as individual incompetence, but was a collective rejection. Far from inculcating notions of possessive individualism such practices sustained a collective Aboriginal identity based on an experience of opposition. The intensification of institutionalisation, interpreted as racial oppression, provided the raw materials which generated a collective sense of identity in opposition to that of the dominating society. It is not that this collective identity was lacking in the era before the 1930s, but that it gained greater significance during the period of institutional control.

There is, clearly, a manifest contradiction here: one finds in operation a programme of state intervention which had the effect of stimulating a collective sense of identity among the Dhan-gadi, though the administration was designed explicitly to achieve the reverse and to individuate the Aborigine as a precondition for assimilation. Such hegemonic forms of control attempted to render Aboriginal identity problematic by transforming unconscious, unreflexive acts associated with cultural norms and behaviours into problematic, conscious and conspicuous ones.

But such hegemonic domination had complex consequences, reflected in the changes associated with the concept of 'shame' or the practice of 'shaming' pervasive among Aborigines. As one man expressed it, 'You know, blackfella terrible shamed fella. You know when you are doing things in the open and you don't want it that way.' The word 'shame' has a wide currency among Aborigines and is used in a number of contexts, usually in a joking way, to comment on some social *faux pas* or some flashness or cheekiness. The regulatory aspects of shaming have a distinctive cultural and structural basis associated with small non-stratified and essentially closed communities with homogeneous rules of conduct (Heller 1982, 216). As Heller (1982, 217–20) has pointed out, shame regulation is associated with acting and being different, based on transgressions of the codes, rules and rituals of conduct of a collective communal authority. It is paradoxical that the separation and social homogeneity engendered by institutionalisation provided the conditions for the perpetuation of such collective community mechanisms of social control. As we have seen earlier, it was the self-regulation by internal authority or conscience, within each individual, that institutional practices sought to achieve through the application of mechanisms of discipline. Whilst the form of such egalitarian community mechanisms of social control remained constant, the content of shaming practices took on more complex and ambivalent meanings associated with their specific social and political context.

In the context of institutional life, shaming took on the role of an oppositional practice which acted to subvert the appropriation of European ways of life among community members. As Fink (1955, 1956), working with Aborigines in New South Wales, described it, shaming operated as a form of internal social constraint on community members. It was very much a part of Aboriginal socialisation whereby an individual 'tries to conform and accept the group's standards as much as possible to avoid being laughed at' (Fink 1955, 37). The practice is, as she suggests, a levelling device which affects people who appear to outdo others or show off, and prevents people in the group from 'doing better' (Fink 1955, 37). What Fink misses, however, is that 'doing better' implied the appropriation of a more European lifestyle. On Bellbrook, for example, this levelling process affected a man who, with the manager's permission, attempted to build up a herd of cattle. It was opposed and subverted by other Aboriginal people on the station. Similarly, another woman complained to me that she and her husband had set up a kiosk on the station which, once again, was subverted by other people on the station. It was not so much that the couple who wanted a kiosk and the man who wanted a herd supported assimilation, but rather that they appeared to support it. Conformity to European standards implied a rejection of Aboriginal identity. In this respect, shaming directed hostility to those who attempted to approximate European values.

However, the notion of shame also embodied in its usage a seemingly contradictory aspect as it was also applied to 'old blackfella ways'. Shame, in this context, is the concrete form to which hegemony aspired—it was part of the process of cultural domination. As they were related to me, such instances usually involved conspicuous aspects of Aboriginality such as the public use of language ('speaking the Lingo'), or eating bush tucker or dancing in 'Koori way'. As one man pointed out to me, although the managers effectively put a stop to cooking on an open fire, many people were already 'too shamed' to cook that way. And again, another man had not allowed his family to eat bush tucker such as wallaby, possum, pademelon or echidna. In this case the necessity of bush tucker as a supplement to European sources of food was restricted to eating white meat—bush turkey, fowls and pigeon. Similar accounts were given of young people who felt embarrassed watching older people 'spinning the leg', as dancing in the Koori way was commonly termed. In this respect then, racism and paternalism had a distinctive hegemonic effect of undermining the Dhan-gadi sense of worth. Certain aspects of Aboriginal identity, the 'old blackfella ways', were rendered into reified objects, which existed outside of them and were set against them like some alien and hostile force.

The most distinctive aspect of this alienation of identity has been the suppression of Aboriginal language. Language is, after all, the most pervasive cultural marker (see Reay 1949, 90–91). The Dhan-gadi language, except for the frequent use of a restricted vocabulary, has been lost. The decline in the use of the language between the generations was explained to me in these terms:

> All them older fellas, the way they're talking, more joking, in the language, none of them talk dirty or anything, more enjoy it if they speak in the language. They can't talk English. They could talk English a bit, but I mean more their own. ...Old Granny C_____, she tell us what to do in the language. That's how we picked it up. You understand it, that's how we know what to do. Spoke to them [parents] only in the home. Outside they spoke English. They shy, don't like to talk it.

'Speaking in the language' had become a covert exercise for all generations. In this regard, the notion of shame is not so much a sanction against 'showing off' but the reverse: a sanction against attracting attention which may render one vulnerable to criticism or ridicule. These aspects of internal group control are also a manifestation of the wider mechanisms of European control and dominance whereby the capacity to remain inconspicuous becomes a virtue.

European contempt and prejudice were such that 'doin things in the open' was always likely to invite European hostility and public embarrassment through ridicule. This is the most significant aspect of shaming, that it is a public form of social coercion. In this it may be differentiated from the concept of guilt as a social process of coercion. The inculcation of guilt to achieve the correction of behaviour is an individual and internalised process seeking to attain self-regulation. As Heller (1980, 221, emphasis added) puts it, 'internal authority is *autonomy*. To obey nothing but our conscience means that we are the authors of our *actions* and of our character...' By contrast, shame and shaming inhibits and represses but is regulated by an external referent. Similarly, guilt is manifested by deviance from an internalised set of norms, while shame is constituted in a tension between a set of habitual acts and values, originally of worth, which have been rendered polluting. In this sense, shame and shaming, as a process, is a social feature of a pariah group and the modes of its external domination.

Conclusion

The imposition of a thoroughgoing form of bureaucratic custodianship on the Dhan-gadi from 1937 onwards was of considerable significance in limiting the possibilities of avoiding European control and determining the use of different political strategies. In effect, the new policy undermined the capacity of the Dhan-gadi to resist European domination by establishing a more effective practice of control, in which the monitoring and surveillance of station Aborigines was greatly increased. In this context, I have suggested that a culture of resistance emerged in some cases as a conjunction between earlier cultural practices (and their perpetuation) and an opposition to the prevailing hegemony, or simply in oppositional claims expressed by denial, distancing and evasion of European authority. Resistance, in this sense, was not a matter of conducting direct frontal assaults on the oppressors. Those Aborigines who threatened the institutional authority were removed from the station or, in cases of violence, were subject to gaoling. Instead, resistance involved strategies to subvert the oppressive aspects of domination.

To understand the historical specificity of such cultural forms, it is necessary to consider the logic of the processes that underpin the state's intervention. A consideration of power in its negative instance, as discriminatory and repressive, does not provide us with a sufficient or adequate understanding. Indeed, it only allows us to understand the use of the total institution for Aborigines as a repressive state apparatus. Instead, I have suggested that the total institution was a cultural and pedagogic apparatus which sought not simply to confine but to transform Aborigines. This was manifestly an act of power. Pedagogic intervention underpinned the logic of institutionalisation. In this respect, we have to consider the notions of power associated with the 'total institution' not simply as negative but also as a positive attempt at disciplining and reforming the patterns and beliefs of the social life of the Dhan-gadi to conform with the wider society.

Therefore, rather than attempting to understand the use of the total institution as an aberration, I have attempted to show the conditions which made it possible and the strategies in which it was situated. In this, I am suggesting that we cannot condemn it in advance as an aberration, distortion or deviation from liberalism because it is in fact grounded in those essential conceptions of knowledge and power so centrally located within liberal discourse. In this respect too, racism can be seen to be an endemic aspect of the wider society, inseparably intertwined with universal and moral imperatives found in liberalism.

Notes

1. My thanks to V Archibald, C Campbell, R Campbell, E Davis, J Kelly, J Knox, S Miranda and JD Quinlan, on whose oral testimony this paper is based. Thanks are also due to Mrs E Davis and Mr JD Quinlan for their patience and support during the period of my fieldwork and to Jeremy Beckett, Bruce Kapferer, Andrew Lattas and Gillian Cowlishaw for their constructive criticisms of the first draft of this chapter.

2. Foucault's characterisation of changes in prison institutions in terms of the techniques associated with the 'leper' and the 'plague victim', this analogy captures precisely the changes in government policy toward Aborigines in New South Wales (see Foucault 1982, 198).

3. Assimilation policy for Aborigines was adopted by all State governments and the Commonwealth government by the 1960s.

4. I should stress that the word 'positive' is not used in a moral or ethical sense here but in reference to an act of power. In contrast, Elkin (1944, 1973), Bell (1959, 1964) and Bleakley (1961), discussed later, do employ 'positive' in its moral and ethical sense when considering the 'positive policy of assimilation'.

5. It was not until some twenty years later, in 1960–61, that a majority decision of the Aborigines' Welfare Board repealed those sections of the Act which 'appeared to discriminate against Aborigines' (Aborigines' Welfare Board Report 1962, 5).

6. The term Koori is the word the Dhan-gadi apply to themselves and other Aborigines rather than the European word Aborigine. Goori or Koori has wide currency among Aborigines along the eastern coastal region of New South Wales.

7. The genesis of such cultural forms had been dealt with and developed largely through the work of a number of cultural Marxists. See Thompson 1977, 1982; Genovese 1974; Sider 1980; Willis 1978a, 1978b; Willis and Corrigan 1983; and Hall and Jefferson (eds) 1977.

8. Hausfeld (1963, 50), a former Welfare Board manager, discussed the problems he faced in an Aboriginal community on the north coast. He stated that he was deliberately given false and misleading information. As he stated, 'At Woodenbong a whole body of material was secret in the sense that it was kept from the outsider...the non-Aborigines'. This included traditional secret-sacred knowledge and more secular forms of information and knowledge.

9. This lack of expertise was compounded by the numerous tasks staff were expected to fulfil. Their duties included the facilitating of raised standards in housing, homemaking, hygiene and education. In addition, they were responsible for the general control and orderly behaviour of the inmates; the specific suppression of gambling and drinking; the allocation of employment for Aborigines on the station; the weekly, and on some stations twice weekly, issue of rations; and the furnishing of comprehensive weekly and monthly reports. In effect, stations were grossly understaffed and poorly equipped. In institutional terms, they were highly inefficient and incompetently run.

10. The Progress Association would appear to have been formed in the late 1950s and early 1960s.

References

Beckett, J.
1964 Aborigines, Alcohol and Assimilation. In M. Reay (ed), *Aborigines Now: New Perspectives in the Study of Aboriginal Communities*, Angus and Robertson, Sydney.

Bell, J.
1959 Official Policies Towards the Aborigines of New South Wales, *Mankind* 5(8), 345–55.
1964 Assimilation in New South Wales. In M. Reay (ed), *Aborigines Now: New Perspectives in the Study of Aboriginal Communities*, Angus and Robertson, Sydney.

Bleakley, J.W.
1961 *The Aborigines of Australia: Their History, Their Habits, Their Assimilation*, Jacaranda Press, Brisbane.

Calley, M.
1957 Race Relations on the North Coast of New South Wales, *Oceania* 15(4), 296–323.
1959 *Dawn: A Magazine for the Aboriginal People of New South Wales*, October, Government Printer, Sydney.

Duncan, A.T.
1969 A Survey of Aboriginal Education in New South Wales, MEd thesis, University of Sydney.

Elkin, A.P.
1944 *Citizenship for the Aborigines: A National Aboriginal Policy*, Australasian, Sydney.
1973 *The Australian Aborigines*, Angus and Robertson, Sydney.

Fink, R.
1955 Social Stratification—A Sequel to the Assimilation Process in a Part-Aboriginal Community, MA thesis, University of Sydney.
1956 The Caste-barrier—An Obstacle to the Assimilation of Part-Aborigines in North West New South Wales, *Oceania* 18(2), 100–10.

Foucault, M.
1982 *Discipline and Punish*, Penguin, Harmondsworth.

Genovese, E.
1974 *Roll, Jordan, Roll: The World the Slaves Made*, Pantheon, New York.

Goffman, E.
1961 *Asylums*, Penguin, Harmondsworth.

Hall, S. and T. Jefferson (eds)
1977 *Resistance Through Rituals*, Hutchinson, London.

Hausfeld, R.
1963 Dissembled Culture: An Essay on Method, *Mankind* 6(2), 47–51.

Heller, A.
1982 The Power of Shame, *Dialectical Anthropology* 6, 215–28.

Morris, B.
1985 The Dhan-gadi and the Protection of the State, *Canberra Anthropology* 8(1–2), 87–115.

New South Wales Aborigines' Welfare Board
1940-68 *Report for the Year Ended 30th June, 1940–68*, Government Printer, Sydney.

Public Service Board
1940 Aborigines Protection: Report and Recommendations of the Public Service Board of New South Wales. In *Joint Volumes of Papers Presented to the Legislative Council and Legislative Assembly (1938, 39, 40)*, Vol 7, Government Printer, Sydney.

Reay, M.
1945 A Half-caste Aboriginal Community in North-Western New South Wales, *Oceania* 15(4), 296–323.
1949 Native Thought in Rural New South Wales, *Oceania* 20(2), 89–118.

Rowley, C.D.
1973 *Outcasts in White Australia* Penguin, Harmondsworth.

Select Committee on Administration of Aborigines' Protection Board
1937–38 Proceedings. In *Joint Volumes of Papers Presented to the Legislative Council and Legislative Assembly (1938-39-40)*, Vol 7, Government Printer, Sydney.

Sider, G.
1980 The Ties that Bind, *Social History* 5(1), 1–39.

Thompson, E.P.
1977 Folklore, Anthropology and Social History, *Indian Historical Review* 3(2), 247–66.
1982 *The Making of the English Working Class*, Penguin, Harmondsworth.

Willis, P.
1978a *Learning to Labour*, Saxon House, Farnborough.
1978b *Profane Culture*, Routledge and Kegan Paul, London.

Willis, P. and P. Corrigan
1983 Orders of Experience: Working Class Cultural Forms, *Social Text* 7, 8–103.

4. Julie D Carter — 'Am I too black to go with you?'

The purpose of this chapter is to discuss how Aboriginal people deal with the negative cultural labels given to them by wider society.[1] Observation in Aboriginal communities shows that derogatory phrases (for example, 'black bastard' or 'lazy blackfella') are frequently found in conversations between children and adults, and indeed it would appear that negative ascriptions are embraced rather than shunned.

Eckermann (1977, 300) identifies the incorporation of derogatory racial remarks as one of the most typical aspects of Aboriginal socialisation: 'From earliest toddlerhood, children are made aware of terms like "black boong", and "black-fellow". The terms *black, coloured* and *dirty* are emphasized again and again'. She goes on to argue that the purpose of this process is to prepare children for the taunting and ridicule likely in their later social experience with Europeans. It also serves as a group identification for the child (Eckermann 1977, 300):

> Teasing by adults and among siblings ensures that a child never forgets that he or she is an Aboriginal; thus colour consciousness is emphasized more as he grows older and social contact makes him aware that he is different from the other children in his group.

Expanding on the work of Eckermann (1977), as well as others who have discussed the incorporation of stigma in the development of Aboriginal identity, I argue that metaphors of stigma are both inverted and transformed to provide an expressive mode of affirming group and individual Aboriginal identity. Stigmatised identity involves the use of derogatory labels by Aborigines as well as Europeans, and reflects the ambivalence of the Aboriginal individual's relationship with the wider society and the oscillation between withdrawal and incorporation.

There is general cynicism within the Australian public about the continuity of cultural traditions among southern Aborigines. As Aboriginal society disintegrated in the nineteenth and twentieth centuries, governments legislated to provide displaced Aborigines with a niche by granting them protection through isolation, and later, assimilated status as members of the wider community. After 200 years of disintegration and apparent assimilation, while scholars have debated whether Aboriginal communities articulate with Australian society through commonalities of class or culture, the general public has continued to see them as an outcast group lacking any common ground with either impoverished whites or Aborigines in remote Australia. But how do Aborigines see themselves? And how do they accommodate the marginalised social identity which wider society accords them?

These questions represent one of the interests which took me to a town on the southern coast of New South Wales which I shall call Bushtown and which encouraged me to articulate the signifiers of Aboriginality as they operated in that particular community. Bushtown seemed very suitable for this kind of enquiry because the town was very publicly Aboriginal. Indeed despite the short period of Aboriginal residency—twenty years—Bushtown is a cultural enclave in the midst of Australian society. The marked Aboriginal profile of the town, together with the high proportion of Aboriginal residents, has provided an ideal environment for raising children to understand themselves to be Aborigines. How this happens has a good deal to do with the character of Bushtown, and the following description sketches the particular features of it as a rural Aboriginal town.

Bushtown

Bushtown consists of about fifty Europeans and 150 Aboriginal people. The latter divide genealogically into five major family groups, similar to the Nyungar 'all one family' groups described by Birdsall (see Chapter 8), linked by intermarriage across several generations. These families share historical links (of birth and residence) with the New South Wales south coast. Before settling in the present location their members made a living by fishing along the coast, in seasonal work such as bean and pea picking, in sawmilling, or as domestics and farm labourers in the district. Many of the older generation have worked beyond the district in areas of New South Wales and Victoria known for regular seasonal employment. Emotionally, however, home has remained the coastal strip of southern New South Wales.

Bushtown is now a permanent settlement despite the disappearance of earlier sources of seasonal employment in the district. The local bean and pea crops have been uprooted, and sawmilling is now a less prosperous industry than before, as well as being considered dangerous (some men have lost fingers using the mill machines). Moreover, the payment of unemployment benefits has freed people from constant travel in search of seasonal work.

Few people of working age in the town are employed; rather, the majority draw social security payments and pensions. Financial resources are distributed and reallocated through sharing (as an obligation of kinship), and gambling at cards, on the horses, and in government lotteries such as Tattslotto or at the TAB. A further source of financial assistance specific to Bushtown's Aborigines is pawning. A non-Aborigine with a long history of co-residence with a number of the families in Bushtown operates an informal pawnshop. This individual is the only non-Aborigine in Bushtown who has extensive personal—and business—interaction with the Aborigines. With an eye for capitalising on opportunities, he will drive individuals to nearby towns at the cost of a few dollars. He also has the only available telephone. His telephone number is given for the purpose of enquiries, and to relatives outside the community as the contact for residents. As a pawnbroker he keeps strict rules for loan repayments, consequently his clients see his service as a last resort, seeking his help only after asking loans of kin or attempting to win money at cards. Several people have lost their watches, cassette recorders and wall clocks to him. Despite his strict business rules his pawn service offers Bushtown people a chance for solvency and is, in an unorthodox sense, a community resource. These strategies for sharing, gambling and pawning enable Bushtown people to operate with some economic flexibility despite severely limited resources.

When the first Aboriginal inhabitants moved to the town in the mid 1960s they occupied abandoned goldminers' and forestry workers' cottages which, because they lacked electricity, sewerage and reticulated water, were cheap. By the mid 1970s there were sufficient Aboriginal people to form an incorporated housing company and to receive funding from the Federal government to build modern, serviced homes as replacements for the nineteenth century shacks. Ten brick veneer homes were completed between 1976 and 1978, and the Bushtown Housing Company was for some time a model for other Aboriginal communities trying similar projects.

The original residential pattern of Aboriginal households in Bushtown was largely *ad hoc*, but the new homes grouped the majority of the families in a specific area separating the Aborigines from the Europeans. The Europeans, moreover, own and/or manage the few businesses in the town, and Aboriginal participation, through employment, is minimal. Only a few of the Europeans who use the town for shopping, collecting mail and so on, actually live there. Most live on farmlets a few kilometres out of the town. The European residents are mostly retired, aged people who keep to themselves and show little interest or involvement with the majority of the Aboriginal townsfolk. The Aboriginal inhabitants provide the bulk of the daily trade with the town's shops, especially the garage and the general store which is also the post office. The flower shop and pottery cater mainly to passing tourists. In the local primary school Aboriginal children are in the majority and the preschool is exclusively an Aboriginal concern.

The Aboriginal residents live daily lives which have more to do with their own community than with the European concerns of the town. There is a dimension to people's lives as Aborigines which is closed to wider Australia and which also contrasts with it. There are a number of points to be made about this boundedness. First, kinship is the reference point of all significant relationships. This is the result of close genealogical ties and intermarriage between the five major families, and is consolidated in daily life by the use of kin terms to address one another. Such terms preclude significant interpersonal involvement with Europeans. Second, social interaction, rules of knowledge and information exchange, conform with the ethnography of the patterns of Aboriginal English in southeast Queensland (Eades 1982). Eades emphasises that among Aborigines, importance is laid on the social context of information exchange. Knowledge is considered a public resource, it is contextual and likely to be elaborated differentially according to who is present and their social relations in the community.

There are also sufficient idiosyncratic speech forms and vocabulary to describe Bushtown Aboriginal English as a code, after Bernstein (1970). Bernstein's notion of language as code refers to the particular use of language to encode articulations which have full meaning only to a specific group. Bernstein analysed this in association with class, concluding that the intention of the code is to produce a system of understanding and communication held in common and capable of demarcating one group from another through in-group feelings and cohesion. People of the town acknowledge the use of language as code when they refer to 'gin talk' or 'blackfella talk', and recognise that conversation between themselves and Europeans proceeds on different patterns. For example, Aborigines refrain from using expletives in the company of Europeans in the general belief that Europeans do not swear and certainly don't approve of it.

A third notable characteristic of Aboriginal social life is the self-conscious identification with notions of sociality and behaviour ascribed to Aboriginality, a world view with definable social values, attitudes and cognitive orientations. This world view is sufficiently shared for adults to impress it upon their children, in the process of educating them for participation in Bushtown's social world. One resident expressed her view of the content of Aboriginality in this way: 'You can always tell a Koori by the way they walk, talk and dress. Not by skin colour.'[2]

Bushtown people also demarcate themselves from the wider society by emphasising the contrast between their social world and the one inhabited by Europeans. But despite such in-group feelings and their marginalisation within the town's economy, they are nevertheless incorporated in Australian society in specific ways. The most obvious point of articulation with the wider society is receipt of government pensions and endowments, which makes Aborigines structurally analogous to other subgroups. The intervention of the dominant society in the lives of Aborigines is also evident in education and the delivery of medical services. The specific nature of the interaction between the closed Aboriginal community and Australian society places Bushtown's inhabitants in a relationship of dependency with the state. Incorporation as dependants of the state has repercussions on Aboriginal social identity, but it is also apparent that withdrawal or separate development from the dominant society has contributed to an ambivalent image. Indeed, the ambivalence is observable through analysis of the speech idioms used in identity development and in intra-community interaction. Both aspects of identity development—of the individual and of the Aboriginal group—are encapsulated in idiomatic expressions described below.

Socialisation of Bushtown's children

There are reasons to suggest that identity development in a closed, tightly-knit, kin-based community presents adolescents—on the verge of asserting a new personal identity—with difficulties about their self-image during prolonged encounters with non-Aborigines. At Bushtown, this experience coincides with the beginning of secondary education, when children leave their primary school to attend high school in a nearby town. The most obvious change for them is withdrawal from the matrix in which they had a publicly acknowledged and secure social identity. With the change to high school this identity is seriously questioned for the first time; no longer are they majority members of the school, but instead they are often divided as a group to form a minority in a predominantly non-Aboriginal school population. No doubt many rural European children making the transition from one-teacher schools to high schools of several hundred students suffer from the effects of this change also, but unlike European children, Aboriginal children often meet for the first time the ambivalent attitude toward Aborigines common in Australian society. Their social identity is challenged and may be undermined. But this frequently painful experience parallels the fundamental Aboriginal experience of separation and incorporation in the wider society. Thus the particular process of identity formation during socialisation prepares individuals for such experiences by including widely used terms about the negative qualities of being Aboriginal. Such aspects are, of course, based on stereotypes about Aborigines.

A child growing up in Bushtown is hardly aware of the closed nature of the community, at least until the beginning of adolescence and the start of secondary school. Most children have a secure childhood under the care of kin, whether parents or maternal grandparents. While it is not uncommon for parents to seek work or recreation outside the town, children generally have continuous residence among their kinsfolk. A child born to Bushtown parents immediately acquires an extensive set of relatives, the closest contact being with maternal kin.

It is not unusual to inherit three generations of kin, nor is it unusual for a child's daily interaction to be almost exclusively with Aboriginal relatives. A child I knew well had both his grandmother and great-grandmother living in the community. As he lived next door, he would often call early in the morning to wake Nan (his maternal great-grandmother) and breakfast there. Moreover, he sometimes slept at her house—if he wasn't staying the night at the home of his father's sister. The playmates of this boy (apart from his siblings) were his cousins—the children of his father's brothers and sisters. Indeed, since the entire community is genealogically inter-related, the boy's social world was wholly kin-based. The importance of kin to children is reinforced by instructing them from time to time in the correct use of kin terms for specific relatives. Few non-Aborigines intrude upon the security of this kin-centred Aboriginal world. Europeans are only likely to be met at the local general store, on visits to the doctor and hospital, and at school. However, in all cases these people are of peripheral interest to the child and since they are not kinsfolk, have no particular social status.

Bushtown children learn their identity from the significant others of their closest associations—their Aboriginal families and relatives. Their awareness of self is intimately connected with a growing awareness of their Aboriginality. The local vernacular for non-Aborigine or white person (Gubba) is often used when explaining to children about community visits from Europeans, whether on council, religious or health business. Children certainly understand the difference between themselves and a Gubba. I observed one little boy abruptly leave the television programme he was watching, rush into the kitchen and call to his grandmother, 'Come and look what the Gubba's doing, Nan!'

Being different from Gubbas is often made explicit in self-conscious stories told by adults about the relative virtues of Aborigines and non-Aborigines. These anecdotes are often about prowess: 'We have more guts than Gubbas.' Furthermore, autobiographical accounts of what life as an Aboriginal child was like fifty to sixty years ago are told to impress children with their present wealth of opportunities, while also indicating the different treatment which was given to European and Aboriginal children.

Differences in social identity are further elaborated by comparing Aboriginal and European personhood. These differences are mainly conveyed as jokes about 'blackfellas'. For instance, on one occasion an adult asked a relative for a substantial loan of money, only to be greeted by comments such as, 'Swallowing money—isn't that typical of a blackfella?' Similarly, jokes about Aboriginal habits merge with jokes about the ways of Bushtown Aborigines. For example, the tendency to set off at a moment's notice on journeys to relatives up and down the coast was characterised as 'the way a blackfella travels'.

Children beginning secondary school generally have a firm sense of identity as Aborigines. Growing up among relatives, children understand not only that social relations are a concomitant of kinship, but that acceptable social behaviour is judged by the standards of appropriate kin behaviour. At the same time, they have also had extensive preparation for social interactions with Europeans. The model which parents use may or may not be derived from personal experience. In any case, expectations about encounters with non-Aborigines are derived mainly from the perception that Aborigines are disliked by non-Aborigines; parents anticipate that interactions in society will be based on stereotypes about themselves.

Part of the protective self that a child develops for dealing with people in the wider society consists of a cheeky assertiveness. Adults tease children to challenge authority figures, principally their parents and, in play-dramas, the police. Toddlers, to amuse adults, are encouraged to poke a finger under the noses of their parents and chant 'La! la! la!' This kind of assertive independence brings a special meaning to jokes about being a 'cheeky black kid', while also refuting the idea that the children might be 'anyone's black slaves'. Such self-confidence is needed, moreover, since the experience of participation in the wider society—secondary education initially— challenges the basic assumptions of early socialisation, specifically by questioning how sociality is conducted and what social value is attached to Aboriginal identity.

Some of the differences experienced by Bushtown children in secondary school were discussed earlier: education outside a known social environment; a minority position in the school population; and separation from playmates who are kin. In addition, there are no permanent figures in their daily timetable, since various subject teachers replace the sole class teacher of the primary school. Moreover, the basis of the child–adult relationship is the authority invested in the teacher's role, rather than kinship. These experiences are not all exclusive to Aboriginal children, but what is particular in their experience of these changes is that being Aboriginal is negatively valued. Parents try to account for the experience during the process of identity development by incorporating negative non-Aboriginal images of Aborigines and Aboriginal behaviour.

Adolescents are emotionally and cognitively involved with the transformation from childhood to adult status. The transition involves a contrast between the contexts of identity formation as a child and the identity options for the adolescent and adult. Adolescents realise that attitudes within the Aboriginal community do not reflect the attitudes of wider Australia about Aboriginal people, which are expressed in the taunts of non-Aborigines about the stereotypical habits of Aborigines. The adolescents come to realise that there is little shared understanding of the social world between themselves and their non-Aboriginal classmates and teachers. Yet children do receive some preparation for this realisation. The teasing of Bushtown children from early childhood, by calling them 'blackfellas', 'black bastards' and so on, has prepared them for the kind of derogatory remarks they are likely to encounter outside.

Ritualisation of stigma

Idioms of stigma in Bushtown thus inure children, through foreknowledge, to hurtful racial interaction, and extend the original capacity of the idiom so that it connotes more than negative stereotypical notions. But there are other explanations for the incorporation by Aborigines of negative and derogatory labels in their self-images. Read (1980) borrows Jean Genet's term 'rituals of stigmatisation' to analyse the ways in which homosexuals subvert the wider society's stereotypes of gender and normality. Genet (see Read 1980, 18) defines rituals of stigmatisation as:

> formally patterned responses to and expressions of *outcast status* that use and distort the shibboleths of *les justes* [wider society] to intensify the experience of stigmatization and of opposition to those who are responsible for it.

Here he emphasises the role of rituals of stigmatisation as strategies for managing a stigmatised social identity. Goffman (1979) has also described in detail, strategies adopted to manage different categories of 'spoiled identity'.

In his ethnography of homosexuals in a tavern in San Francisco, Read (1980) suggests that certain of their behavioural styles are specifically aimed at subverting cultural myths about minority groups held by the dominant society. These cultural myths are representations of what certain minority groups are assumed to be (limp-wristed, softly spoken, 'feminine' men), rather than what they are. This reading of certain homosexual behavioural styles as ritualised stigma is relevant to the awareness within Bushtown that interactions with Australian society are more likely to be based on cultural myths about what Aborigines are, than on the assessment of individual cases. As Read also points out, Genet's work illustrates that the members of such groups, as a stigmatised minority, invert the stigma, making it a virtue. Doing so recognises, in fact, 'The absurdity of conventional ascriptions and emphasizes existential understandings of living in an absurd world' (Read 1980, 17).

Gilbert (1977, 1) describes the content of stigma inversion for Aborigines. He identifies the product of the process of sanctioning stigma, and making a virtue of it, as a romanticised myth of Aboriginality, held as 'true' by Aboriginal people:

> Aborigines share freely; they have a strong feeling of community. They don't care about money and lack the materialism of white society. They care more deeply for their children than do white parents and so on.

His interviews with a variety of Aborigines across Australia and his experience of the diversity of their living conditions, in his opinion, belie the reality of this myth. But the inverted cultural myth—if we accept Gilbert's evidence that it is only an ideal—serves the same purpose as the rituals of stigmatisation. The behavioural reactions to outcast status can turn a stereotype into a virtue; for example, crowded housing can be interpreted as a concern for others and unconcern for material conditions.

The ritualised teasing and shaming of Bushtown Aboriginal children during socialisation can be seen as a mechanism for the management of stigma, and begins a process of inuring people to unpleasant encounters with Europeans. But it is also a process of strengthening the corporate identity of Aboriginal people. The expression 'I don't like cheeky black kids' is one example of this dual emphasis. The expression implies first that independence in black children will be considered as cheeky, and second that all black children are likely to be cheeky according to European stereotypes.

Idioms in Bushtown ritualise stigma by providing the expressive and symbolic means to affirm ethnicity. The original meaning of each expression is invested with metameanings. Idioms, I suggest, are manipulated as strategies to manage stigma, and to carry meanings about being Aboriginal at a number of levels. Expressions of 'spoiled identity' (Goffman 1979) can belong to any one of the following categories of expression:

1. a reference to ethnic identity;

2. an idiom of cultural style and sociality;
3. an insight about the socio-economic marginality of Aborigines as a group; and
4. an indication of the content of Aboriginality as constructed from the wider society's stereotypes of Aborigines.

Some examples of each will show what is meant.

References to ethnic identity

Idioms sometimes combine parts of the body with colour—in this case black—where colour is used as a signifier of group identity, as in 'Stop it, or I'll smack ya black bum'. A similar correspondence is evident in the expression 'I will/won't kiss his black arse!' There are other examples. On the occasion of a group of people preparing to go shopping in a nearby town, some uninvited passengers tried their luck for seats by asking, 'Am I too black to go with you?' The metaphorical image of 'too black' is both a veiled damnation (a sign of outcast status) and defiance (assertion of group cohesion). I mean by this that it is both an appeal and a reminder of membership in the same pariah group. To invoke it when making requests is to appeal to others, as members of the outcast group vis-a-vis the wider society, and through claims to the bonds of in-group solidarity between individual members. Moreover, when speaking of themselves collectively, Bushtown residents use the term 'dark people' whose meaning is interchangeable with Koori. The inverse of the latter, is Gubba (white/non-Aborigine).

Idioms of cultural style

An example of this type of idiom has been mentioned already: the readiness to travel at short notice with minimal luggage is considered 'blackfella way'. In another case, adopting certain behaviours, such as drinking and swearing with people, is often considered as 'mixing it with them', with the implication that these behaviours are particularly characteristic of Aborigines.

Insights about socio-economic marginality

Idioms in this category articulate Aboriginal recognition of their structural position in Australian society. Requests for a member of the household to help with particular chores may be deflected with the reply, 'I'm not your black slave'. The same notion is expressed when people speculate on the spending of a windfall from the lottery or horseracing: 'I'll buy a house, a car, video and a black maid'. In a different context the same perception conveys ideas about wider social attitudes to Aboriginal households: during a game of cards, one of the players, an Aboriginal woman married to a European and living outside the community, jokingly remarked to her neighbour, 'We don't need to say "excuse me" here—it's only a black household'.

Indications of Aboriginality through stereotype

Sometimes these stereotypes incorporate references to the pre-contact Aboriginal lifestyle. By referring to pre-contact lifestyles in such ways, Aborigines draw attention to the historical differentiation of their culture. When a debate over housing allocation became tense, the threat to 'Go bush and live in a *mia-mia* and eat goanna like a real blackfella' brought laughter and a more relaxed exchange.

Tricking

The analyses of both Genet and Goffman indicate that the intensification of the experience of stigmatised identity and the inversion of meanings associated with idioms of reproach, expose the absurdity and rationalisation of difference. The most obvious exposure of this kind occurs when Aborigines 'trick' non-Aborigines in some way. They do so with an implicit assessment that they are sharper and more quick-witted than non-Aborigines. Tricking is a self-fulfilling confirmation of this. Tricks can be minor and involve manipulation of information to improve the chances of renting a house, receiving assistance, having someone 'shout' drinks out of turn, and so on. Tricking reverses the picture Aborigines understand non-Aborigines to have of them—a picture of them as uneducated, not very bright and easily taken in. Tricking is in fact a joke against non-Aborigines; a process of ridiculing the stereotypes non-Aborigines have about Aborigines by making fools of non-Aborigines. It is particularly clever because the process is hidden from the victims who often fail to realise it is they who are uneducated, and easily manipulated.

Tricking isn't only of interest as an illustration of the way differences are rationalised and made ridiculous in cultural myths. Examples from Bushtown also suggest that the process of inverting stigma has helped to develop a concept of Aboriginal identity and its social attributes which is indeed superior to the identity that whites have of themselves.

Conclusion

Both Read's (1980) ethnography of homosexual life and my study of Bushtown show that the expression of stigma is one way of invoking category distinctions between in-group and out-group, Bushtown and the wider society, Aboriginal and non-Aboriginal. When endowed with in-group meaning, stigma is transformed, even transcended. Hence Aborigines who joke about being 'lazy black bastards' among themselves are fully aware that the same expression used by non-Aborigines has a different meaning. But as it is used within the Aboriginal community there are no necessarily negative connotations. I suggest that subverting the 'naturalness' of the claims within Aboriginal stereotypes, by incorporating them in speech idioms and in the process of identity formation, is one of the ways in which Aboriginal people live their social lives with some self-respect, come to terms with the ambiguity of their identity as a minority group, and assume some control over the formation of their own group identity.

Notes

1. This chapter is based on seven months during 1982–83 when I lived in a coastal New South Wales Aboriginal community. I thank the Australian Institute of Aboriginal Studies for a grant to cover the expenses of field research. Several people contributed with helpful criticisms and suggestions on drafts of the paper. I wish to thank particularly Nic Peterson, John Morton, Jerry Schwab and Ray Wood.

2. In part the content of this view, as Tugby (1973) suggests, may be the contrast Aborigines observe between themselves and others, that is, non-Aborigines. Leaving this issue aside, I argue a case here on the basis of people's perceived experience of being Aboriginal in Bushtown.

References

Bernstein, B.
1970 Social Class, Language and Socialization. In P.P. Giglioli (ed), *Language and Social Context*, Penguin, Harmondsworth.

Eades, D.
1982 'You Gotta Know How to Talk...' Information Seeking in South-East Queensland Aboriginal Society, *Australian Journal of Linguistics* 2(1), 61–82.

Eckermann, A.
1977 Group Organization and Identity Within an Urban Aboriginal Community. In R.M. Berndt (ed), *Aborigines and Change*, Australian Institute of Aboriginal Studies, Canberra.

Gilbert, K.
1977 *Living Black: Blacks Talk to Kevin Gilbert*, Penguin, Melbourne.

Goffman, E.
1979 *Stigma*, Pelican, London.

Read, K.
1980 *Other Voices: The Style of a Male Homosexual Tavern*, Chandler and Sharp, California.

Tugby, D.
1973 Introduction: The Aboriginal Looking Glass. In D. Tugby (ed), *Aboriginal Identity in Contemporary Australian Society*, Jacaranda Press, Brisbane.

5. Jerry Schwab — Ambiguity, style and kinship in Adelaide Aboriginal identity

In traditional Aboriginal societies identity was rarely ambiguous. Each individual's identity was constituted in the social realm through kinship ties and passage through a variety of distinct roles and statuses, in the spiritual realm through fundamental responsibilities and direct linkages to the Dreaming, and even geographically in binding associations with particular places and regions. When Europeans began to arrive, the traditional social systems, which so clearly established the identities of Aborigines, were elastic enough to account for (and often include) these new arrivals, thus overcoming the ambiguity—at least temporarily—of the Europeans' positions in the Aboriginal social order.

As the numbers of Europeans increased and as disease and violence, especially in the southeast of the continent, decimated the Aboriginal population, many Aboriginal societies began to fracture under the strain. Some were forced and others were lured from their traditional lifestyles. Many Aboriginal people were subjected to mission and government policies which variously attempted to convert, destroy, displace, isolate and eventually assimilate them.

While pockets of traditionally-oriented Aboriginal communities have managed to survive, though certainly not unscathed, in the less accessible centre and north of the continent, the majority of Aboriginal people today reside in 'settled' Australia, descendants of the people who experienced the most severe cultural disruption. While some might consider it remarkable that Aborigines survive at all in 'settled' Australia, what is truly remarkable is that among these people there remains a culture which is still distinctly Aboriginal. This is not to say that the content of this Aboriginal culture is identical in every respect with traditional Aboriginal culture, nor that its expression by Aborigines themselves is always achieved simply and effortlessly. While incorporating continent-wide features as distinct, local configurations, both of which spring from and continue to be related to traditional patterns, Aboriginal culture in 'settled' Australia exists and is manifest in sometimes subtle and localised symbolic forms. It is not the basic Aboriginality of these varied localised forms which is problematic for Aboriginal people; that is taken for granted by most. However, the articulation of the various localised systems of shared and patterned meanings is sometimes difficult to express. Nonetheless, the persistence of Aboriginal culture is assumed and recognised by most Aboriginal people. For example, many recent autobiographies and family histories published by Aborigines who have grown up in 'settled' Australia, of which James Miller's *Koorie: A Will to Win* (1985) is one of the most recent, have nothing to do with the invention of a new culture nor the recovery and resurrection of a culture which was lost and is now found. Rather they are affirmations of, and attempts to articulate, the existence and continuity of distinctive Aboriginal cultures in places where they had long been said (by some anthropologists, among others) to be extinct. To most anthropologists working in Australia today, the claims by some that the majority of Aborigines have rediscovered their Aboriginal heritage en masse at a time when it is politically or economically advantageous to do so, seem absurd. The logic of such assertions is difficult to follow given that Aborigines remain on the bottom rung of the national economic ladder.

Identity among Aborigines in 'settled' Australia is complex and multilayered. While it rings true on one level, the conception that all Aboriginal people are one is considered far too simplistic a notion by most Aboriginal people. Within and between communities, Aborigines have always recognised both cultural unity and diversity. Social scientists have now begun to pay attention to this unity in the consideration of ideological phenomena such as Aboriginal 'core values' (Crick 1981) and Aboriginal 'commonality' (Sansom 1982) which, it is said, appear in Aboriginal communities throughout the country. These cultural features come as no surprise to the people living in these communities—they are assumed. However, where there is a recognition by Aborigines of pan-Aboriginal components of identity, there is also a recognition that diversity exists, a diversity which in certain circumstances introduces an element of ambiguity.

The focus of this chapter is on the nature of Aboriginal identity in Adelaide, South Australia, with attention to the ways in which Aborigines in this setting conceive, portray, express, and interpret that identity. As will be shown, identity among most Aborigines in Adelaide is fundamentally a matter of kinship. At the same time, the influx of Aboriginal people from interstate and distant country areas has created a situation where kinship often cannot provide a ready map of identity. The actual and potential ambiguities of this situation will be explored, as will the cultural mechanisms by which such ambiguities are sometimes, but not always, resolved. The more general questions of how Aborigines in Adelaide identify themselves as Aborigines, and by what means individuals are identified by the community, will also be considered. As an avenue for exploring these questions, the chapter will focus on a small number of Aboriginal teenagers who were residents in an Aboriginal boys' hostel in Adelaide during the early 1980s. While the boys' personal histories and individual backgrounds are not meant to appear typical of all Aboriginal people in Adelaide, their attempts to portray and articulate their own and each other's identities as Aborigines do highlight some of the salient features of the process whereby Aboriginal identity is defined, not just for them but for other Aborigines in Adelaide as well.

Adelaide, Aborigines and identity: an overview[1]

According to the 1981 census, the Adelaide metropolitan region has a total population of approximately 882,520 including an Aboriginal and Torres Strait Islander population of approximately 3,217.[2] Though Aborigines came and continue to come to Adelaide from a number of locations and for a wide variety of reasons, the majority of Aborigines in Adelaide today trace their roots to one of a small number of former reserves and mission stations within a few hundred kilometres of the city. Among these reserves, Point Pearce on the Yorke Peninsula and Point McLeay on the lower Murray River have contributed the greatest numbers of Aboriginal people to the Adelaide Aboriginal community.[3]

Identity among most Aborigines in Adelaide is clear and explicit because it is based in large part, as it was in the past, on a local ground of kinship. Sense of self, as well as relation to and identification with other Aborigines in Adelaide, is at root a result of growing up among Aboriginal kin. While not all local Adelaide families are related, nor immune to long standing feuds and factionalism, they are familiar with one another. They share a common history, a history conceived, most importantly, as one of subjugation and discrimination at the hands of Europeans. There remains, however, a great sense of strength and pride in their survival despite what they commonly perceive to be the continuation of that subjugation and discrimination. It is the common emphasis on the importance of kinship, coupled with a shared sense of history, which is at the base of identity for most Aborigines in Adelaide, as the following case study illustrates.

Case 1

A local Aboriginal organisation in Adelaide had organised a week-long series of speakers, music, films, and lunches for the older members of the community, and each morning a bus arrived carrying thirty or so people who had been picked up at home and brought to the hall where they joined others who had arrived independently. The series became quite a social event and attracted dozens of younger people as well. As most of the people were 'locals', there was often more attention paid to visiting and catching up on news than to the official programme. Indeed, to most of the older people, that was the official programme.

On the first morning I was visiting with an elderly Aboriginal couple, Max and Mary Hill, whom I had not seen for several weeks. As we sat and talked during the morning literally dozens of people came to hug, kiss, and chat with Max and Mary. Most, but not all, were members of families which had originally come from a nearby reserve, Point Pearce, at which Max and Mary had grown up, but which they had left thirty years before. (Today, a significant number of Adelaide Aborigines whose families had come from there, Max and Mary included, continue to refer to Point Pearce as home, even though few were born there and not many have actually lived there.) The majority of younger people addressed Max and Mary as 'Uncle', 'Aunty', 'Nana' or 'Papa'. Most of these were genealogically related to Max and Mary in some way, but the few who were not addressed them as kin nonetheless. Occasionally, however, a person arrived at Max and Mary's table who was not immediately recognised by them.

In one case, a middle-aged woman came up to Max, kissed him on the cheek and said, 'G'day Uncle, how ya goin luv?'[4] Max looked carefully at her face and with a small smile which seemed to reflect puzzlement and only partial recognition, said, 'Are you one of the Atkins girls?' 'That's right Uncle, I'm Dora,' she replied, obviously happy Max was on the right track. 'Timmy's girl?' he asked, still not sure. Dora nodded and smiled. Max grinned and said, 'That's right. Dora! You're the middle one.'

Max turned to me, laughed, and with his memory sparked and an opportunity for one of his famous stories at hand, said, 'Let me tell you about these Atkins girls!'

The pervasiveness and importance of kinship for most Adelaide Aborigines is in constant evidence and serves as the base for individual and social identity. Kin terms are in almost continual use both as they reflect actual relationships and as indicators of affiliation and affection where no traceable kin relationship exists. For example, in the case mentioned above, Dora was not actually Max and Mary's niece. Dora was born on Point Pearce Reserve, and her parents, before their deaths many years ago, were well known to Max and Mary. Dora's use of the term 'uncle' when addressing Max reflects an extension of kinship to include persons whom Europeans in similar relationships might not consider kin. Certainly Europeans can and do make such fictive extensions, but less frequently than do Aborigines in Adelaide where such extensions serve to anchor both individual identity and the Aboriginal community's identity.

The social world, for most Adelaide Aborigines, revolves around the extended family, a feature of life which is invariably mentioned by them as a difference between Aborigines and non-Aborigines. Adelaide Aborigines may identify themselves as Aboriginal to Europeans, but among other Aborigines one's identity is distinctly familiar and social—a person is, for example, 'one of the Smith girls' or 'one of those Millers'.

For certain individuals, identity in Adelaide is not always so clearly and explicitly a matter of kinship. While the majority of Aborigines are still members of families which have lived in the city for many years and before that on nearby reserves, sometimes for generations, there are a significant number of Aborigines who are relative newcomers. Where the majority of new arrivals were once from one of the nearby reserves, increasing numbers have come to Adelaide from outside the State—often only temporarily at first—for education, medical treatment, or employment, and have chosen to stay. Some come from traditionally-oriented communities to perform and teach art, song, and dance, or to attend national political meetings, while many visit Adelaide merely for recreation. This influx of people with diverse non-local backgrounds has resulted in increasing ambiguity and has complicated the nature of Aboriginal identity in Adelaide.

The bases of contemporary identity

The importance of kinship as the primary basis of Aboriginal identity in Adelaide cannot be over-emphasised. Within the community, and from the perspective of a member of one of the established families who identify themselves as 'from' one of the major reserves, an individual's identity is perceived in terms of five conceptual categories:[5] kin; persons from home; known persons; recognised persons; and unknown persons (see Figure 5.1). According to this model each individual is classified as a member of one, and only one, of these categories.

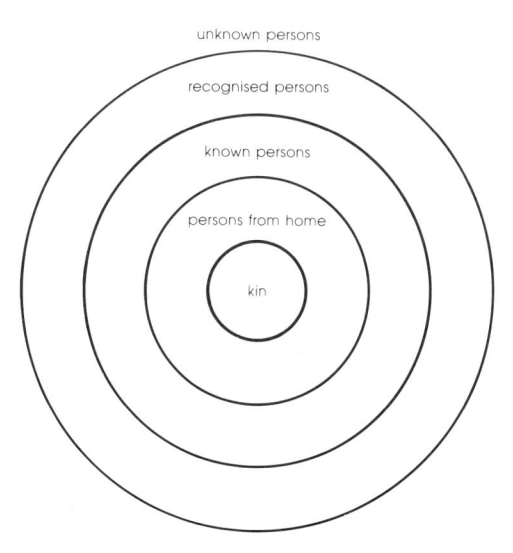

Figure 5.1 Conceptual categories in the Aboriginal recognition of Aboriginal identity in Adelaide.

The category 'kin' includes the members of one's family, but most importantly consanguineous kin. The category 'persons from home' refers to the members of other kin groups which trace themselves back to the same geographic place of origin, usually a particular mission or reserve, often incorporating a tribal referent.[6] It is generally felt that members of this category share a special bond which is not only historical but affective and spiritual as well. The boundary between 'kin' and 'persons from home' is somewhat flexible as can be seen in the extension of fictive kinship, most often to senior members of the community who come from the same reserve. The category 'known persons', includes members of kin groups from one of the other major local reserves or missions. 'Known' refers here to membership in an identifiable local family, and does not necessarily imply that the individual in question is known personally. 'Recognised persons' include individuals and families who have established themselves in Adelaide and who, though they are not members of one of the major kin groups from one of the major reserves, are recognised and acknowledged by most as legitimate members of the Aboriginal community. It is important to note that such persons have almost invariably waited many years before receiving recognition. Identification of individuals within this category by the wider community reflects a measure of acceptance by the community and a movement to this category from the category 'unknown persons'. This category includes all other Aborigines who, for whatever reasons, find their way to Adelaide and have not been acknowledged by the community as having a legitimate place in that community. Into this category fall persons from traditionally-oriented, interstate, and distant rural communities. The movements of individuals from the 'persons from home' to the 'kin' categories and from the 'unknown' to the 'recognised' categories represent the only avenues of movement within the model. These avenues, however, are obviously very different from each other.

In a very real sense, for the majority of Aborigines in Adelaide, kinship remains the foundation of identity. While the perception of individuals outside one's immediate kinship network involves the recognition of real social distance (especially for those classed as unknown persons or recognised persons), this is not to say that persons outside that network are necessarily considered less Aboriginal; however the nature of their social identity does become increasingly ambiguous. Where, on the local level, identity is cemented by the obligations and responsibilities of kinship, beyond the local kin group that social cement is less binding and often non-existent. Unknown persons, for example, may be seen to be Aboriginal, but the content of that identity is more abstract and has less to do with a recognition of kin than with a recognition of kind; dispositions toward and expectations of the two categories are quite different. The implications of this situation for individuals who are outside the local kin groups are significant. Such persons will not be immediately accepted into the community on the basis of their Aboriginal ancestry alone, since that is identity of a secondary, more abstract order.

Style and identity

While kinship is at the base of identity for most in Adelaide, identity is also portrayed, expressed, and articulated through a distinctive Aboriginal style which creates and reflects much of the tone and mood of life for Aborigines in Adelaide. Where kinship is fundamental and concrete, style is flexible and fluid, open to a wide range of expressions and manipulations. (Obviously individuals can and occasionally do ignore responsibilities to kin, but the ties to kin in Adelaide are never truly cut since such a denial is offensive to the whole community and the social reverberation of such an act is long lasting.) Indeed, it is this flexibility in style and the possibility of its manipulation which provide an avenue for movement toward recognition in the Adelaide community, movement from the status of unknown person to recognised person. At the same time, understanding and participating in the local Aboriginal style sometimes provides a means by which persons can overcome the perceived ambiguity of their identities.

The distinctive style used by Aborigines in Adelaide consists of a whole complex of components which together afford a symbolic presentation of identity, directed both outward to non-Aboriginal society and inward to the Aboriginal community. These components together provide both a means of identification and an orientation. While a detailed analysis of the major components of this distinctive style and the extent of its applicability outside Adelaide requires more space than is available here, it is useful to look briefly at a few salient components.

Perhaps most prominent among these is the retention and use of what Adelaide Aborigines term 'the Lingo' or, sometimes, 'the Language'. Made up of a limited number of Aboriginal words and phrases—remnants of languages that no longer exist in their fullest forms—interwoven with English, the Lingo provides a powerful vehicle for the expression of local Aboriginal identity. Though once considered archaic and slightly embarrassing by some local Aborigines, the Lingo is recognised today as something unique to Adelaide Aborigines, something which provides tangible evidence of identity.

Many older members know of words which are no longer used, as well as words which by usage or pronunciation identify speakers as to their places of origin. The word *Gunia*, for example, is widely used by Adelaide Aborigines to refer to whites even though it is identified as a Narangga word and so more rightfully belongs to the descendants of the Narangga people, most of whom claim Point Pearce on the Yorke Peninsula as home. The Ngarrindjeri people from Point McLeay have a different word for whites, *Karinkerie*, but the tendency appears to be for younger persons especially to use *Gunia* regardless of where they and their families came from. Such distinctions are made less frequently today and the lexicon from which most draw includes a collection of Narangga, Ngarrindjeri and west coast words as well as words of obscure geographic or tribal origin. Still, the Lingo is seen to be distinctly characteristic of Adelaide Aborigines.[7]

The Lingo is widely used throughout the community and people often express pride in the fact that Adelaide Aborigines still retain portions of their languages while Aborigines in other cities (most believe) have all but lost theirs. The Lingo is functional, communicating particular information between individuals, but it is something more than just a functional alternative. Its significance today lies mainly in its ability to identify the speaker as a member of the Adelaide community and often more specifically as a member of a particular tribal group. There are limitations, however. For speakers of the Lingo who are members of local kin groups its use publicly confirms their identification with the community, but when used by individuals who are not known to the community its message may be more ambiguous. For example, I was told of an Aboriginal bureaucrat, originally from interstate, who was addressing a group of Adelaide Aborigines, peppering his speech with the Lingo. Though he obviously intended to show his identification with the community, many of the local people complained afterward that his use of the Lingo was condescending and offensive.

Aboriginal style is expressed in a variety of other forms as well. While some of these are quite obvious, including the utilisation of particular styles and colours of clothing and accessories and the identification of particular types of music which are considered Aboriginal in flavour, style also exists in more subtle forms, and includes things like deportment, body language, and etiquette.

Style itself, however, is but a visible manifestation of a pervasive cultural system, a system which provides a particular orientation through which the world is viewed. This orientation includes a set of values, attitudes and understandings, seen as unique by Aborigines, which give form and texture to everyday life. A respect for and emotional affinity with traditionally-oriented Aboriginal groups, a recognition of the importance of kinship, an emphasis on the concepts of sharing and caring, and an awareness of the importance of the land rights movement as a key symbol for all Aboriginal people are a few features of this orientation. Much of this orientation, however, has a very local flavour and assumes, most importantly, a competence and facility with local knowledge such as the ability to recognise powerful people, to avoid stepping on the wrong toes, to see the divisions between community factions, and to be aware of local political issues which are of importance to the community—in short, to recognise, respect, and abide by the local version of commonsense.[8]

Aboriginal identity in Adelaide, as I have attempted to show, is strictly structured as a result of the constraints of kinship. This is not to say, however, that identity is static. Every individual is able through choice and especially through action to influence the way they are perceived by others within the community. Those perceptions, I would argue, are greatly dependent—especially for persons outside established local kin groups—upon the individual's facility with and grasp of local style. In order to illustrate these points it will be useful to draw upon some case material. The case studies below are concerned with three Aboriginal boys attempting to come to terms with their own and each other's identities within an institutional setting, which first needs to be described.

The Kaurna Family House[9]

Established in early 1983, the Kaurna Family House was a response to the need for accommodation for Aboriginal teenagers in Adelaide. It was set up and supported by an Aboriginal Christian group which sought, it said, to provide a caring Aboriginal family environment for Aboriginal boys who were homeless or who, for various reasons, were unable to live at home with their families. The boys who lived at Kaurna House were generally between the ages of thirteen and seventeen and most were juvenile offenders, referred to the House (with the boys' consent) by the courts.

Adelaide, like most major cities, includes an area which is frequented by delinquent youth. In Adelaide that area is the entertainment strip, Hindley Street, which includes several movie theatres, adult bookshops, game parlours, hotels, restaurants, and fast food outlets. The bright lights and readily available alcohol and drugs is a magnet which attracted, without exception, the boys from Kaurna House. The area provides all the opportunities for excitement and entertainment that led the boys to Kaurna House in the first place—alcohol and the sniffing of liquid paper, fights, cars to break into and steal, older relatives drinking in the hotels, and girls.

According to the Kaurna House staff, each boy's needs were assessed, and his capacity to live and develop within the structure of the House and its programmes considered, before acceptance into the programme. The boys were only considered for the Kaurna House programme if no more suitable placement could be found. While most boys came to the House via the courts, referrals also came by way of government and private agencies, boys' families, and sometimes individual boys made requests themselves. Staff preference was for placements of at least three or four months, but short term emergency care was sometimes provided.

On occasion boys were expelled from the programme for continued violations of House rules or because they had been arrested for criminal activities and placed in State detention centres. However, because the Kaurna House programme operated on the principle that there is no such thing as a bad person and that no boy should ever be permanently barred from the House, it was not uncommon for boys to have been legally placed in the House more than once, even after expulsion. Kaurna House operated for less than two years and during that time provided accommodation for approximately twenty-five boys, of whom six or seven had remained in the programme (with few or no expulsions) for periods of more than twelve months. The average placement, however, lasted about three months.

The Kaurna Family House was designed to provide the boys with a sense of family and community, a place where individuals worked together to support and help one another. The staff tried to provide an environment, they said, which was expressly Aboriginal, with an emphasis on stable, supportive family living. This Aboriginal emphasis was to be achieved by the employment of Aboriginal staff whenever possible, participation in the wider Adelaide Aboriginal community, and activities which promoted 'Aboriginal cultural experiences'. During the summer of 1984, for example, the boys made an extended camping trip to Uluru (Ayers Rock). Though the preference was for Aboriginal staff, the inclusion of non-Aboriginal persons was also encouraged in parts of the programme. Kaurna House was not, it was often said, a haven for runaways, and boys were encouraged to visit and receive visits from their families. Ultimately, it was hoped, many of the boys would return to their families.

Life at the Kaurna Family House was carefully structured by the staff so that most of the boys' time was taken up with supervised activities. The boys were required to attend school until they reached school leaving age and were encouraged to continue beyond that point. At any one time approximately half the boys living at the House were in school. Boys who had left school were expected to seek employment, and maintain jobs once they were secured. Most were unsuccessful in their attempts to find employment outside, but the Aboriginal Christian group which operated the House was able to provide jobs—for those who could find no other employment—in the group's secondhand clothing shop.

In the late afternoon, when the boys returned to the House from school or work, they were required to engage in what the staff defined as 'constructive activities'—homework, music practice, letter writing, reading, and so on. During this time, variously scheduled during the week, the school boys met with tutors provided by the State who assisted them with their homework and gave remedial help if necessary.

After the evening meal, served family-style, the boys were expected to complete a variety of housekeeping tasks which were assigned on a rotating basis. These tasks included washing up, cleaning the showers and toilets, cleaning the dining and lounge rooms, and picking up the rubbish outside the building. On occasion a 'gardening night' or a 'clean up night' might be called and staff and boys were expected to do more thorough cleaning and maintenance. Usually, however, these tasks were completed quickly and the rest of the evening was spent in some organised, scheduled activity. These evening activities included a variety of excursions, some occasional, such as concerts or films, others ongoing, such as silk-screening, leatherwork, weight-lifting, and swimming. By 10.00pm the boys were expected to be in their bedrooms and by 10.30pm lights were to be turned out.

Weekend activities were only slightly less structured, but again the emphasis was on supervised activities and outings. On the weekends, however, boys who had shown themselves to be trustworthy were given a limited amount of freedom and unsupervised time away from the House. These boys were expected to abide by House rules while away, and no boy was allowed the privilege of roaming the city at will. At no time, for example, were the boys to enter hotels, drink, or frequent areas of Adelaide—especially the local trouble spot, Hindley Street—which were specifically off limits. All time away from the House, whether supervised or not, was to be accounted for and approved by staff before a boy left.

In order to gauge the progress the boys were making while resident at Kaurna House, and to encourage positive progress, a point system was employed by the staff, with points awarded or taken away from each boy during the week. Points were gained by what the staff defined as 'stable and positive behaviour', for example control of a drinking or drug problem, progress at school, leadership, taking responsibility, banking and spending money 'sensibly', taking pride in personal appearance, and employing 'good' manners. Offences against neighbours, being drunk or on drugs, assault, damaging the building, or breaking bail or bond conditions could not only significantly lower a boy's position on the scale but could, and sometimes did, lead to a boy's expulsion from the Kaurna House programme. Other activities such as leaving the House without permission, coming home late, failing to go to school, being a 'loudmouth', or poor personal grooming, could result in a loss of points. Each boy's weekly point total was calculated by staff together with that boy and posted after the weekly House meeting. In general, the higher the boy's points, the greater his freedom and independence. Toward the bottom of the scale, boys not only lost privileges such as pocket money but could be sent to bed at 9.00pm each night. If a boy remained for some time at the bottom of the scale he could be asked or forced to leave the House. On very rare occasions, boys remained for so long at the top of the scale that they were released from the point system.

Identity and ambiguity

For most of the boys who lived in the Kaurna Family House during its two years of operation, their identity as Aborigines was incontrovertible and a source of great pride and strength. These boys had grown up in Adelaide, or adjacent towns, as members of families which were well known to the Aboriginal community and to each other. There were, however, a few boys at the House who, for various reasons, were unknown to the community. These boys' identities as Aborigines were in many ways ambiguous. The following cases both illustrate the ways in which the local boys came to terms with that ambiguity, and provide insights into the nature and increasing complexity of Aboriginal identity.

Case 2
Peter was placed at Kaurna House at the request of his grandmother who claimed she could no longer control him. He was thirteen years old with a long record of arrests for break-ins, car stealing, and other similar offences, a record which was fairly typical of other boys at the House. Though he was a familiar face to the Aboriginal teenagers who frequented Hindley Street, he was not generally accepted by them. Consequently, while most of the Kaurna House boys knew Peter before he came to the House, it was not as though he could simply fit in among old friends as did most of the other boys upon their arrival. Indeed, during the few weeks he lived at Kaurna House Peter never won the acceptance of the other boys.

The boys at the House almost continually harassed and insulted Peter and he returned the abuse. Peter's inability to fit and win acceptance appeared at first to be best explained by his abrasive personality, but it quickly became apparent that this was merely a defensive reaction to the other boys' constant ridicule. It was soon obvious that the basis of the other boys' rejection of Peter was really very simple: they did not believe he was actually Aboriginal.

Raised by his grandmother, who had only a few very tenuous links to the Adelaide Aboriginal community and who was not Aboriginal herself, Peter's identification as Aboriginal had virtually no basis in local kinship as far as the boys in the House were concerned. He was clearly not a member of any well known Aboriginal family and he was continually harangued as a 'whitefella' who had no right to claim an Aboriginal identity. Further complicating matters for Peter was the fact that he was very light skinned and lacked Aboriginal features—a fact the other boys were quick to note. In what appeared to be an attempt to assert his identity, Peter almost continually employed the Lingo. Eventually, however, as things grew worse, Peter's use of the Lingo only elicited laughter and began to irritate the other boys.

One evening as the boys were watching television the conflict came to a head and a fight broke out between Peter and one of the other boys, Tony, who had been harassing Peter all day for various reasons and decided the time was ripe for assaulting Peter where he was most vulnerable.

'You're not *Nunga* [Aboriginal], Peter, you're just a *Gunia* [white] fella,' Tony said in a voice loud enough to make clear to the other boys his insult. Peter tried to give the appearance he hadn't heard Tony's comment and continued staring intently at the television, saying nothing.

'You shouldn't even be here. This is a place for blackfellas,' Tony tried again.

'Piss off,' Peter shouted without averting his eyes from the television.

'Why's a whitefella like you want to be here with us blacks?' Tony bantered.

Peter could no longer ignore the insult. 'Larry,' he said, turning to one of the other boys, 'tell this dickhead I'm as Aboriginal as him.' Larry had been the most tolerant of Peter and had even cited Peter as an example to me of how Aborigines can be very light skinned and still be Aboriginal. By this time, however, Larry seemed to have lost his sympathy for Peter and, apparently uninterested in his defence, chose to ignore him.

'My father's black,' Peter shouted, aware now that he was on his own.

'Yeah? Where's he from, Africa?' Tony taunted. This got an enormous laugh from the other boys who could sense a fight developing.

'You're just a whitefella,' Tony said in a definitive tone.

At this point Peter jumped from his chair and a fist fight broke out, the other boys cheering, not surprisingly, for Tony.

Later, the head of staff angrily told the boys he was sick and tired of Peter being picked on and called *Gunia*. He was Aboriginal and otherwise would not have been admitted to the programme in the first place. (This staff member later told me that he had been shown documents by court officials and Peter's social worker which gave Peter's family history and that his father definitely was Aboriginal.) Any further name calling would result in all of the boys losing points and thus privileges, he warned.

Later that night Peter ran away and committed two break-ins. The Kaurna House staff decided to give him another chance and he was back at the House the next day.

About two weeks later Peter left the Kaurna House programme. He had become even more abusive toward the other boys and to the staff at the House and finally the decision was made to remove him from the programme. During his final two weeks Peter was alternately sullen and abusive. Unable to establish himself, it appeared Peter chose to leave the House and his uncomfortable position there by continual abuse of the staff, the other boys, and the House rules; rather than show the other boys he could no longer handle Kaurna House, he chose to show that the House could no longer handle him.

Case 3

Andrew was seventeen years old and was from a small town a few hundred kilometres away from Adelaide. He was placed in the Kaurna Family House by the court in the hope of 'rehabilitating' him and removing him from the 'bad' influence of friends back home. Though Andrew had visited Adelaide before, he had never really lived in the city for any extended period of time.

Adopted as toddlers by non-Aboriginal parents, Andrew and his sister were not in contact with any Aboriginal family they might have. Though his non-Aboriginal family had not, he said, discouraged his friendships with other Aborigines at home and had encouraged pride in his ancestry, he had grown up in many ways completely outside the small Aboriginal community at home. In Andrew's case those friendships happened to be with Aboriginal boys who were involved with car stealing and joy-riding, eventually leading him, via the courts, to Adelaide and Kaurna House.

Andrew's identity as an Aborigine was somewhat complex. Though his physical appearance left no doubt as to his Aboriginal heritage (he referred to himself as a 'full-blood'), he had grown up in what was essentially a non-Aboriginal world. Andrew claimed that he had been immediately accepted by Aborigines in Adelaide, including the boys at Kaurna House, but once admitted he sometimes felt awkward and a little out of step.

One evening, shortly after Andrew's initial arrival at the House, I was discussing the Lingo with the boys and was making a list of words and phrases. Andrew had obviously not heard many of the words and so was especially attentive. After Andrew asked one of the boys to repeat a word for him, another boy took the opportunity to explain to me that Andrew was having to 'learn' to be *Nunga* and having to learn the Lingo from scratch. It was funny, he said, that even though Andrew looked more Aboriginal than most of the people in Adelaide, he hardly knew any Lingo.

In the weeks that followed, before Andrew left the House, I often observed him asking the other boys what the words for various things were. During that time Andrew learned a great deal of the Lingo though he used it less frequently and perhaps more self-consciously than did the other boys.

Andrew's pride and confidence in his identity seemed to flourish while at Kaurna House, and he was keenly interested in everything Aboriginal. On one occasion Andrew presented me with a gift, an Aboriginal flag he had drawn and painted on a large piece of paper. Above the flag was written 'Nungas Rule', an expression common at the time among Aboriginal teenagers in Adelaide and frequently seen as graffiti. After Andrew left the room I noticed he had apparently made a mistake in painting the flag. The Aboriginal flag is composed of a black field over red, united by a yellow circle (representing Aboriginal people on the land, united by the sun), but Andrew had reversed the red and black fields. When I pointed this out to one of the other boys after Andrew had left the room, he remarked defensively, 'Yeah, he's just learning.'

Case 4
Kenny came to the Kaurna Family House from an Aboriginal community in the northern part of South Australia when he was fifteen years old. He had been involved in petrol sniffing and vandalism and was sent to Adelaide by his family, the community council, and the courts. The Kaurna House programme was made available to Kenny because a senior staff member of Kaurna House was well known in Kenny's community and had offered the House as a place where Kenny could get away from the sniffing.

When Kenny arrived at Kaurna House he seemed to be somewhat dazed and shocked and seldom spoke more than a few words at a time. Most staff members believed him to be brain damaged from petrol sniffing and, while he was never any 'trouble', they worried that he was hopelessly beyond reach.

After a few months, Kenny began to open up slightly and the staff began to realise that their initial diagnosis was probably in error. Not only was Kenny bright and clever with a dry sense of humour, but he was in many ways mature beyond his years. His initial solemnity and reserve reflected more his homesickness and discomfort in unfamiliar and overwhelming conditions than it did the effects of petrol sniffing. Initially a curiosity and puzzle to the other boys, Kenny eventually gained a great deal of (usually unspoken) respect. Most of the other boys were secure in their identities as Aborigines, of that there was really no question, but Kenny provided another reference for that identity, a tangible reference from a more traditional society. Kenny, it was pointed out to me by the other boys, spoke his traditional language and would one day return to 'go through the rules' (initiation) and become a man. Kenny's people, they said, lived more like Aborigines in the 'old days', alluding to a world of hunting and spiritual power, and an absence of whites.

The boys were fascinated by Kenny's ability to speak his language, Pitjantjatjara, but Kenny was self-conscious and refused to speak it, though he was often requested to, for their enjoyment. Consequently, when Kenny received a phone call from home or from relatives visiting Adelaide, the boys would gather out of sight in the hallway so as to hear him converse in Pitjantjatjara. Similarly, Kenny could seldom be drawn into discussions of what the other boys imagined to be a very traditional, almost magical life at home. On one occasion the boys were talking about visitations by ghosts and spirits. I asked Kenny if he had ever seen a ghost and he laughed and said, 'No'. Later, he caught my attention when the other boys were not looking and mouthed silently, 'I'll tell you later.' About a week later, he brought up the subject when we were alone and talked at great length about ghosts he had seen. When I asked why he could not talk in front of the other boys he answered that he was too embarrassed, that they would only laugh. I suspect the real reason he was reticent was not that the other boys would laugh, but that their intense interest made him very uncomfortable.

Conclusion

The cases of the three boys from the Kaurna Family House illustrate some of the key features and complexities of identity among Aborigines in Adelaide. All three of the boys were unknown to the majority of the Aboriginal community in that none of them were identifiable as members of any local kin group. Kenny had come from a traditionally-oriented community and Andrew, raised by non-Aboriginal parents, was from a distant country town. Peter's relation to any local group was disputed and in effect denied.

Given that none of the three could establish an identity on what was the most basic level in Adelaide, kinship, the different treatment of the three by the local boys residing at Kaurna House presents a problem which does not appear to be explained simply by conflicts of personality. The answer, I believe, has to do with their portrayals of their own identities as expressed in the manipulation of local style.

Peter, it seemed, was well versed in many of the components of that style. He was articulate in the Lingo, shared the attitudes and participated in the lifestyle of other delinquent Aboriginal boys, and understood a great deal about the structure of the local Aboriginal community. What he did not seem to understand was the less tangible complex of values, attitudes, and orientations shared by members of the local Aboriginal community. Most significantly, Peter did not understand that he could not force himself into the local community. It seemed obvious to everyone but Peter that the establishment of a local Aboriginal identity was not simply a matter of attempting to adopt the local style and then demanding acceptance, but involved waiting for recognition by the community. In other words, a person can demand recognition as a member of the local community only if that person's relationship to the community is based on kinship. Paradoxically, assuming that such a relationship already exists and the responsibilities of that relationship have been upheld, such a demand is totally unnecessary. To press for recognition when there is no basis in local kinship for such a claim is to ensure its rejection. This is, first, because there is no felt responsibility on the part of the community to consider the demand and, second, because the demand itself exposes the actor's ignorance of Aboriginal style. Recognition, if it comes at all, is given, not taken.

Andrew, on the other hand, made no such demands for recognition but quietly adopted and respected the local cultural style. While Andrew may not yet have been recognised as a member of the Adelaide community, he had done nothing to close the door on some form of eventual recognition. Andrew's experience draws attention to the nature of the recognition by the community of those Aborigines who have come from outside and have decided to stay: the process often takes several years, is never complete, and requires participation in the local cultural style. One man, for example, who came to Adelaide from interstate over eight years ago and is deeply involved with and committed to a variety of Aboriginal community projects, says he is only now gaining some recognition as a legitimate member of the Adelaide community, and only within a particular section of it. According to him, to be accepted as an Aborigine is easy, to be accepted as a member of the Adelaide Aboriginal community is 'bloody hard'. After eight years, he admits, he has a long way to go and will most likely never be fully accepted.

Kenny's case provides some of the most interesting insights of all. Kenny, as a member of a traditionally-oriented community, had every intention of eventually returning home and professed no desire to gain acceptance as a member of the Adelaide community. In fact, Kenny was proud and secure in his own identity, even if somewhat self-conscious in displaying it among Aboriginal people in Adelaide. Kenny's presence in the Kaurna Family House, however, had an interesting effect on the other boys. His apparent shyness and self-consciousness seemed only to confirm the other boys' perceptions that 'tribal people', as they called them, were somehow closer to the spiritual essence of Aboriginal identity than they. This perception was coloured with pride, respect, and perhaps a little fear, but not, I think, envy. For these boys, it seemed, Kenny never represented anything like Aboriginality in a pure form, as something they should have possessed; rather he appeared to substantiate the continuing vitality of Aboriginal culture, a culture they too participated in but in a different way. Kenny's tribal identity seemed to confirm their own identities, not deny them. This confirmation, however, was in the abstract; though Kenny served as a reference point for their own identities, the boys realised that in many very important ways Kenny's world was fundamentally different from theirs.

Finally, it is interesting to consider one other factor in the cases of Peter, Andrew, and Kenny: skin colour and physical features. I do not believe the fact that Peter was ultimately rejected by the other boys and the fact that he was not recognisably Aboriginal are merely coincidental. For a person who comes to Adelaide from outside the local community, skin colour and physical features provide the most immediate flag of that person's identity. If a person is clearly and immediately physically recognisable as Aboriginal but is not linked through kinship to the Adelaide community, that person is at a distinct disadvantage. If a person cannot be recognised physically by other Aborigines, that disadvantage is potentially compounded.[10] On the other hand, if a person is a member of a local group, physical appearance, for the purposes of community recognition anyway, has no meaning.

Notes

1. The fieldwork on which this chapter is based was carried out between May 1983 and September 1984 and was supported by research grants from the Australian National University and the Australian Institute of Aboriginal Studies. The names of individuals, locations, and other identifying features have been changed in an effort to provide some anonymity. My thanks to Barbara Schwab, Julie Carter, David Martin, Howard Morphy, John Morton, Nicolas Peterson and Robert Tonkinson for their valuable comments on an earlier draft.

2. Aboriginal population figures for Adelaide, as for the rest of Australia, are a matter of constant debate. These statistics for 1981 are from the Australian Bureau of Statistics (1982) and represent one of the most recent estimates.

3. For a discussion of the history of the movement of Aborigines into Adelaide from outlying areas as well as a comprehensive demographic profile of the Adelaide Aboriginal population see Gale (1972) and Gale and Wundersitz (1982).

4. The conversational material presented here is not verbatim transcription but has been reconstructed from detailed fieldnotes written during or soon after the individual incidents.

5. Judy Inglis, working in Adelaide about twenty-five years ago, described a basic categorisation of 'insiders' and 'outsiders' (1961), a dichotomy which is no longer entirely accurate. Many of the individuals Inglis described in 1961 as outsiders have gone on to gain a great deal of respect within the local community and are now seen to be legitimate and valuable members of that community although they have not gained full acceptance within the Adelaide Aboriginal community.

6. One middle-aged woman explained that Point McLeay was on the Murray River and her people were river people, people with an aversion to the salt water. This is in marked contrast to the other major reserve near Adelaide, Point Pearce, which is on the seashore and whose people are identified and identify themselves as a salt water tribe. This contrast is often pointed out by members

of both groups and invoked as one explanation for the traditional and continuing tension between the two groups.

7. The Lingo is obviously much more than simply a cache of Aboriginal words which Aborigines in Adelaide draw from. Its use requires a complex knowledge of pronunciation, sentence construction, cadence, inflection, and rules of usage.

8. Adelaide has a reputation among Aborigines across the country as an extremely parochial community, and I often heard individuals from outside the community comment that Adelaide was a 'closed' community.

9. 'Kaurna Family House' is a pseudonym, Kaurna being the name of the original inhabitants of the Adelaide Plains, the area which now includes the city of Adelaide. This description of the history and structure of the Kaurna Family House programme is based on interviews with boys and staff at the House, observation, and the Kaurna House Handbook which details the programme.

10. It is important to note, however, that many Aborigines in Adelaide would reject this notion outright. Several people have told me that Aboriginal identity has nothing to do with skin colour. One person, in fact, told me the very question was a typical whitefella question and was meaningless to Aborigines. At the same time, several other Aborigines in Adelaide have told me that in their own personal experiences physical appearance is painfully significant. 'It's easier,' one man said, 'to be black if you're black.'

References

Australian Bureau of Statistics
1982 *Persons and Dwellings in Local Government Areas and Urban Centres, South Australia*, Government Printer, Adelaide.

Crick, M.
1981 Aboriginal Self-Management Organisations, Cultural Identity and the Modification of Exchange, *Canberra Anthropology* 4(1), 52–81.

Gale, F.
1972 *Urban Aborigines*, Australian National University Press, Canberra.

Gale, F. and J. Wundersitz
1982 *Adelaide Aborigines: A Case Study in Urban Life 1966–1981*, The Aboriginal Component in the Australian Economy 4, Development Studies Centre, Australian National University, Canberra.

Inglis, J.
1961 Aborigines in Adelaide, *Journal of the Polynesian Society* 70(2), 200–18.

Miller, J.
1985 *Koorie: A Will to Win*, Angus and Robertson, London.

Sansom, B.
1982 The Aboriginal Commonality. In R.M. Berndt (ed), *Aboriginal Sites, Rights and Resource Development*, University of Western Australia Press, Nedlands.

6. Diana Eades

They don't speak an Aboriginal language, or do they?

Growing numbers of people in 'settled' Australia who identify as Aboriginal, speak varieties of English as their first language. The fact that such people speak little or none of their traditional Aboriginal languages is often used by non-Aboriginal people as evidence that these people are 'not really Aboriginal'. Thus the choice of language variety plays an important role in questions of Aboriginal identity, and therefore in issues of needs and rights in areas such as politics, land rights and education.

In this chapter, I draw on my research in southeast Queensland,[1] which sheds new light on the relationship between language and identity. While many Aboriginal people may speak English as their first language, the context of conversation has significant Aboriginal cultural and social aspects which lead to distinctively Aboriginal interpretations and meanings. While the chosen language code is frequently English, there are important continuities in the ways language is used. By focussing on aspects of language use I will illustrate some of these continuities, which are significant both in the issue of Aboriginal identity and also in developing more effective cross-cultural communication.

Discussions of Aboriginal Australia in the discipline of sociolinguistics have mainly worked from the assumption that language reflects or expresses social and cultural realities. Studies have tended to be restricted to isolated topics in language use, most notably the two areas of kinship terminology and special language varieties. While these topics are important, a broader and interactive view of language illuminates new and important dimensions of cultural continuity. Interactional sociolinguistics works from the assumption that language is much more than a reflection or expression of society and culture; it is a dynamic and creative instrument of social action. Such a theoretical framework is a powerful tool in understanding why people interact with each other in the way they do, their intentions and interpretations. Such a theory can also explain aspects of cross-cultural mis-communication in interactions where Aboriginal and non-Aboriginal speakers are using varieties of English.

The framework of this chapter is ethnographically-based, interactional sociolinguistics. The ethnographic study of society is a necessary pre-requisite for understanding language. We need to understand the socio-cultural contexts of speakers and situations, and look beyond isolated instances of language use to the use of language within interactions. Language is impossible to separate from context—it is continually both reflecting and creating aspects of context.

Aboriginal people in southeast Queensland

Almost all Aboriginal people in southeast Queensland today are of mixed descent, and there is still much intermarriage with non-Aborigines. Non-Aboriginal people frequently fail to see beyond skin colour and superficial aspects of lifestyle (including choice of language), and hence mistakenly assume that Aboriginal identity in areas like southeast Queensland is largely tokenistic. But the sense of Aboriginal identity remains strong. Although a few people (as elsewhere in Australia) have found it necessary to deny their Aboriginal identity and origins, publicly at least, in order to escape anti-Aboriginal discrimination, it is rare for Aboriginal people to renounce their responsibilities and rights in their Aboriginal society.

Aboriginal people in southeast Queensland belong to over-lapping kin-based networks sharing social life, responsibilities and rights, a common history and culture, an experience of racism, and ethnic consciousness. Social relations are characterised by ongoing family commitments within groups. Barwick's summary of Aboriginal identity (1974, 154 and see Chapter 2) is highly appropriate here: 'To be Aboriginal is to be born to, to belong to, to be loyal to a family.' When people talk about being Aboriginal, they invariably talk about Aboriginal family relationships. Place of residence, travel, social networks, leisure activities and personal loyalties all revolve in some way around one's kin, as other authors in this volume have found. It is significant that Aboriginal kin involves a wide network of people many of whom are related only distantly in non-Aboriginal terms.

One of the most important obligations or expectations of kin is that they maintain contact. Although people participate in mainstream Australian social life in many day-to-day activities, they place the highest priority on seeing relatives. The most serious complaints and accusations about people's behaviour usually concern some aspect of family interaction, such as: 'She never visits her people'; or 'He talks bad to [swears at] his mother when he is drunk.' Such interactional failings generally cause much more concern and bad feeling than incidents such as an illegitimate pregnancy, being sacked from a job, or failing an exam.

While the greatest responsibility is frequently to the nuclear family, family responsibilities are generally applied within a wide range of kin. This applies to the maintaining of social contacts, but also to such areas as the rearing of children, the support of ill or very old people, and the sharing of material resources.

There are many examples of the way in which the wages and benefit payments of Aboriginal individuals are shared between related households. Direct continuity can be seen from pre-contact times, when extended families were provided for by the labour of some of their members, and a young man killing a kangaroo, for example, would be obliged to share certain portions with specific kin. What is more significant than the extent to which resources such as money, housing and car, are shared, is the expectation that they will be shared. This is certainly an area in which both Aboriginal and non-Aboriginal Australians perceive a great cultural difference. It is impossible adequately to understand Aboriginal values, attitudes, intentions and actions without understanding the fundamental pivot of social relationships, particularly between relatives.

Many non-Aboriginal people, for example, find it hard to understand why Aboriginal households invariably have a television set (usually colour), despite serious poverty and extreme lack of material possessions in some instances. But this is an indication of the Aboriginal concern with entertainment not just as a private experience, but as a group activity, rather than, say, with labour saving devices or attractive furniture and furnishings. Perhaps a link could be drawn between contemporary Aboriginal television watching and pre-contact Aboriginal ceremonial life, in which there was generally great passive participation (Christie 1982). Contemporary Aboriginal television watching can also be described as passive participation in that people constantly interject during shows, address actors, and discuss programmes with each other.

Similarly, contemporary Aboriginal attitudes to employment need to be understood in the light of the priority on developing, maintaining and strengthening complex and over-lapping social relationships. Aboriginal unemployment is high. Few Aboriginal people in southeast Queensland subscribe to a work ethic, and although many people are employed at times, their participation is often peripheral. Many place no importance on continual employment, and work is generally regarded as an economic necessity, rather than as part of a life-time plan. Because of the shared financial obligations within family networks, individual unemployment has neither the disastrous financial consequences nor the negative social stigma common to mainstream Australian society. Here again Aboriginal families subordinate financial and employment priorities to the important aspects of social relations.

Non-Aboriginal readers who have dealings with Aboriginal people may be surprised at some of the features discussed in this chapter. It is important to point out that the majority of Aborigines in 'settled' Australia are biculturally competent. Many people choose to operate within white norms in many of their dealings with non-Aborigines, and to use Aboriginal norms, such as those discussed in this chapter, in their own in-group interactions. However, this choice is by no means universal, and much cross-cultural interaction is affected by different norms of interaction, in areas such as those discussed here.

Aboriginal languages in southeast Queensland

Aboriginal people in southeast Queensland today primarily speak varieties of English. There is probably no-one from this area of Australia who today speaks an Aboriginal language as a first (or primary) language. Many Aboriginal people are competent users of a number of varieties of English, from which they choose according to aspects of the conversational context.

Many people speak Standard English, particularly in their interactions with white Australians in formal settings, such as education, government, health and legal arenas. However, while many Aboriginal people throughout Australia are fluent speakers of Standard English, cultural factors affecting language use can lead to differing interpretations, as I will show below. As well, most Aboriginal people speak different varieties of Aboriginal English in different Aboriginal contexts. But there is considerable variability in the Aboriginal English spoken in southeast Queensland, as throughout Australia.

Aboriginal English reflects grammatically the structure of traditional Aboriginal languages. For example, the plural '-s' marking on nouns in English is frequently absent in Aboriginal English (eg 'one dog', 'two dog'). This is a reflection of the traditional Aboriginal languages in which plural is rarely overtly marked. Such features have led to a widespread tendency among non-Aboriginal Australians to regard Aboriginal English as a deficient variety of English, but it is important to point out that Aboriginal English is in no way an inferior language. It is a perfectly adaptable, rule-governed language. Some grammatical variations are simpler than the corresponding Standard English structures, such as the plural markings on nouns, and the equational sentence structure which differs from Standard English equivalents by the absence of a verb 'to be' (eg 'Where Johnny?'), but other variations are more complex. For example, the second person pronoun in Standard English is 'you', regardless of its reference to singular or non-singular participants. But, in Aboriginal English, there is a distinction between: 'you' (second person singular); 'you two, you-n-(h)im' (second person dual); and 'you mob' (second person plural). These pronouns also reflect the grammatical category distinctions of traditional Aboriginal languages.

Many Aboriginal people, speaking varieties of both Standard English and Aboriginal English, use Aboriginal language words, for example:

'Move your big *jinung* [foot].'
'Dog *goonung* [faeces] over there.'
'Look out—*boolimun* [policemen] coming.'

This style of speaking is common throughout Australia and is an important 'badge' of Aboriginal identity (see Chapter 5).

The indigenous Aboriginal languages (such as Gooreng Gooreng, Waka Waka, Wooli Wooli, Kabi Kabi and Batjala) are still spoken in some restricted contexts, mainly by older people. For several generations people were actively discouraged from, and on some government reserves even punished for, using their Aboriginal languages. Today it is quite rare for non-Aborigines to hear Aboriginal languages being spoken in southeast Queensland. However, Lingo (the local Aboriginal name for these languages) is still fulfilling a social function. It is used mainly by older people, either to chastise someone, or else to exclude someone from their conversation—be they a non-Aboriginal researcher, a policeman, or an Aborigine from another part of Queensland. It is also used as a polite, euphemistic form of language to talk about private topics such as pregnancy or urinating. It is not uncommon for older people to switch from speaking English to short but fluent conversations in Lingo and then back into English. These traditional Aboriginal languages in southeast Queensland are thus not dead, even though they may be barely elicitable by linguists. They are fulfilling a social function in some restricted contexts.

Language as a part of culture

The Aboriginal priority on developing, maintaining and strengthening social relationships is both reflected in, and created by, the way people speak to each other, whether the language variety is English, Aboriginal English or Lingo.

We saw above that it is important for Aboriginal people to know a wide-ranging group of relatives, to know in detail how they are related, and to maintain contact with many relatives. There are several aspects of language use which indicate the importance of these family obligations. It will be seen from discussion of these aspects that they do more than indicate the importance of these obligations, or reflect an existing reality. It is partly through the use of certain ways of speaking that these family obligations are actually fulfilled and maintained. These ways of speaking are creative social actions integral to the continuity of Aboriginal society and culture. This creative aspect of language usage is illustrated here with kinship terms of address, and the conversational avoidance of certain relatives.

Use of kin terms

Within the extended family, there is widespread use of English terms of address, such as 'cuz' (cousin), 'aunty' and 'uncle'. Unlike the situation in most non-Aboriginal Australian families, the use of these terms is not restricted to children. 'Aunty' and 'uncle' tend to be used between any Aboriginal adults and their higher generation relatives. Some young Aboriginal adults, particularly those who marry non-Aboriginal spouses, stop using 'aunty' and 'uncle' and this causes considerable concern. Such behaviour indicates not only lack of respect for older relatives, but also cultural breakdown. It is important in Aboriginal culture to acknowledge respect due to older people, even by mature adults. Age brings power and wisdom in Aboriginal culture in 'settled' Australia, just as in traditionally-oriented Australia (Berndt and Berndt 1964).

While it is generally English kin terms which are used, there are some continuities with traditional language kin categories and terms of address, such as the following examples, discussed by Williams (1981), which are English translations of traditional labels: 'cousin brother' is used sometimes by parallel cousins to address their male parallel cousins; and 'daughter' is used to address an old woman by her great-grandchildren.

The use of 'cuz' appears to be frequent between same-generation relatives, no matter how distant. Its use is an important part of ongoing Aboriginal culture in places like southeast Queensland, where Aboriginal people live and work in such a large-scale society. Links with one's own kin are still seen as important and as able to transcend non-Aboriginal social structures into which Aboriginal people are drawn. For example in bureaucratically structured Aboriginal organisations and government departments Aboriginal people work, have meetings, and decide policies with a wide range of other Aboriginal people from all over Australia. But within these bureaucratic structures and ways of operating many elements of Aboriginal culture persist. One such element is the loyalty to kin. Thus the use of the term of address 'cuz' in a meeting or a tutorial in a tertiary institution, for instance, both maintains and reminds Aboriginal participants of a speaker's relationship to another participant and the accompanying rights and responsibilities. Whereas in pre-colonial times this might have encompassed food provision and child-raising, in the 1980s it includes such dimensions as loyalty in voting, and assistance with assignment work, as well as financial and family responsibilities.

Avoidance behaviour

It is not only the actual words people use which reflect and create continuities of Aboriginal culture. In contemporary Aboriginal society, we see continuities of traditional norms concerning who an individual can speak to and in what ways.

Avoidance behaviour between particular in-laws in Aboriginal societies is well documented in the anthropological literature (eg Berndt and Berndt 1964). In many Aboriginal societies special language varieties were used between certain relatives (see Dixon 1971; Harris 1970). Haviland (1979) describes avoidance speech behaviour between certain relatives in Hopevale (a North Queensland community) as part of a range of avoidance behaviour which includes eye contact, posture, and restrictions on physical contact and on the sharing of food and possessions.

Older people in southeast Queensland today remember that there was strict avoidance between a man and his mother-in-law until about the 1950s. They remember that in their childhood a man would never directly address, face toward, or give food to, his mother-in-law. Conversations between a man and his mother-in-law would take place through a third, intermediary person in a stylised way. One woman told me how her mother never ate at the family table when her husband was present. On these occasions she ate at the small table made specially by her husband for his mother-in-law to eat at.

While many Aboriginal families today no longer observe such strict avoidance, there is still some continuity in that many men avoid direct conversations with their mothers-in-law. The literature would indicate reasons to interpret such avoidance as not simply identical with the frequent mainstream antagonism, but as based on long standing Aboriginal traditions of respect-based avoidance. One such form which I have frequently observed in a particular country town, concerns a man in his sixties with a bad leg who often walks about two kilometres to town. On the way he often passes his mother-in-law's house where he sometimes rests. However, he never enters the house, but rests in the shed out the back. They rarely, if ever, speak to each other.

We have glimpsed the way Aboriginal culture is created and reflected through ways of speaking. To put it another way, the use of language is an integral part of social action which is distinctively Aboriginal. Even though English is the language spoken by Aboriginal people in many parts of Australia, social aspects of the way it is used reflect and help to maintain and create a culture which is Aboriginal and which shows continuities with traditional Aboriginal cultures.

Further examination of the language-culture relationship

Ethnographically-based interactional sociolinguistics enables us to go beyond the realm of kinship terminology and avoidance languages in the examination of the language–culture relationship and the continuity of Aboriginal culture. In this section I focus on the way Aboriginal people in southeast Queensland use English to achieve certain social ends—namely making and refusing requests, seeking and giving information, seeking and giving reasons for actions. But to understand these inter-related uses of language we first need some insight into aspects of the socio-cultural context of speakers. We will look first at the public nature of Aboriginal social life, and the role of indirectness in social interactions.

The role of indirectness

Aboriginal social life is very public. Traditional Aboriginal society has no walls and, as Hamilton (1981, 97) puts it, 'No particular value [is] placed on privacy in camp'. Although Aboriginal people in 'settled' Australia live in quite different physical settings from those in traditional Australia, their social life is still very public. In the cities, towns and reserves people live very close to one another and their day-to-day activities are public. Small houses accommodate large families, or many members of an extended family, and by non-Aboriginal standards are frequently over-crowded. There is a communal, non-private nature to this style of living. As well, much day-to-day living takes place in open, outside areas, such as the main street of towns, in public places, and (in country towns particularly) on the verandahs of houses. The importance of verandahs in country town and reserve Aboriginal social life cannot be over-emphasised. Here people regularly sit for long periods, observing the comings and goings of others around them and passing on reports of other people's activities. Modes of transport are highly public too. Because people often walk, they are easily observed and they often bear reports between households. Cars frequently travel with full passenger loads, stopping at different houses to exchange passengers and news. The fact that many cars are also noisy enables people's movements to be easily observed. As well as this close lifestyle in physical, spatial terms, Aboriginal people live close lives socially, through complex and wide-ranging kin ties which are constantly maintained and strengthened in social interaction.

In such a public society, we can ask whether there is any privacy at all. To answer this question we need to look at norms and expectations of Aboriginal relationships. Here we find a dimension of personal privacy not common in non-Aboriginal Australia. The Aboriginal way of interacting indirectly preserves a considerable degree of personal privacy. In a number of aspects of conversation, Aboriginal people tend to be much more indirect than non-Aboriginal people. Even where the same language variety (eg Standard English) is used, there are cultural differences in usage which both reflect and continually create and maintain indirectness in social interactions.

Several researchers have discussed the norm in traditional Aboriginal societies of avoiding direct confrontation and respecting a greater personal privacy than is usual in non-Aboriginal society. Von Sturmer (1981, 29) says that for whites talking to Aborigines, 'the need for caution and circumspection' is 'the primary consideration'. Similarly, Harris (1977) reports that one of the most significant factors of conversations in Milingimbi (Arnhem Land) is the avoidance of direct verbal confrontation. The work of Liberman (1981; 1982a; 1982b,1) examines the way Western Desert Aborigines structure discussions so that consensus can be preserved:

> The preservation of this consensus is achieved by the unassertiveness of participants, avoidance of direct argumentation, a deferral of topics which will produce disharmony, and above all, by an objectification of discourse which is effected by a serial production of summary accounts of the particpants' deliberations.

I have observed similar conversational strategies among Aboriginal people in southeast Queensland. In many interactions these people do not express a firm or biased opinion, even if they hold it. They may discuss a topic generally while gauging others' views, before stating their own. If people find their views on a topic to be at odds with others in a conversation, they will tend to understate their own. In minimising confrontation and argument, the speaker leaves open the possibility for further comfortable discussion. What Liberman (1982b, 2) explains as 'a strict refusal to force a way of thinking upon others' can also appear as a refusal to state one's position openly in a particular discussion. Thus, many meetings in which Aboriginal and non-Aboriginal people discuss contentious issues involve more than the expected cross-cultural tension. Part of the tension is due to the different ways in which different or conflicting viewpoints are presented. It is an appropriate communicative strategy in European–Australian meetings to present clearly a viewpoint which is directly contrary to that of the previous speaker. Aboriginal speakers are more likely to present some similar viewpoint first, leaving the more significant conflicting viewpoint for a later opportunity. Because of the differences in timing, misunderstanding often occurs. Aboriginal speakers often feel they are not given enough time to speak, and to develop their viewpoint. As well they often feel that non-Aboriginal participants are confrontationist in the way they present their ideas. Non-Aboriginal speakers often feel that Aboriginal speakers are not clear in expressing their views—Aboriginal indirectness and circumspection is often interpreted as inarticulateness and the lack of a logical argument.

Von Sturmer's (1981, 29) discussion of Aboriginal caution and circumspection also points out the strategy of 'not presenting oneself too forcefully and not linking oneself too closely with one's own ideas'. He discusses the use of the expression 'might be' (as a modal qualifier) to distance the speaker from the certainty of the idea he is presenting. Similarly Aboriginal speakers often preface their views with comments such as, 'This is just what I think.' Disclaimers such as these point to a fundamental cultural view that an Aboriginal person can speak only for themselves. Western-style democracy and notions of representation impose many difficulties on Aboriginal ways of expressing opinions.

The importance of indirectness in much daily conversational interaction is shown by examining the way Aboriginal people in southeast Queensland use English for the following communicative functions: to seek and give information; to make and refuse requests; and to seek and give reasons.

Seeking and giving information

I have elsewhere discussed the ways in which Aboriginal people in southeast Queensland obtain information. To summarise briefly, information-seeking is part of a two-way exchange in which people give information in order to get information. A distinction is made between orientation information and substantial information. Orientation information is defined as 'information which clarifies a topic' (often the current topic of conversation). The information sought comprises background details about people especially, but also about the time, place and setting of some situation or narrated event (Eades 1982, 72–73).

Direct questions are used to elicit orientation information, for example: 'Where you from?'; or 'Who's his mother?' However, the form of the question frequently presents certain information, but with question intonation (or a following interrogative tag). This form of question, referred to in some studies of Aboriginal English as 'uninverted question forms' (eg Dwyer 1974, 17), is a linguistic strategy consistent with the indirectness typical of much Aboriginal conversation. Rather than directly ask for information, the questioner presents some proposition for confirmation or correction, for example: 'That's his brother?'; or 'Grandfather used to live at Tirroan?' These orientation questions play an important interactional role in Aboriginal society. They are an essential part of the development and maintenance of social links.

In constantly finding out about another's kin, movements, and country, an Aboriginal person is creating or maintaining closeness. Such a process is common between Aboriginal people all over Australia, whether in English, or English related languages, or traditional Aboriginal languages.

The common Aboriginal question, 'Where are you going?' (or its language equivalent, such as *Woonju ngin yun.gim* in Gooreng Gooreng) is interactionally equivalent to 'Hullo', 'Hi' or 'Gidday' in non-Aboriginal Australia (Eades 1982). It is common for Aboriginal people to greet each other with this question. Orientation questions serve an important role in developing and maintaining social links, in locating participants in a conversation in a socio-spatial relationship, and indeed in finding out information (Eades 1982). We will see further that orientation questions can also be intended and interpreted in other ways, for example, as requests or inquiries after the reasons for actions.

While questions can be used to seek orientation information, they are not used to seek substantial information, such as important personal details, a full account of an event, or the explanation of some event or situation. In these situations indirect strategies are used: the speaker contributes some of their own knowledge on a topic and then leaves a silence, to lead the person with the knowledge to impart information. Important aspects of substantial information-seeking are the two-way exchange of information, the positive, non-awkward use of silence, and often considerable time delays (frequently several days) between the initiation of substantial information-seeking and the imparting of information.

Making and refusing requests

Aboriginal people rarely make direct requests. The most common ways of asking someone either to do something, or to give or loan something, involve indirect, multifunctional forms. That is, a question might serve several of the functions outlined above, including that of a request. For example, the standard Aboriginal way of asking for a ride is to ask a car owner an orientation question, such as 'You going to town?' or 'What time are you leaving?' These questions are multifunctional, structurally ambiguous and, depending on the relationship between speakers, communicatively ambiguous. That is, these questions can be interpreted as part of the information-seeking involved in socio-spatial orientation, but they can also be interpreted as a request for a ride. Appropriate interpretation cannot be made without an understanding of the relationship between speakers. But even if speakers understand such questions as requests for a ride, the ambiguity enables a person to refuse a request in a similar indirect fashion, for example by saying, 'might be later', or 'not sure'. In this way, Aboriginal people can work out requests and refusals without directly exposing their motives.

Such indirect strategies are of course not restricted to Aboriginal conversations. Non-Aboriginal people use such ways of making requests and refusals in sensitive situations. What is significant about the Aboriginal use of these strategies is that they are not restricted to sensitive situations, but are the usual everyday ways of interaction, in which indirectness is the norm.

Seeking and giving reasons

One of the most striking features of language use by Aboriginal people in southeast Queensland is the virtual absence of the reason-seeking question 'why'. People use 'why' and 'what for' to make complaints, as in: 'What you come to me for? I got no money.' But there is no direct way of questioning a person's reasons. However, this is not to say that Aboriginal people are not curious, as they are constantly using ways of speaking to find out reasons for states of affairs. In seeking reasons, people elicit statements of fact, which they accumulate over time and interpret as reasons. The multifunctional forms discussed above also serve to seek reasons for actions. In seeking information, speakers are also seeking the evidence with which they can assume reasons for the actions of others.

For example, in trying to find out why a teenage girl was late home, her granny would never ask: 'Why were you late home last night?' Instead, she would begin by establishing her granddaughter's whereabouts: 'Where you went last night?' or by assuming her whereabouts and querying this fact: 'You were at the pub last night?' Then to find out why the granddaughter was at the pub, her granny would ask: 'Bill there too?' By using a series of orientation questions, the old woman would establish reasons for the granddaughter arriving home late. There is no obligation on Aboriginal speakers to answer questions such as these, however the granddaughter would be well aware that her granny was trying to establish reasons for her actions and she would usually give some answers to enable her granny to establish some acceptable reasons. But the responsibility is on the person interpreting reasons, and the person being questioned does not have to account directly for their reasons. Again multifunctional forms make the requests for reasons indirect and ambiguous and give people considerable privacy. They are never confronted with an inescapable request for a reason, such as the question 'why'.

It is clear that strategies for seeking reasons for actions are indirect. A further technique which lessens direct verbal contact is the inquiry about reasons by a third person. Again the style of questioning is basically the presenting of an assumed fact or facts to a third person in an interrogative mode. Of course, this third person may then assume this fact to be true, and pass it on to a fourth person and so on. Indeed, because reasons are assumed so regularly, unfounded explanations are frequently circulated. However, because these explanations are expressed as facts or assumed facts, rather than as facts with undeniable reasons, speakers are not held accountable.

In reporting facts learned from another party, Aboriginal speakers have a range of expressions available which indicate the speculative nature of the reporting statment. When the speaker is disclaiming responsibility for the truth of the statement, one of the following is frequently used:

must have—as in 'He must have been after that woman';
must be—as in 'They must be still at the pub';
reckons—as in 'Kit reckons that man's still at the pub'; and
might be—as in 'They gone fishin?' 'Might be'.

(These qualifying forms are also used to protect one's commitment to future action; see Eades 1983.)

Non-verbal actions, such as observation, are important strategies for finding out reasons for the actions of others. In Aboriginal society, there are no sanctions against direct observation of the observable actions of others, including staring. The situation is rather the reverse in white society where there is a strong prohibition against staring at the observable actions of others. This prohibition is further supported by the privatised nature of white society. Much interaction takes place in enclosed areas and is secluded from public observation, as indicated by the expression concerning 'the four walls'. However, there is a wide range of contexts in which it is quite appropriate to question others' actions and reasons directly. On the other hand, in Aboriginal society people have direct and uninterrupted observational access to many day-to-day interactions, but the direct questioning of reasons is prohibited.

Just as the seeking of reasons uses multifunctional forms, so too does the expression of reasons: While the Standard English reason connectors, such as 'because' and 'to', are sometimes used by Aboriginal speakers, it is much more common to give reasons for actions simply as statements, or by using the multifunctional connector 'and'. For example, a woman advising another woman to be careful on a long trip, and to keep the driver awake, said,

> You get too tired, you wanna camp on the road you know. Don't travel, he might go to sleep, he must be knocked up too you know. Camp on the road. I'll give you a stick. You give him a poke in the ribs, keep him awake.

This extract could be translated with Standard English reason connectors as,

> If you get too tired, you should camp on the road you know. Don't travel, because he might go to sleep, because he must be knocked up too you know, so camp on the road. I'll give you a stick so you can give him a poke in the ribs to keep him awake.

As there is frequently no unambiguous linguistic marker of reason, Aboriginal speakers depend on aspects of context to interpret statements as reasons. Specifically they rely on that element of context which is derived from their sharing of experiences and knowledge.

Linguistic forms which express reasons, then, also serve other communicative functions at the same time. In particular, while giving information, speakers are also expressing reasons for action. Being structurally (but not usually pragmatically) ambiguous, this way of expressing reasons leaves speakers not directly accountable for their motives. In Aboriginal conversations the responsibility for the interpretation of an utterance as a reason rests with the hearer. The speaker has no responsibility to encode an utterance as a reason. The hearer must interpret structurally ambiguous utterances in the light of knowledge shared with the speaker, but the speaker is free to keep utterances pragmatically ambiguous and leave the hearer with insufficient knowledge to disambiguate.

Thus in the expression of motives and reasons, speakers have a great personal freedom and privacy. It is the responsibility of hearers to infer causal links between statements. If hearers do not share enough knowledge with the speaker to do so, they need to initiate investigations, in the indirect ways discussed above.

An example To illustrate the seeking and giving of reasons, let me quote at some length an interaction which I witnessed and taped in a country town in southeast Queensland. It is a good example of Aboriginal indirectness in the giving and seeking of reasons. Central to the Aboriginal style of seeking reasons are:

1. observations of movements, preferably from some public position—in this example, the verandah;
2. the gathering of evidence over time;
3. indirect questioning which overtly does not query anything more than the orientation of participants to events;
4. the norm that a person being questioned has no obligation to provide information, and can subvert the questioning with non-cooperative replies, such as untruths and, in this example, vague replies or silence; and
5. the repetition of assumed and observed facts to a third person.

Features 1 and 5 above are part of the public nature of Aboriginal life, while features 3 and 4 contribute to the privacy of Aboriginal individuals.

In a house where I frequently stayed in a small country town, Janey (an elderly woman) had been keenly observing the movements of Sally (her teenage granddaughter). In gathering evidence and making assumptions, Janey had made at least a few factual errors of which I was aware. For example, one day Sally was in town for quite a longer period of time than usual. Janey remarked to me, 'She must have met Tom.' Now Janey was encouraging Sally to marry Tom, so she was pleased with any evidence of their being together. However when Sally came home she told me she had had lunch with a girl friend. It seemed she had not seen Tom at all. A few days later Janey and I went out early in the morning. When we returned in the mid afternoon, no-one was home. Janey told me, 'Sally must have gone out with Tom.' We resumed our positions on the front verandah and observed the comings and goings in the town. After some time we saw Molly's (Sally's sister's) car coming up the road. Janey was surprised because Molly's car usually came to bring Sally home. Janey said to me, 'There Molly. Where Sally? Sally sitting there? Have a look.' I confirmed that Sally was there. When the car pulled up, Sally came up to the verandah and immediately told us, 'I won on the races today.' This was followed by a short conversation on Sally's winnings in which the first person singular pronoun was used several times, indicating that her actions were not with Tom. In fact, Tom was not mentioned at all.

In the next exchange, which is quoted below, Janey tried to establish the reason why Sally didn't go with Tom. Janey's linguistic strategy was that of orientation questioning. In lines A and C she queries assumed information; in line E she repeats information given by Sally; and in line G she uses a standard form of question (discussed in Eades 1982). Janey begins,

A. 'Oh youself, youself went there?'

B. 'Yeah.'
C. 'Didn you go with Tom out there?'
D. 'No, he went fishin with Mick.'
E. 'Tom did?'
F. 'Yeah.'
G. 'Where they went?'
H. 'I dunno—somewhere.'
I. 'Oh.'

Janey was successful in finding out a reason why Sally and Tom did not go out together, but she was not successful in finding out why Tom went fishing. Sally successfully avoided giving any further information with her non-committal answer H. (Note that while the relationship between grandmother and granddaughter in Aboriginal society places the granddaughter under certain obligations, such as cooking for her grandmother, they do not extend to giving information. The right to deny information appears to cut cross all kin obligations.)

The conversation turned to Janey telling Sally about our day and then the three of us played with Sally's baby. But the reason for Sally and Tom not going out together was still a concern to Janey. After some time, when Sally took her baby inside to bath her, Janey said to me in a surprised tone, 'Wonder she didn go with Tom.'

Later that afternoon Tom arrived and Janey was able to continue her indirect investigations. Again she used orientation questioning, filling in background details in A and using the audience participation strategy of repetition in C and E. Again the person being questioned (Tom) was under no obligation to provide factual information. Janey asks,

A. 'Catch any fish, Tom?'
B. ' No, I didn get there.'
C. 'Eh?'
D. 'I didn get there.'
E. 'You didn go there?'
F. 'No.'
G. 'Oh, I thought you went with Mick and Anne.'
H. (Silence)

Tom made no further comment and then had a very quiet conversation with Sally on the steps of the verandah, which Janey observed. Later Janey joked with me about 'them two fighting'. Her comments to me about the situation were not made in an ambiguous causal manner, but knowing the southeast Queensland Aboriginal mode of giving reasons, I understood that Janey had determined the reason Sally and Tom had not gone out together was because they were having a disagreement.

Conclusion

Many non-Aboriginal people feel that people like Janey and her family are 'not really Aboriginal', because of their relatively light skin colour and superficial similarity to many non-Aboriginal Australians in such aspects as language, dress, housing and employment. A traditional linguistic or static sociolinguistic analysis would do little to demonstrate continuities in Aboriginal ways of believing and acting in places like southeast Queensland. But, ironically, while many people in 'settled' Australia deny any real or distinctive Aboriginality, many people, both Aboriginal and non-Aboriginal, perceive communication differences and difficulties (Eades 1984). For example, Aboriginal people often complain that whites are rude, nosey, impatient and ask too many questions. And whites often complain that Aboriginal people are shy, ignorant, slow and uncooperative.

In this chapter, I have used ethnographic interactional sociolinguistics to explain some of these differences, thus providing evidence of continuing Aboriginality in southeast Queensland. Furthermore, I have shown that it is impossible to understand language without understanding its social and cultural context. This chapter has examined some significant aspects of the social and cultural context of Aboriginal people in southeast Queensland today, which reflect continuities from traditional Aboriginal cultures. These aspects, such as the importance of responsibilities to kin, the priority of social relationships, and the need for indirectness in interactions, are both reflected in, and continually created by the ways in which people interact. Speaking is an important part of such interaction. It is in everyday conversational interaction, such as the giving and seeking of reasons for actions, that we can see significant evidence of Aboriginal cultural continuity. Understanding such cultural continuity is essential to any effective communication between Aboriginal and non-Aboriginal people in 'settled' Australia.

Notes

1. This chapter is based on the research for my PhD thesis (Eades 1983) which was carried out between 1978 and 1983 with a number of Aboriginal families in southeast Queensland. I am indebted to the people who shared their culture and lives with me. In particular, my thanks go to Michael Williams and his relatives for enabling me to be involved in the family research and for teaching me so much about Aboriginality. Many colleagues provided comments on my writings, and in particular I am grateful to Ian Keen for his encouragement and helpful criticism on both the thesis and this chapter.

References

Barwick, D.
1974 The Aboriginal Family in South-Eastern Australia. In J. Krupinski and A. Stoller (eds), *The Family in Australia*, Pergamon, Sydney.

Berndt, R.M. and C.H. Berndt
1964 *The World of the First Australians*, Ure Smith, Sydney.

Christie, M.
1982 Teaching Purposeful Reading to Aboriginal Children, *The Aboriginal Child at School* 10(2), 11–26.

Dixon, R.M.W.
1971 A Method of Semantic Description. In D. Steinberg and L. Jakobovits (eds), *Semantics*, Cambridge University Press, Cambridge.

Dwyer, J.
1974 The School and the Aboriginal Child, *The Aboriginal Child at School* 2(1), 3–19.

Eades, D.
1982 You Gotta Know How to Talk...Information Seeking in South-East Queensland Aboriginal Society, *Australian Journal of Linguistics* 2(1), 61–82. Reprinted in J. Pride (ed), *Cross Cultural Encounters: Communication and Miscommunication*, River Seine Publications, Melbourne.

1983 English as an Aboriginal Language in Southeast Queensland, PhD thesis, University of Queensland.

1984 Misunderstanding Aboriginal English: The Role of Socio-cultural Context. In G. McKay and B. Sommer (eds), *Applications of Linguistics to Australian Aboriginal Contexts*, Applied Linguistics Association of Australia, Occasional Papers No 8, 24–33.

Hamilton, A.
1981 *Nature and Nurture: Aboriginal Child-rearing in North-Central Arnhem Land*, Australian Institute of Aboriginal Studies, Canberra.

Harris, J.
1970 Gunkurrng, a Mother-in-law Language. In S.A. Wurm and D.C. Laycock (eds), *Pacific Linguistic Studies in Honour of Arthur Capell*, Pacific Linguistics C13, Canberra.

Harris, S.
1977 Milingimbi Aboriginal Learning Contexts, PhD thesis, University of New Mexico.

Haviland, J.B.
1979 Guugu Yimidhirr Brother-in-law Language, *Language in Society* 8, 365–93.

Liberman, K.
1981 Understanding Aborigines in Australian Courts of Law, *Human Organization* 40(3), 247–55.
1982a Some Linguistic Features of Congenial Fellowship Among the Pitjantjatjara, *International Journal of the Sociology of Language* 36, 35–52.
1982b Intercultural Communication in Central Australia, *Working Papers in Sociolinguistics* No 104.

Von Sturmer, J.
1981 Talking with Aborigines, *Australian Institute of Aboriginal Studies Newsletter* 15, 13–30.

Williams, M.
1981 Master's Qualifying Report, Griffith University.

7. Jeremy R Beckett

Kinship, mobility and community in rural New South Wales[1]

The setting of this chapter is the far west of New South Wales of the late 1950s, a region of semi-arid plains, mainly given over to sheep grazing and supporting only a sparse population. The region's only large town is Broken Hill, a mining centre of about 30,000 inhabitants; the rest are small commercial and servicing centres for the pastoral hinterland: only Bourke, Cobar and Condobolin exceed 2,000, while the three townships of the Corner (the extreme northwest of the State), together boast no more than 250. East of the Bogan and south of the Lachlan Rivers, sheep grazing gradually gives way to wheat farming, while at Mildura and Griffith there is fruit growing. The population of these areas is less sparse and the towns are larger; however, they figure only marginally in the present account.

In or around most far western townships one finds a number of people who are known, locally and officially, as Aborigines. In fact, few of them are of full Aboriginal descent, the remainder having European ancestry; however, in most situations the important distinction lies between those who have some Aboriginal ancestry and those who have none. The latter are white people; the former are dark people (the polite euphemism), 'Abos' or 'darkies'. The stress on colour is not altogether misplaced. Most Aborigines are physically distinct, ranging from very dark to a swarthiness which might in other places indicate Mediterranean origin; however, there are some who are physically indistinguishable from whites but retain Aboriginal identity because of their known kinship with darker people or their adherence to Aboriginal ways.

Although one may speak of an Aboriginal way of life, this implies little that is tribal. The old tribal groups are dispersed, while local populations are of mixed origin; no boys or girls have been initiated for fifty years or more; the old rules of kinship behaviour, including prescribed marriage, are not merely disregarded but forgotten; indigenous languages are scarcely spoken, even at home, and are not being learned by the rising generation. The eating of wild foods, such as kangaroo, is perhaps the only conscious carryover from tribal times. Loss of their indigenous culture has not, however, made them any more ready to adopt the white Australian way of life, as some advocates of assimilation seemed to think it should. Instead of emulating the industry, thrift and regard for property and comfort of middle class Europeans—with whom they had little contact—they took as their model the nineteenth century pastoral workers, whose way of life presented many parallels to their own. This 'nomad tribe'[2] took little account of property or thrift, preferring to squander their earnings in prodigality and drunkenness; they changed their jobs frequently, affecting a sturdy independence, and took what was almost a pride in enduring rough food and conditions; generosity to friends was perhaps their cardinal virtue. Few Europeans live this way today, and those who do are not highly regarded by the more settled section of the population; however, it has been carried on by Aborigines for several generations, with the difference that they are more or less settled in one place and have large families. The white citizens of outback townships expect from their neighbours a minimum standard of material possession and comfort, cleanliness and sobriety. Not all Europeans conform to this standard, but almost all Aborigines fall short of it. Dirtiness, fecklessness, drunkenness and sexual immorality form a central part of the 'no-hoper Abo' stereotype commonly held by white country people. The camps of scrap iron humpies and ill kempt government cottages, which fringe so many country towns, are said to 'give the place a bad name' and endanger public health; no white person would go there except on business or for some nefarious purpose.[3] The entry of an Aboriginal family into the body of the town is regarded with misgiving, unless respectability is firmly established.

Racial antagonism is perhaps strongest in a place like Wilcannia, where the Aboriginal–European ratio is of the order of 300:600 and where the Aboriginal population is largely a post-war phenomenon. Antagonism is less in the Lake Cargelligo district where the ratio is 300:1,500 and where the Aborigines live segregated on a government settlement (Murrin Bridge) ten miles from town, but this may be only because contacts are so limited as to provide insufficient base for any positive attitude. In either case, there is a marked separation between Aborigines and non-Aborigines. Far west Aborigines are integrated into the regional economy as wage-labourers and consumers, and into the governmental system as persons subject to ordinary laws as well as, at the time of writing, to special 'protective' laws, and the attentions of a special agency devoted to their 'welfare'; however, there are many areas of Australian institutional life where few if any Aborigines penetrate. Bridge situations, which might lead to closer rapport between Europeans and Aborigines, are few and in fact friendships are rare and intermarriage even more so.[4] The separation is reinforced by the lack of common interests, which makes communication difficult, while initial antipathy and suspicion disincline either side to seek each other out.

Aborigines throughout the far west—indeed, throughout the southern half of Australia—share a common culture, but they are not organised in any overall way. Even local communities rarely engage in any joint enterprise; the nuclear family is the largest group functioning regularly. This low level of organisation is possible because Aboriginal society is very much dependent upon European society, particularly as regards the economy and the maintenance of law and order. The

Kinship, mobility and community in rural New South Wales

norms of Aboriginal society govern interpersonal rather than intergroup relations, and are mostly concerned with casual, short term types of interaction. In the absence of any wider coordinating principle, face-to-face relations are of primary importance among Aborigines, and local communities are only saved from isolation by the direct contacts their members make in the course of moving about the countryside. Mobility is consequently of considerable social importance.

Since coming under white domination, far west Aborigines have moved about a good deal, though mostly within the region. Some of these moves have been involuntary, dictated by the authorities or economic circumstances; others have been voluntary. These last follow a pattern which is largely the product of factors within Aboriginal society. Mere proximity need not be a major factor—an Aborigine may go 200 miles to a place where he is known, rather than ten miles to a place where he is not. Usually, being known means having kin who will receive him and act as sponsors in the local community. The area within which he moves—his 'beat', as I shall call it—is defined by the distribution of kin. I shall show that the typical beat is gradually expanding.

Uprooting, segregation and dispersal

The tribes of the far west were often distinguished only by their use of a particular named language or dialect, however, the approximate territories of these linguistic groups are known,[5] and tribal identification gives some indication of local origin during the early period.

The Darling River forms the major division in the area (see Map 7.1). To the southeast lived the Wiradjeri speaking tribes, the Ngiemba around Cobar, the Wongaibon (also sometimes called Ngiemba) between Cobar and Ivanhoe, and the Wiradjeri (Wiradjuri) proper along the Lachlan River and to the south and east. At the lower ends of the Lachlan and Murrumbidgee lived a number of small groups such as the Ita-Ita and Waimbu-Waimbu, about whom very little is known. Along the Darling, from about Wentworth to Bourke, lived the Bagundji speaking peoples, and back from the river to the north, along the Paroo, and to the northwest as far as the South Australian border, lived a number of tribes who spoke dialects of the same language, most of whom have now died out. In the corner region, around Tibooburra, were two more tribes, the Maliangapa and Wonggumara, who were again distinct though related to others across the Queensland border.

Jeremy R Beckett

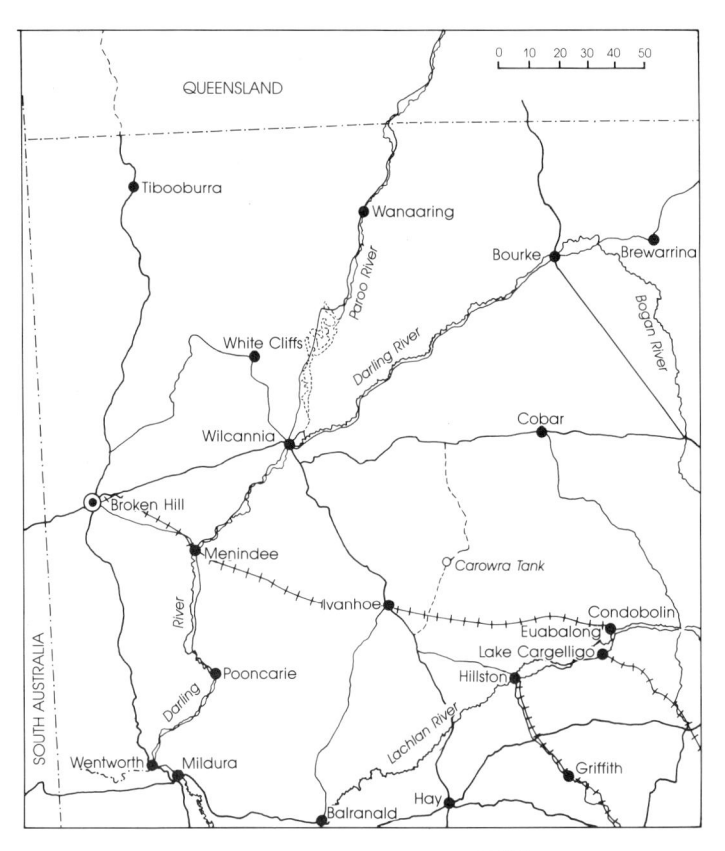

Map 7.1 The far west of New South Wales.

The major linguistic divisions seem to have been correlated with cultural differences in kinship organisation, ceremonial and mythology,[6] though how far these differences inhibited contact is hard to tell. According to native tradition, Wongaibon fought with the Lachlan River people, and both they and the Ngiemba fought the Darling River people, but again we do not know whether these hostilities were sufficiently continuous to inhibit contact. Certainly, trade linked widely separated tribes.

Europeans settled the far west early in the second half of the nineteenth century, though the settlement was very sparse for some years. Because the settlement was mainly pastoral, and Aboriginal spearing of stock provoked violent clashes in other pastoral areas, we may guess that the same occurred in this area. Bean (1911, 259), speaks of shootings along the upper Darling and there is an Aboriginal tradition of a massacre near Menindee, but information concerning this early period is very sparse. In 1883 the New South Wales government produced the first of a series of reports on the conditions of Aborigines in the far west (Protector of Aborigines 1883). By this time a *modus vivendi* had been reached, corresponding to the phase of intelligent parasitism described by Elkin (1951, 31). Aborigines camped around the small townships and large station homesteads, living partly from government handouts, partly from what they earned from doing casual stockwork and odd jobs; however, when they wished it was still possible for them to take to the bush, living on wild foods in the traditional manner and organising the old ceremonies (Beckett 1958). Depopulation, resulting possibly from shootings, and certainly from epidemics, had reduced the Aborigines to what was seen as manageable numbers—indeed, it had exterminated some tribes altogether—and they continued to decline for some years.

Table 7.1 Location of Aboriginal population in the far west, 1883 and 1915.

location	population in 1883	1915
Tibooburra	153	17
Milparinka (near Tibooburra)	80	33
Wanaaring	109	32
Wilcannia	189	5
Menindee	-	21
Pooncairie	37	26
Cobar	17	28
Ivanhoe	-	43
Mosgiel (near Ivanhoe)	99	109
Hillston	80	32
Lake Cargelligo	31	-
Euabalong	66	76
Condobolin	145	53
	1,006	475

The distribution of Aboriginal population in 1915, the last year in which the New South Wales government published detailed figures (Aborigines Protection Board 1916) is set out in Table 7.1. The figures for 1883, the date of the first survey, are added to indicate the rate of decline over the period. Up to about 1920 the tribal remnants were mostly living on or near their old territories. The possibilities for travelling had increased, however; those still interested travelled into Queensland and South Australia in search of ceremonies; others, more interested in modern things, travelled long distances as drovers or moved about from station to station in search of stockwork. One or two men never returned from their travels and a few strangers married local women and stayed, but the overall scene was fairly stable. However, the inter-war period was to bring a more serious upheaval.

The pattern of life described above was disrupted by two main factors: pastoral subdivision and the Great Depression. The subdivision of large pastoral property began during the 1900s and was resumed after the war as a means of settling ex-servicemen. In the far west, the vast sheep runs with their village-like homesteads, employing large numbers of workers and supporting small Aboriginal camps (Bean 1945, 73–76), were replaced by small family blocks which employed only a few men and could not afford to maintain Aborigines. The evicted Aborigines drifted away to live on the fringes of townships.[7]

The plight of the Wongaibon, who were the largest group in the far west, was sufficiently serious for the government Aborigines' Protection Board to establish a controlled settlement for them at Carowra Tank, providing a minimum of shelter, food for the indigent, medical care and education (Aborigines' Protection Board 1927). Similar settlements had existed for some time in the more closely settled areas, including one at Brewarrina and another at Darlington Point (near Griffith), but they had not hitherto been considered necessary in the far west; nor were the other groups in the region sufficiently large to justify the establishment of further settlements.

During the early 1930s there was serious unemployment throughout the area and for various reasons the Aborigines were particularly affected. Being ineligible for unemployment benefit (Bell 1959, 350), they were reduced to seeking government rations, and families who had previously lived independently were obliged to settle at Carowra Tank—among them a number from Hillston and the Darling River.

In 1934 the Carowra Tank water supply failed and the people were abruptly shifted to a new settlement outside Menindee. The Protection Board also seized this opportunity to bring Aborigines living at Menindee and Pooncarie under its control. As employment opportunities improved, after the outbreak of war, a number of these families resumed their independent existence and drifted up to Wilcannia. In 1948 the Aborigines' Welfare Board (the successor to the Aborigines' Protection Board) transferred the Menindee settlement 200 miles east to Murrin Bridge, near Lake Cargelligo, but while most of the Carowra Tank people were content to 'go with the mission' most of the Darling River people were not, preferring to live independently at Menindee or joining their countrymen in Wilcannia. At least ten marriages between the two groups had occurred during the period of co-residence, and when the ways parted most, though not all, husbands followed their wives' people.

The government also forced a number of Tibooburra Aborigines to move some 300 miles across to its settlement at Brewarrina, during the depression. However, as soon as employment conditions improved the majority moved back west to Bourke, Wilcannia and the corner region. The population of the corner region has been declining for many years, and the Aboriginal section of it has also been emigrating, mainly to Wilcannia and Bourke. The Wilcannia population, which has now swelled to about 300, consists mainly of Aborigines from the lower Darling, Tibooburra and the Paroo. By about 1950, then, the Aboriginal population of the far west had almost all been uprooted from their tribal territories. Few have gone outside the far west

Table 7.2 Origin of 'married' Aboriginal residents of Murrin Bridge and Wilcannia in 1957.

origin	population at Murrin Bridge	Wilcannia
Condobolin	5	-
Euabalong	3	-
Hillston, Darlington Point	12	-
Balranald, Denilaquin	5	-
Carowra Tank, Murrin Bridge	58	11
Darling River	9	30
Wilcannia	1	20
Paroo River, Tibooburra	-	15
elsewhere	1	5
	94	**81**

region, but there has been a general movement from the smallest townships and back country, to the more populous centres.

Since 1950, the main centres of Aboriginal population in the far west have been Wilcannia, Bourke, Brewarrina, Murrin Bridge (near Lake Cargelligo) and Condobolin, each with more than 200 Aborigines. Euabalong has had about fifty, and Hillston, Ivanhoe and Menindee, slightly fewer. Most originate within the region, though not necessarily at the place where they are now resident, and few from within the region have gone far afield.

In Table 7.2 the 1957 married populations of Murrin Bridge and Wilcannia are broken down according to origin. Only persons who are or have been married,[8] and thus have families of their own, are included; children up to the age of sixteen or seventeen almost invariably live with their parents; over that age, until marriage, young people wander about so much that some cannot be said to be permanently domiciled anywhere. Married people do move, but infrequently, and they can generally be regarded as being domiciled in a particular locality. Determining origin can be difficult when a person has lived in a number of places; however, Aborigines generally associate one another with particular localities which are generally where their early years were spent.

A little over sixty-three per cent of those living at Murrin Bridge originated in or around Carowra Tank (ie persons of Wongaibon descent), or the younger generation, at Menindee and Murrin Bridge settlements (most of whom are also of at least part-Wongaibon descent). Of the thirty-four outsiders, eighteen were married into this core group. This composition had changed very little by 1964, despite some turnover of population, except that there had been a slight reduction in the number of outsiders not married into the core group.

The Wilcannia population is a coming together of several stocks, of which the largest part, thirty-seven per cent in 1957, came from the Darling River (Bagundji). A little over eighteen per cent came from the back country, some from around Tibooburra (Maliagnapa) and a few from the Paroo (Barundji). A further twenty-five per cent, offspring of the others, considered Wilcannia their home. All those originating elsewhere were married into one of these stocks. Here again, this composition had changed very little by 1964, except that a few more outsiders (mainly from Murrin Bridge) had married Wilcannia people and settled there.

It can be seen from Table 7.2 that both populations consist largely of persons originating from one or two centres. In Table 7.3 are details showing the extent of

Kinship, mobility and community in rural New South Wales

dispersal of the people from these centres in 1957. About fifty-five per cent of the Carowra–Murrin Bridge stock resided at Murrin Bridge; the remainder were scattered about in twos and threes, most of them within the area confined by Lake Cargelligo–Menindee–Wilcannia–Euabalong. Ten lived outside it, but only three of them outside western New South Wales. This distribution had not changed significantly by 1964, except that rather more young people had gone to live in Wilcannia, as already noted.

Table 7.3 Distribution of 'married' far west Aborigines in 1957.

residence	origin of popultion			
	Carowra Tank, Murrin Bridge	Darling River	Wilcannia	Corner
Condobolin	2	-	-	-
Euabalong	5	-	-	-
Hillston	1	-	-	-
Griffith	1	1	-	-
Murrin Bridge	58	9	1	-
Ivanhoe	3	1	1	-
Menindee	2	5	-	-
Mildura-Wentworth	3	3	-	-
Wilcannia	11	30	20	15
Broken Hill	-	-	-	1
Tibooburra, White Cliffs, Wanaaring	-	-	-	6
Bourke, Brewarrina	-	-	-	8*
far west sheep stations	9	2	-	5
Sydney	-	-	-	1
Queensland	3	-	-	1*
	98	51	22	37*

* Note: these are estimates only.

Almost sixty per cent of the Darling River people lived at Wilcannia in 1957, while the rest were distributed within an area confined by Wilcannia–Murrin Bridge–Wentworth. Only one lived further afield. This distribution had not changed substantially by 1964, except that a few more had moved down to Wentworth district, and a few up to Bourke. The people originating in the corner area were and are more widely dispersed. Exact numbers of those living in Bourke and Brewarrina are unfortunately not available, but the majority seem to be living in these two towns and in Wilcannia.

Substantially, the distribution of population living in, or originating from the far west is the function of factors within Aboriginal society, although European society does impose some limitations. Transport itself is not a serious problem. A regular train service links the townships along the Broken Hill–Condobolin line. Back from the railway, travel is slow, uncomfortable and expensive, except for those few with cars, but it is generally possible to get wherever one wants in the long run, and Aborigines are not averse to spending substantial sums on taxis. Moving the contents of a European house might be difficult and expensive, but Aboriginal possessions are generally so few as to constitute little impediment. Representatives of the Aborigines' Welfare Board are empowered to expel undesirables from a controlled settlement (ie Murrin Bridge), but I know of only one instance in which it was done. Movement into Murrin Bridge is also limited by the lack of vacant houses and the refusal of the Board to permit the erection of temporary dwellings such as tents and scrap iron humpies. Elsewhere there is little restriction on the erection of such dwellings and, since most Aborigines are content to live in them, accommodation presents little problem.

Economic factors may perhaps discourage Aborigines from visiting certain places. Their pastoral skills are scarcely exportable to the city, but wherever sheep are raised or unskilled casual labour is employed there should be opportunities for them. There are firm, though seasonally variable limits on the amount of such labour that any locality can utilise, and when supply exceeds demand employers tend to favour workers who are already tried. However, pastoral workers do not always expect to live close to their place of work. Their families must live near town so that the children can attend school (as they are required by law to do) and since many stations are isolated, they must resign themselves to being absent from home for weeks at a time. Under these circumstances, it may not matter greatly whether they work 100 rather than fifty miles away.

External factors do not, then, closely determine the distribution of Aboriginal population, and we must look for clues within Aboriginal society. Overall, we can discern two clear trends; first, the tendency for people of the same origin to be concentrated in one or two main localities; and second, the tendency for people to live near some, though not necessarily all, of their kinsfolk.

In 1957, the following patterns of cohesion among close kin were apparent. Attachment to parents was fairly strong. Of thirty-seven men who had one or both parents living, fourteen resided elsewhere. Of forty-eight women, similarly placed, only eleven (twenty-four per cent) resided elsewhere, and of these one had been forcibly removed (from Murrin Bridge) while three lived only ten miles away. In the case of marriage between persons from different settlements, one or other spouse has to live away from his or her parent—thus five of the eleven women and three of the fourteen men living away from a parent were living near parents-in-law. Of thirty-nine sets of married siblings (each numbering two or more persons), twenty-six (sixty-six per cent) were dispersed; however, only twelve out of seventy-six married men who had siblings alive (and a much smaller proportion of women) resided where none was present. Three Aborigines who had kin somewhere resided away from them but near affines, while five lived near neither kin nor affines, having moved outside the far west region.

Kinship behaviour and mobility

The clear tendency for Aborigines to reside near at least some of their close kin can be explained by an examination of kinship relations. In terms of stability and sentiment, the relationship between mother and children is by far the strongest. Women scarcely ever desert their children, and most never leave home at all. Their lives are very largely taken up with domestic duties and it is they who obtain and prepare the food—an important consideration in a society where the supply of meals is often uncertain. In short, the mother is the pivot of the home. The bond is continued in later life, and old women, whose children have grown up, spend their lives visiting one after another, including those who have gone to reside elsewhere. Once widowed, they move in with a son or daughter and often exercise considerable authority over the next generation. The position of fathers is more variable. Divorce is fairly frequent[9] and in these cases the father generally leaves home, though he may maintain some connection with the children. Men who do pastoral work, the majority, are necessarily absent from home for long periods, and their homecomings may be marked by drunkenness and discord (Beckett 1964). Nevertheless, children generally retain some regard for their fathers, and provide a home for those who are widowed. The status of elderly parents is perhaps bolstered by the pension which they receive and which constitutes a small but regular addition to an otherwise uncertain household budget.

Genealogical knowledge goes back one or, at the most, two generations, but since many families are numerous a large number of kin may still be recognised within this narrow span. Moreover, children often use kin terms for persons to whom they know themselves to be related, though ignorant of the precise link. Vernacular kin terms have now fallen into disuse and are not known to the younger generation. In their place, the standard English terms are used, though probably used more frequently than in most white communities.

The traditional norms of kinship relations have also been abandoned, and there is now very little difference between the norms of behaviour appropriate to the various categories of kin. Briefly, these norms govern the choice of spouses, the sharing of property, particularly food, and the provision of hospitality. Sexual intercourse with first degree kin is universally considered shameful, though it seems to occur very rarely; but it is also said that mating with any consanguineal kin is improper. Where genealogies are no deeper than three generations the prohibition cannot extend beyond second cousins, but in practice, marriages between more distant kin are extremely rare. This can be safely concluded, even without genealogies, since, as I show later, so many have taken their spouses from other local groups with whom there was previously no contact. A recent marriage between second cousins once removed[10] evoked no comment, but this is the only 'test case' available to me. In principle, the prohibition is so generally accepted that little attempt is made to justify it. Aborigines sometimes suggest that 'close' marriages produce unhealthy children, but this may well be a *post hoc* justification. The old rules forbade marriage with close kin, even when these were in the correct kinship category, but whether this has carried over into the contemporary situation or whether there is an unexpressed disinclination for marrying those with whom one already has defined rights and obligations, is hard to say.

Discussing traditional Aboriginal attitudes to property, Elkin (1951, 165) has written, 'the goods are to use or to give away or to exchange (mostly ceremonially); food is obtained to eat and to share according to rules'. Today, the ceremonial function is defunct and the rules are forgotten, but the general principle still holds. The obligation to share food, clothes and—more doubtfully—money, with kin who are in need is loosely defined and frequently evaded, but it is nevertheless recognised in principle and is of great social importance.

The sharing of food was important in 'nomadic times' because the fortunes of the chase were uncertain and a regular supply of meat for each family could only be ensured in this way. Today, wild food is a minor item of diet but food supplies are uncertain for other reasons. Aboriginal workers can earn quite substantial wages, but the supply of housekeeping money is irregular; many return after several weeks' work with their wages in a lump sum, which, in the flush of momentary opulence, is quickly dissipated in purchases of liquor, small luxuries, handouts to kin and foodstuffs. The foodstuffs will also be shared with other households in need at the time. Men may spend several idle weeks at home before returning to work, by which time money and food are exhausted and the housewife obliged to go borrowing. In theory at least, some of those whom she has helped are now well equipped and ready to reciprocate, although there is no strict accounting.

In practice there are some who borrow more than they lend and a few who are little more than parasites, but even these generally get what they want. Women may call the adults bludgers[11] but confess that they 'don't like to see the little children going short'. Families may opt out of this system if they wish. Indeed, it is necessary to do so if one intends to adopt a European way of life, which involves accumulating property, but they will be called 'flash'[12] and will be placed in a humiliating position if they ever find themselves in need. In a context of irregular work and improvidence, then, sharing food is an economic necessity as well as a civic virtue, and there is a crucial dependence between households.

There is little diffidence in asking for help and great reluctance to refuse. However, requests are generally addressed to kin and relatedness is implicitly or explicitly regarded as a charter. Those who have known one another for many years but are not related may also recognise similar rights and obligations, but with less certainty, while strangers are virtually excluded. An Aboriginal family, then, unless it is prepared to be entirely self-reliant, must live near some kinsfolk with whom it can engage in sharing relations. Persons of Carowra Tank origin living at Murrin Bridge have a very wide range of kin; but those living in Wilcannia are not completely isolated, even if they have no links with the Darling River people. The need is to live near some but not necessarily all of one's kin.

The right to ask, and the obligation to provide hospitality, only arise in the case of people coming from other places, either as transient visitors or as intending immigrants. In either case, hospitality is provided for long periods without overt complaint and with very little attempt to make the guests 'pay their way'. Again, these rights are recognised mainly among kinsfolk although strangers are occasionally sponsored by a friend who has met them elsewhere.

Aborigines are generally unwilling to go where they are not known, for a number of reasons. Prior to 1962 the law forbidding the supply of liquor to Aborigines prevented them from seeking accommodation in hotels, and even now some landlords would refuse to accept them as guests. Thus the hospitality of other Aborigines is the only alternative. Finding work in a strange locality may also be harder, particularly for Aborigines who are shy in the presence of Europeans, and there is always the risk of being charged with vagrancy if one is unemployed. Aborigines in other regions succeed in overcoming these problems and become quite self-reliant after one or two experiences as servicemen or as long distance drovers, but few in the far west have served in the armed forces and little long distance droving is now carried on. A number have been sent to a state capital for medical attention, but they seem to have seen little and made no social contacts there. My suggestion that a spontaneous visit should be made to a city evoked the almost standard response: 'I'd get lost.'

Far west Aborigines often strike the stranger as shy and they are undoubtedly hesitant about going where they would feel out of place. However, they like to travel where they are known, that is to say, where they have kin or close affines who, even though not personally acquainted, can be asked to provide hospitality. Considerable value is attached to seeing a bit of the world, even though that bit is only a tiny township which scarcely differs from the one left, and there is a steady traffic between the main centres of Aboriginal population, particularly of old women visiting their married children and young people 'taking a trip'. Single boys and girls travel a good deal: their lack of domestic responsibilities renders them particularly mobile, but some may also be in search of a spouse from another place.

The rule against marrying kin drastically reduces the number of eligible partners in some places, notably at Murrin Bridge. The population there is very much interrelated and a large proportion of the Carowra Tank–Murrin Bridge people are the descendants of three sisters. Boys and girls of the third generation find themselves with a choice of only two or three eligible partners for whom, of course, the competition is intense. Had they been cut off from outside contacts the old rule would certainly have broken down, but contacts—first with Hillston, later with the Darling River (due to the merging at the Menindee settlement) and recently through intervisiting with Wilcannia and other places—have reduced the strain upon it. Of 119 current marriages involving at least one Aborigine who originated in the far west, eighty-nine (almost seventy-five per cent) were contracted with a spouse who originated from a different locality or—in a few instances—who was a European.

When I returned in 1964, after an interval of seven years, the pattern was essentially the same. Of twenty-six marriages occurring in the interim, sixteen were between persons who normally resided in different localities, having resulted from one partner visiting the locality of the other. Three more were between persons who, though currently living in the same locality, had originated in different ones; while a further four were between persons whose respective parents originated in different localities, though they themselves belonged to the same locality. In short, the process of migration and visiting within the region has resulted in intermarriage between localised groups which were originally almost endogamous.

All Aboriginal people have 'beats', areas which are defined by the situation of kin who will give them hospitality, within which they can travel as much or as little as they please, and where they are most likely to find spouses. Proximity is only a minor factor. When first working in Murrin Bridge, I was impressed by the fact that most of the people knew far more about Wilcannia (200 miles away) and visited it more frequently, than they did Euabalong (only ten miles away) or Condobolin (only thirty). One explanation is that the Murrin Bridge people have lived near these last two places only since 1948, whereas their contacts with the Darling River people go back to 1934 and before. However, one might expect links to have developed after a decade. In fact, over the last seven years only one marriage has been contracted with Condobolin and only one with Euabalong, as against six with Wilcannia.

A child acquires kinship connections through both parents; if the parents originated from different localities the child's own constellation of kin[13] is likely to be more widely dispersed than either one of theirs. If the child again marries someone from another locality, his or her children's kin constellation will be still more widely dispersed. Consider the following case:

> Gloria is a Murrin Bridge resident whose mother comes from Carowra Tank and whose father comes from Hillston. Most of her maternal kin live in the same settlement, but she has a mother's brother in Mildura and a mother's sister's son in Wilcannia. Her father's kin live in Hillston, Griffith and Condobolin.
> Gloria has married Mervyn, a Wilcannia resident, whose mother comes from Tibooburra and whose father comes from the Darling River. His maternal kin live in Wilcannia and Bourke, while his paternal kin live at various points along the lower Darling and at Murrin Bridge.

The marriage is hypothetical—no one yet has kin so widely dispersed as the offspring would have—nevertheless it is most likely to become a reality before long.

Assuming that genealogical knowledge becomes cumulative, and that Aborigines continue to provide visiting kin with a *pied-a-terre*, beats will tend to become more extensive with each new generation. If we further assume that the prohibition on marriage with kin persists, there will be an increasing tendency to seek further afield for marriage partners. For example, a child of Gloria and Mervyn might find a spouse in Bourke, whose kin lay further to the north and east, or in Mildura, whose kin extended south into Victoria. In short, if our assumptions hold, the social insulation of Aborigines in the far west is breaking down, and will continue to do so with increasing rapidity.

Of course, these assumptions may not hold, for the Aboriginal kinship system is subject to both internal strains and external pressures. Fundamental to the system is the use of genealogy as a means of classifying people. It is particularly appropriate in homogeneous societies whose members are otherwise distinguishable only by gender, age and personal idiosyncrasies. Contemporary Aboriginal society is precisely of this character and it generates strong pressures against incipient economic, political or religious differentiation. Gradations of skin colour are also without significance in the far west. Increasing concern with colour, as in Brewarrina (Fink 1957); living standards, as in Moree (Reay and Sitlington 1948); or religion, as on the north coast (Calley 1964), would reduce or modify the use of kinship as a means of classification and a framework for social relations. Such developments would, moreover, conflict with the types of rights and obligations which now make up the substance of kinship relations. Those claiming superiority on grounds of lighter skin colour would scarcely welcome visits from darker relatives; those trying to accumulate property would not welcome the importunings of feckless kin. Similarly, those who have joined some puritanical religion will wish to stand apart from those who remain addicted to drinking and gambling.

Even if these major changes do not occur, it is still not yet certain whether genealogical knowledge will become cumulative or whether more remote ties will be forgotten with each new generation. Till now, genealogies have usually been shallow. However, those kin who are the most remote geographically are not necessarily the most remote genealogically, so that the extension of kin ties over an ever-widening area need not be prevented by the loss of some connections. It is also uncertain whether marriage will be prohibited even with genealogically remote kin, or whether, in emulation of white people, even cousin marriage will come to be considered permissible. Such changes could reduce one of the pressures toward seeking spouses from other localities, but if young people continue to travel for other reasons the probability of their marrying non-kin would be higher than if they stay at home. Since travel in itself widens the choice of marriage partners, it is this rather than any marriage rule which is the primary determinant of inter-locality marriages.

Yet another assumption made in these prognoses is that more distant groups of Aborigines will be content to marry the far westerners, and that their social systems are essentially the same. From the handful of studies already done in surrounding areas, there does seem to be a broad uniformity—most Aborigines live more or less apart from Europeans, while among themselves social relations are organised on kinship lines. Some are even more mobile than their far west cousins, but the majority seem to confine their journeyings to a set beat. However, there are differences in marriage preferences. For example, the main groups of Victorian Aborigines, whose unity derives from common local origin, prefer to marry among themselves, although they recognise a prohibition on first—and sometimes also second—cousin marriages (Barwick 1963, 256–64). This preference seems to be based on an unwillingness to go to live among strangers and the expectation that the other spouse would be unhappy away from his people. Other groups, such as those at Moree, base a like preference on their adherence to higher living standards (Reay and Sitlington 1948). To these too, far west Aborigines would scarcely be acceptable. However, the areas immediately on the periphery of the far west do not seem to be so exclusive, and it is with them that intermarriage is most likely to occur over the next generation.

Kinship, mobility and community

Far west Aborigines distinguish two main classes of humanity: European and Aboriginal, concerning each of which they have fairly well developed stereotypes. Aborigines are deemed to have a common culture in which open-handedness, particularly toward kin, is valued, and any form of exclusiveness or superiority disapproved as an attempt to ape Europeans. However, while it is expected that all Aborigines will conform to these norms, personal responsibility is accepted only for those who are 'known'. One is known wherever one has lived and wherever one has kin; where one has kin one can also visit and meet the other local people face-to-face. There are no other means whereby one can become known, even by repute. If we are to speak of an Aboriginal belonging to a community wider than the local residential group, it is his or her beat—the localities where there are kin who will provide a *pied-a-terre*. In this sense, each individual a personal community, but inasmuch as people are closely inter-related and tend to marry into the same local groups, communities tend to coincide. Few far west Aborigines are known outside the region, and few living elsewhere are known within it.

No far west Aborigine has achieved any reputation among Aborigines living outside the region, and only those few outsiders who have received some notice in the mass media—for example, the painter Namatjira and the popular recording artist Jimmy Little—have achieved any reputation within it. The marked lack of interest in outsiders is an important factor in Aborigines' lack of political unity. The Welfare Board has for some years encouraged New South Wales Aborigines to elect a representative, but the elections have been conducted on a State-wide basis and it has never been possible to find a candidate known to everyone. For many years the Aboriginal 'representative' has come from other parts of the State, leaving the far west people without any sense of being represented at all. The only one whose name is remembered and occasionally mentioned, Bill Ferguson, was related by marriage through his brother to the Carowra Tank people. For much the same reasons, probably, the religious revivals among Aborigines of other regions have never spread to the far west. The ideologies of 'hot Gospel' sects and the various groups now working for Aboriginal rights in the more closely settled areas, implicitly at least transcend locality and kinship,[14] but it seems as though they must be transmitted initially along the roads provided by kinship.

Notes

1. Reprinted with revisions with kind permission from the *International Journal of Comparative Sociology* 6, 1965. Previously entitled 'Kinship, Mobility and Community among Aborigines in the Far West of New South Wales'.
2. 'Nomad tribe' was the name given to Australian pastoral workers by the author Anthony Trollope, when he visited Australia during 1870 (Trollope 1873, 69); see also Ward (1958, 9).
3. A more detailed account of race relations in the far west can be found in Beckett (1964).
4. In 1957, four Aboriginal women were married to or living with European men around Wilcannia; there were no Murrin Bridge Aborigines married to or living with Europeans, though in neighbouring Euabalong five women and three men were involved in mixed marriages.
5. Australian tribal boundaries have been drawn by Tindale (1940), utilising a number of sources. See Beckett (1958) for a re-drawing of some of the boundaries in the corner area.
6. There is a voluminous though often superficial literature on the culture and social organisation of the tribes of the far west, mostly dating from the late nineteenth and early twentieth centuries, see Greenway (1963).

7. A similar upheaval seems to have occurred on the north coast of New South Wales (Hausfield 1963).

8. Aborigines distinguish between those couples who are legally married and those who are simply 'living'. However, the distinction is of no practical significance and I include both types of relation under the heading 'married'.

9. In 1957 approximately twenty per cent of Wilcannia and Murrin Bridge Aborigines who had ever been married (formally or informally), had also been divorced.

10. The boy married his mother's mother's sister's (and also mother's father's brother's) daughter's daughter's daughter. His father claimed to have been unaware of the connection until I pointed it out.

11. 'Bludger' is popular Australian slang for a parasite.

12. 'Flash' is nineteenth century Australian and Cockney slang applied to anyone affecting showy or superior ways.

13. Piddington (1961, 16) has chosen the word 'constellation' from several suggested by Firth (1956, 16) 'to apply to the aggregate of effective kinsfolk centred round a given individual'.

14. In this connection, the words of Sydney Aboriginal spokesman and 'freedom rider', Charles Perkins, are very relevant: 'Aborigines used to be very quick to say to someone— 'You're a Barrowville boy, or you're from Queensland or you're a Kempsey boy'. If the kinship ties weren't there they wouldn't have much to do with you. But now there's a growing feeling that we're all part of one people' (Lipski 1965).

References

Barwick, D.E.
1963 A Little More than Kin: Regional Affiliation and Group Identity Among Aboriginal Migrants in Melbourne, PhD thesis, Australian National University.

Bean, C.E.W.
1911 The 'Dreadnought' of the Darling, Angus and Robertson, Sydney.
1945 On the Wool Track, Angus and Robertson, Sydney.

Beckett, J.R.
1958 Marginal Men: A Study of Two Half Caste Aborigines, Oceania 29, 91–108.
1964 Aborigines, Alcohol and Assimilation. In M. Reay (ed), Aborigines Now: New Perspectives in the Study of Aboriginal Communities, Angus and Robertson, Sydney.

Bell, J.H.
1959 Official Policies towards the Aborigines of New South Wales, Mankind 5(8), 345–55.

Calley, M.J.
1964 Pentecostalism among the Bandjalang. In M. Reay (ed), Aborigines Now: New Perspectives in the Study of Aboriginal Communities, Angus and Robertson, Sydney.

Elkin, A.P.
1951 Reaction and Interaction: A Food-gathering People and European Settlement in Australia, American Anthropologist 53, 164–86.

Fink, R.A.
1957 The Caste Barrier—An Obstacle to the Assimilation of Part-Aborigines in North-West New South Wales, Oceania 28, 100–10.

Firth, R.
1956 *Two Studies of Kinship in London*, University of London, The Athlone Press, London.

Greenway, J.
1963 *Bibliography of Australian Aborigines and the Native Peoples of Torres Strait to 1959*, Angus and Robertson, Sydney.

Hausfield, R.H.
1963 Dissembled Culture: An Essay on Method, *Mankind* 6(2), 47–51.

Lipski, S.
1965 The Freedom Riders, *The Bulletin* 87, 4434.

Piddington, R.
1961 A Study of French Canadian Kinship, *International Journal of Comparative Sociology* 2(1), 3–22.

Reay, M. and G. Sitlington
1948 Class Status in a Mixed-Blood Community, Moree, New South Wales, *Oceania* 18, 179–207.

Tindale, N.B.
1940 Distribution of Australian Aboriginal Tribes: A Field Survey, *Transactions of the Royal Society of South Australia* 64, 140–231.

Trollope, A.
1873 *Australia and New Zealand*, George Robertson, Melbourne.

Ward, R.
1958 *The Australian Legend*, Oxford University Press, Melbourne.

8. Chris Birdsall   All one family

In his paper entitled 'Southwest Aboriginal Society', Howard (1980, 98) writes of the Nyungar people,

> In the face of such a hostile environment Aborigines have had to build protective barriers and to rely on norms of social solidarity. Whites, supposedly for the Aborigines' own good, have been trying to destroy these barriers and change these norms for over a century. So far, southwestern Aborigines have been able to resist such external pressures and to maintain their identity and a style of life which is in many ways distinct and not without merit.

The extent of Nyungar success in maintaining their identity and their distinct style of life may be measured in part by their capacity to retain their own form of social structure within the towns of their adopted country, hundreds of kilometres distant from their traditional regions in the southwest. It is the purpose of this chapter to examine the bases of social identity and the form of kinship organisation that have enabled the Nyungar people to maintain themselves as a distinct socio-cultural group within the wider Australian society.

The Nyungar people are native to southwestern Western Australia. Through the pressures of the assimilation policies of previous decades and the search for work, they have become widely scattered along the coast, as far north as Broome (see Maps 8.1 and 8.2). They are now a people of the towns and cities whose first language is English.[1] Although little now remains of their original language, the Nyungar people retain knowledge of the names and locations of some of the original tribes, some myth cycles, naming practices, and aspects of the spirit world. As well, they remain a distinctive socio-cultural category, maintaining a particular system of kinship organisation. This system of kinship organisation is the basis of Nyungar social structure, one feature of which is the pattern of geographic dispersal of the Nyungar people. Within their southwest territory many Nyungar people have maintained an attachment to and residence within particular regions for many generations. Each of these regions is identified with and occupied by the members of particular extended kin groups. According to their own accounts, they have habitually dispersed themselves around and in the towns of these regions while still maintaining an integrated extended family type of kinship organisation among the related family groups.

The northward movement of the Nyungar people has taken place comparatively recently in their history, beginning at the time of World War II. During this time, the Department of Native Affairs suffered the transfer of a significant proportion of its personnel to other, war-related areas of administration. Because of this, the department was unable effectively to administer the provisions of the 1936 Aboriginal Administration Act. As a result, Aborigines experienced more relaxed conditions than previously and were able to move about more freely in search of employment (Howard 1980, 94). In their northward progress, the Nyungar people colonised the new territory in a particularly Nyungar way—as in the southwest, the extended family group was dispersed among a particular set of towns, and the unity of the family group was maintained over the distances.

All one family, lines and runs

Nearly all Nyungar individuals claim membership in one or another of a number of large groups based on cognatic descent from a known ancestor. Often little is known of the early life of this individual apart from his or her parentage. Such an individual was quite often born of a union between a white man and an Aboriginal woman, whose name is remembered, although not the details of her life history. In the telling of the family history, this woman appears as a shadowy figure about whom 'we don't know too much, just her name, that's all'. Her child appears as a fully adult man or woman with children but no known siblings: 'We know he had a lot of half-sisters and brothers, but we don't know their names or who their father was.' Such a genealogy may look like that shown in Figure 8.1.

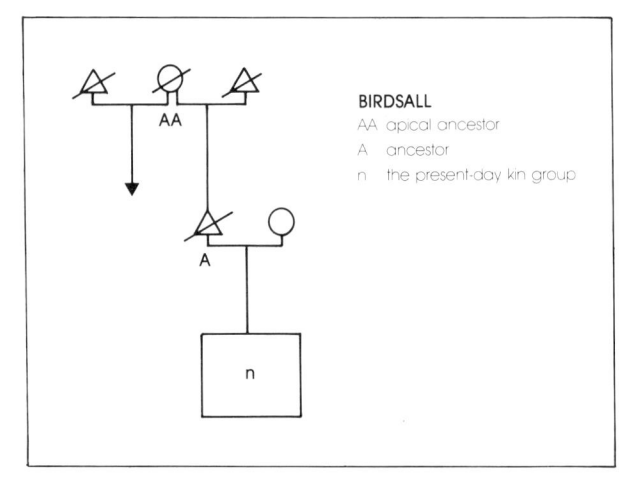

Figure 8.1 Cognatic Kin Group One.

In other cases, however, knowledge of this apical ancestress is quite detailed, including knowledge of her unions previous to and succeeding the one resulting in the founder of the present-day kin group. Such a genealogy may appear like that in Figure 8.2.

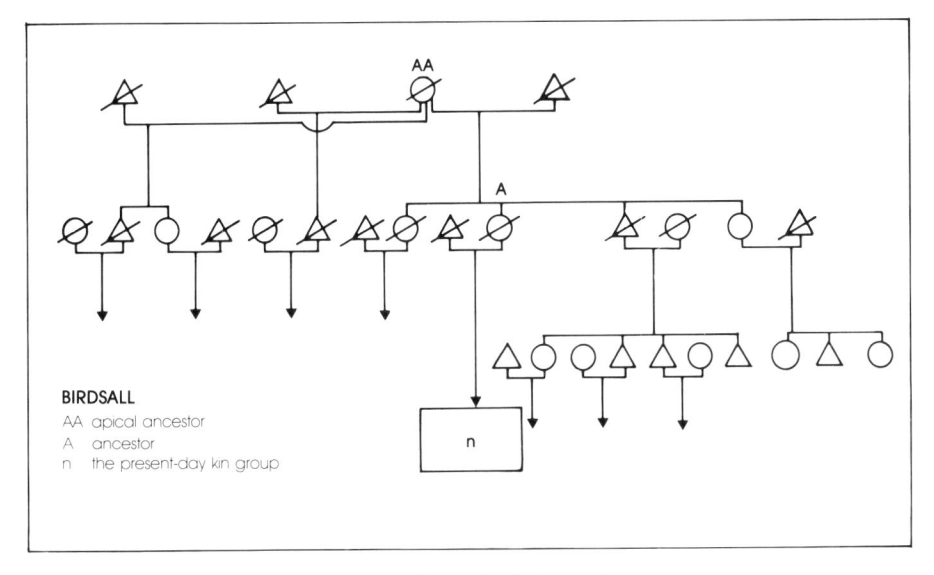

Figure 8.2 Cognatic Kin Group Two.

There is thus great variation among these large kin groups with regard to knowledge of their origins. Whatever the depth of their knowledge of family history, detailed questioning of individuals regarding their family connections always elicits a statement along the lines of, 'It all goes back to this old girl. That's where it all started, and now, we're all one family.' This phrase, all one family, is commonly used in such discussions to refer to the large kin group. Every such group has a surname which is used when people are discussing the kin group affiliation of individuals, as the following discussion illustrates:[2]

> 'Who's that woolly-headed boy, that one there, headed for the post office?'
> 'That's Arnold Halfpenny.'
> 'Who's he in with?'
> 'He's one o them Calleys.'
> 'From down Pingelly way?'
> 'No, not them Calleys. These the Northam Calleys. Northam, York, Quarading, Merredin, Goomalling; all through there.'

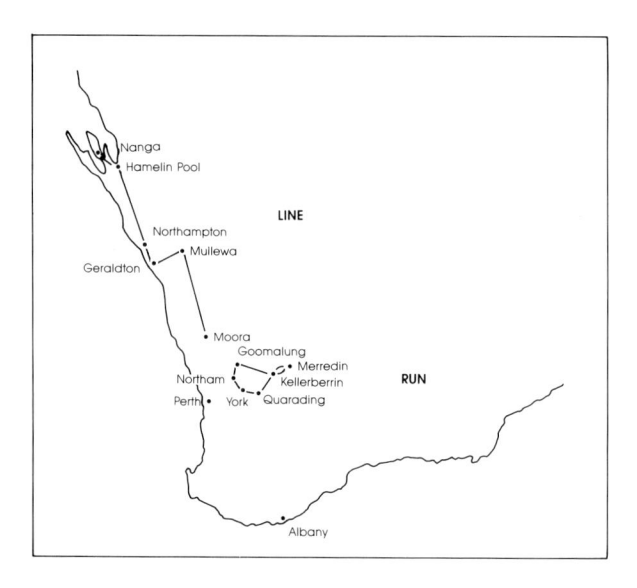

Map 8.2 Hypothetical examples of a run and a line in the southwest.

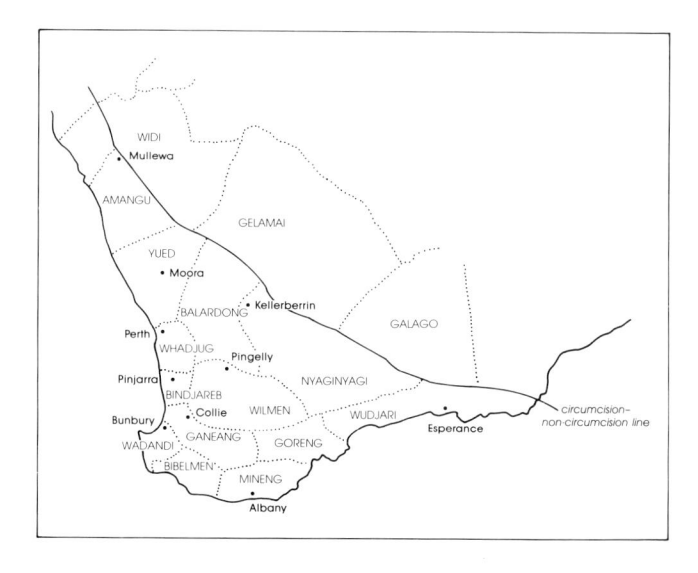

Map 8.1 Tribes of the southwest, after Tindale (1940), as amended by RM Berndt (1980).

The members of the kin group, the all one family, only use the surname to refer to themselves when they are explaining to a complete outsider who they are and what kin group they are affiliated with, or as the Nyungar people would put it, who they are 'in with'. The all one family generally numbers between 200 and 300 individuals who, as is shown in the above discussion, may be widely dispersed throughout various regions of the southwest. Many of these individuals may not see one another from one year to the next, but they will still take care that their exact genealogical relationship, according to Nyungar reckoning, is known. The all one family is divided into a number of sections of approximately forty to 150 people. These sections have no specific term but are variously and interchangeably referred to as 'lots', 'mobs', or simply 'that part of the family'.

Such sections are groups of individuals usually descended from a set of 'sibling-cousins', who are usually women in late-middle to old age. The sibling-cousin set, which often numbers no more than four individuals, is in the third ascending generation. These women work to hold their family together as a community through close and continuing cooperation over the years. Above this group, in the fourth ascending generation, is the oldest living member(s) of their parents' sibling-cousin set. This individual, who may be a man or a woman, has ordinarily passed or is passing the point of taking a fully active role in his or her family's social life, and has become a living symbol of the common bond of kinship which is the basis of Nyungar social organisation. It is within these sections of the larger all one family that the greater proportion of social interaction takes place. The individual's closest friendships are found and his or her greatest loyalty and commitment are given to this group of kin, who form a discrete community within the wider framework of Australian society (MacIver 1948, 8).

The family community is ordinarily not localised in one town, but is dispersed throughout a set of towns, usually within one region of the southwest. Often, the family community can claim a long history of association with their claimed region, verifiable by local mission records of births, deaths and marriages from the last century. The set of towns within a particular region is referred to by the Nyungar as a 'run', equivalent to the 'beat' referred to by Beckett (see Chapter 7). The concept of a run has no meaning unless it is attached to a particular family community, and a run is usually spoken of in the possessive; for example, our run, their run, or his run. The towns of a run form a rough circle and Nyungars often speak of travelling around their run.

However, not all Nyungars can claim a long history of association with their claimed set of towns, for many Aboriginal people were transported to missions and settlements far distant from their places of birth, as has been documented by other researchers (eg Biskup 1973; Howard 1981; Rowley 1970; Haebich 1982). In such cases, individuals have attempted to return to their old homes many years after being transported, despite having married and had children among the people of the region to which they were transported. These people have had to work their way home over many years. Often they will have settled in one town and moved on after a few years' residence. Not all their children will have followed them to the old home; a few were always left behind. Some married or single people in one or another of the towns *en route* simply decided that they liked it in one of these towns and stayed behind to take up residence. This process creates a 'line' of towns rather than the circular formation of towns in a run. Unlike the run, however, these towns do not represent ancestral claims to an entire region; rather, they represent a path of migration. Correspondingly, one does not travel around the line; rather, one travels up or down it. Moreover, the towns of a line tend to be far more distant from one another than the towns of a run.

Despite the differences in historical origin and geographical form and location (see Map 8.2), the members of the family communities occupying the towns of a line face essentially the same problems as those who occupy the towns of a run. These are the problems of maintaining continuity of social organisation and unity of the family as a community over the distances of time and space that separate its members from one another. The only way to accomplish a solution to these problems is to engage in regular and frequent travel among the towns of the claimed region. However, the practice of frequent travel presents a heavy drain on the limited resources of the Nyungar people. On account of their poverty, it is difficult and costly for the Nyungars to mount these journeys. This is particularly so for those of the lines because the distances involved are so much greater between their towns than between the towns of a run. To an outside observer it would seem to make better sense, economically anyway, to travel less often or not at all.

It is not lack of opportunity to engage in regular social contact with others that motivates people to travel. Nyungars are well represented in the populations of the towns in these claimed regions and, in general, the Nyungars of a town are well known to one another. And so, usually, no shortage of opportunity to interact with other Nyungar people exists. Given all this, the question becomes, Why is it important to the Nyungars that they individually remain part of a family community? With this question in mind, let us consider some aspects of the dynamics of Nyungar family organisation and the ways in which Nyungar people establish social identity.

Family and identity

Nyungar people make three sets of claims in identifying themselves. They claim membership in an all one family, they claim special knowledge of a set of towns recognised by other Nyungars as belonging to one of the family communities comprising that all one family, and one particular town in this claimed set is specially claimed as identifying the individual. Of foremost significance is the claim to family membership, because regional and town identity derive from family membership. Without membership in a family community, the individual cannot fully participate in Nyungar social life. Further, such an individual lacks the bases of social identity by which Nyungar people mark themselves off from the rest of the world and, to a lesser extent, from one another.

Nyungar social life is bound by an institution of reciprocal obligation. Rules of common practice define, who owes whom, and what sort of service on the basis of age and kin relationships. Such rules therefore do not operate systematically among people who have no consanguineal or affinal links. Consanguineal links moreover are fully operative only between people who have a 'rearing-up relationship', that is, the individual must have been reared-up by or with one of the senior women of the family community. Affinal links to members of a family community are operative only if the individual marries a person who has such a rearing-up relationship within the family community.

The means by which rearing-up links are established between kin is the regular practice of sending or taking children to live with their mothers' kin for varying periods of time throughout their childhood. This practice has an important role in teaching children that they live in a world where responsibility and relationships are generalised rather than privatised. For example, primary responsibility for children rests with the mother, but certain others have controlling interests in their welfare, chief among whom are the maternal aunts and grandmothers.[3] Children are taught that aunts are 'the next best thing to your mother', and likewise that the children of aunts are to be regarded no different from siblings. Often the means used to teach this is the obligation to share goods with kin. For example, when one child has a packet of lollies and the child's cousin wants a share, he or she will be instructed to share in the following terms: 'Give some to sister now, good girl', or 'Give some to budga-boy' (younger brother).

In a Nyungar extended family the oldest child in a group of children is held to be responsible for the younger ones when the group is out of sight of adults. This child is duty bound to 'tell' if the younger ones misbehave. If a younger child takes harm or does harm, the older one may be punished, but when such punishment is meted out, the older child has no compunction in surreptitiously redistributing the punishment among the younger ones. The children thus learn very early that they are accountable for their actions to each other, because individuals' actions have consequences for the entire group.

The membership of the sibling-cousin set is established relatively early in individuals' lives and is limited to those who were reared-up together. In being reared-up together, children acquire a commonality of life history. They share their childhood and are known to one another as they are known to no-one else. The basis of individual social identity is partly founded in this experience of having been reared-up as part of a sibling-cousin set. Furthermore, over time the members of this group foster and continuously evoke for one another an individual style of social interaction. It is only within this group that the individual is able to exhibit the full flowering of his or her social being, because only this group has the knowledge necessary to evoke and support the individual's personal style.

It is expected that sooner or later, the child will come to prefer certain of the mother's kin over the rest, and will ask to visit these particular people more often than other kin. Feelings are not hurt by this, nor are the child's wishes in this regard thwarted. Rather this is seen as an important act of choice reflecting some little understood aspect of the child's inner being. Specifically, it is said to be the child's will directing the basis of what is later to become the child's town-based identity.

The mother's influence in directing a child's choice of certain kin over others is great, however the child must be seen by others to give expression to this choice so that the interpretation of the child's will can be publicly declared. For example, a child may be said to be 'a real Carnarvon girl, that one, right from when she was just a little one. She always was wantin to go to Carnarvon, go to Carnarvon, always wantin to go stop with Elsie and them.' Individuals will similarly declare this of themselves.

The individual who claims to be a Nyungar of a particular town, often regardless of birthplace, must maintain that basis of identity through residence or through regular visits to the town. Often, if the individual is too long in the south, living in Perth for example, the person's Carnarvon sibling-cousins will often taunt him or her when they next meet, saying that, for example, she is no longer a Carnarvon girl: 'You a city-slicker now.' 'Don't call me a city-slicker,' comes the retort. 'No city-slickers here. I grew up in this town.' Sometimes the individual can be so long absent from the town that kin will declare, for example, 'No, she's not from here no more. She's a Mullewa girl these days.'

There is a heavy investment of time involved in maintaining membership in a family community. One must regularly visit and be visited by kin both within one's town of primary residence and among the other towns of the run or line. An individual who fails to visit regularly will eventually lose his or her place in the constellation of kin relationships, and may be deprived of a part of the basis of his or her social identity, in particular the claim to be a Nyungar person of a specially claimed town. In losing this, the person is symbolically deprived of a close relationship with sibling-cousins who live in that town. These are the people with whom the person was reared-up and who helped foster a self-image based in the role as a member of that sibling-cousin set. This role must be enacted if it is to be retained by the individual. Visiting, regularly and often, is the means to accomplish this.

Visiting, and style of travel

Visiting from one town to another always occurs in the context of 'business'. The kind of business depends on the age and gender of the individual and role relationships within the family community (Bott 1957, 3). Also dependent upon age, gender and role relationship, is the actual style of travel; that is, whether travel is undertaken with a group or alone, the composition of a group, the type of transportation employed and the degree of self-determination in making the decision to travel.

When travelling from town to town young men can travel (by car) either alone or in a group. Such a group generally would be composed only of other young men. Young women very rarely travel alone. 'A man can always look after himself—it is said; 'A woman can't. A woman goes with people who are not her relations, they'll never take up for her or give her a home. They don't have to.' Outside the world of the family community, then, there is potential for danger from which a woman cannot protect herself; the danger of attack from strangers, the danger of having no-one to take her side and the danger of finding herself destitute with no one to turn to for the basic necessities of life. She must stay within the family community in order to be assured of protection from these dangers. But it is not necessarily the men who protect her from danger. More often, the people who come to her aid are her sister-cousins, her aunts, her grandmother and her mother. In travelling from town to town, women will ordinarily travel in a three-generational group composed of one or more of their mothers or their mothers' sister-cousins, their own sister-cousins and their children. The older women prefer this mode of travel, though they can also take the bus. Younger people prefer not to travel by bus, and describe it as 'Going in with all the old womens.'

Travel frequency: an exemplary case

McNish is the name I use to refer to a large all one family among whom I conducted field research between September 1980 and December 1982. This all one family numbers more than 300 individuals, divided into two family communities. One of these family communities is composed of a group of southwestern people occupying a run, while the other is a northern coastal group occupying a line. I refer to this McNish line-community in the following discussion.

The family community numbers 162 individuals. Their line includes Perth, two wheatbelt towns and three northern coastal towns. These northern towns figure largely in the discussion that follows and so I have adopted pseudonyms for them: Bayshore, LaMarr and DeLand. The majority of the family community lives principally in Perth, Bayshore and DeLand. The data in Table 8.1 refer to all the travel engaged in by the McNishes, over an eight-week period between 6 June 1982 and 25 July 1982, which took in the town of Carnarvon.

In this eight-week period, thirty-eight people engaged in twenty-four separate trips, travelling to, from or through the town of Bayshore. Thus at some time during

Table 8.1 McNish family journeys, 6 June–25 July 1982.

location	total family population	number travelling through Carnarvon	percentage of town population
DeLand	46	6	13.0
Bayshore	38	16	42.1
Perth	51	12	23.5
other (wanderers and ramblers)	4	0	0.0
	23	4	17.4
	162	38	23.5

this period 23.5 per cent of the McNish family community was known to be in transit somewhere along the line. (This figure includes only people travelling through Bayshore, and there were in fact more people travelling during this period, whose travel did not include Bayshore. Firm data could not be obtained on the travels of these people and so they have been omitted in this case.)

Twenty-three members of the family community do not principally reside in any of the towns along the line. They are said to wander or ramble among all the towns. They have no homes of their own and regard themselves as being equally at home among any and all of their kin up and down the line. They travel more or less continuously. Five of these people are young men aged seventeen and over who have left their mothers' homes in search of jobs, wives and adventure. Not all young men do this, but it is an optional mode of behaviour that any young unmarried man may from time to time engage in.

The remainder of the wanderers and ramblers are referred to by their kin as the 'drunkers' or the 'no-hopers'. These are people aged twenty-three and over who have never 'settled down'. That is, they have never shown any interest in establishing themselves in a home, or in looking after their children (who are often reared-up by their kin), or in establishing a stable marital relationship. They tend to get drunk 'too much'. For these reasons, they are a constant source of worry to their kin, as well as being a continual drain on the resources of the family community.

On a trip

As used by Nyungar people, the term 'trip' refers to travel engaged in to accomplish an objective. When that objective is accomplished, the trip is over. Nyungars rarely speak of going on holiday. This expression was sometimes used in reference to children's school holidays, or in jest, as in the following extract of conversation:

> 'Yeah, well, I think I need a holiday.'
> 'Yeah Aunty? Where you thinkin of goin?'
> 'I think I might go to Bali. Leave all you fellas behind.'
> 'Yeah? Hey you fellas. Aunty Dorie's goin to Bali, and she's not takin any of us along.'
> 'Yeah? What you goin to do in Bali all by yourself, Aunty?'
> 'Oh you never know what I might get up to. Nobody there to see, I might do anything.'

A trip may take several forms. A woman, for example, may wish to travel from Perth to DeLand for some purpose but may not be able to find transport past Bayshore. She may wait in Bayshore (for a day, a week or a month) until she can get transport, whereupon she will resume her trip. When she gets back home to Perth, her trip will be over. The separate legs of the trip are not counted as individual trips despite the time spent waiting. However, if while she was waiting for a lift to DeLand she were to avail herself of an opportunity to go to a third town for a visit and then back to Bayshore, that would be a separate trip. If she decides that she will not get transport to DeLand within what she deems a reasonable period of time, she will give up her objective and return to Perth. This entire period of travel she will refer to as a 'wasted trip'.

Reasons for travel depend on the individual's time of life and role relationships within the family community. For example, a woman with grown children and grandchildren will travel in order to ensure that her daughters are rearing-up their children properly. If any of her daughters have become 'drunkers', have abandoned or are neglecting or abusing their children, the woman must exercise her authority to rescue her grandchildren from their unfit parents. These older women also have the responsibility to oversee the conduct of their daughters' marriages and they will interfere if they consider it necessary. They will be particularly concerned for any of their married daughters who have gone to live among their in-laws. It is said of a woman who goes to live among her in-laws that she has no protection. 'She goes with her man to live with his people, who's to stop him beltin into her or her kids if he wants?' These older women, the senior women of the family community, must travel many times a year, conducting extensive visits among their kin, in order to meet their obligations to the family community.

Travel and the secrecy of affairs

Senior women are never secretive about their reasons for travel. For example, one of the senior women (Mary) of the McNish family had an adult daughter who began to neglect and abuse her child when it was aged three years. It was therefore necessary for the child's grandmother to travel from Perth to DeLand to take her grandchild away from the unfit mother. Everyone up and down the line of that family community knew that as soon as she could get a ride, Mary was going to DeLand to get her grandchild. The young people, the adolescents and the young unmarried adults are in contrast highly secretive about their movements. They do not broadcast either their intentions to travel or their reasons for travel.

After Mary heard that her grandchild was in danger, it took her some months to arrange a lift from Perth to DeLand. Seeing no other options, she eventually approached me and proposed that I should take her as 'this business with Daphne' was very important, and if I was really interested in the Nyungars I should want to see for myself how such business was conducted. Mary offered to arrange a relief driver for me, as the journey from Perth to DeLand measures a distance of well over 2,000 kilometres.

The relief driver was to have been her youngest son David, aged twenty years. She made this arrangement a month ahead of time and periodically made him renew his promise to be 'our driver', exhorting him to make no other plans. She began to suspect his promises when, the fortnight before we were to leave, David went out and bought himself a car. He assured his mother that he had only bought it because it was such a good deal that he felt he couldn't afford to pass it up. Mary tried to ensure his participation in her project by wringing a further promise out of David. He would leave his car with one of his older sisters so that she could use it to get her licence and buy her own car. In the end, David did not go with his mother to DeLand. The day before we were to have left, he left in his own car with three of his male sibling-cousins for the town of LaMarr which lies mid way between Bayshore and DeLand.

The reason David did not drive his mother and me to DeLand was that at that time he was in love with a LaMarr girl and had been courting her since he had turned seventeen, though he had met with opposition from the girl's family. The problem was that the girl was very fair compared with David and her family was concerned that she should 'do better' for herself than marry a relatively dark skinned boy like David. For this reason, they made it plain to David that his attention to their daughter was not welcome. Despite this considerable opposition, David and the girl persisted and when she became pregnant by him they thought at last her family would have to agree to their marriage. However, the girl was under-age and her parents not only refused their consent, but her mother forced the girl to obtain an abortion.[4]

David's response to the news that his girlfriend had been made to have an abortion was to go around to his prospective mother-in-law's house and punch her in the face several times. He left town immediately thereafter. When he arrived at his mother's house in Perth, he gave her and his older sisters no explanation for his sudden departure from LaMarr. He had had a good job in that town and would not say what had happened to make him quit. All David would say was that he was tired of LaMarr, it was 'a ugly ol town', and he'd rather 'go riding round with the boys', his male sibling-cousins. David never told his mother or his sisters what had happened until he was ready to return to LaMarr.

His mother demanded to know why he could not go with her and see this girl at the same time. He told her to think about how it would look to people if he were to arrive in town driving his mother, two of her nieces and their children and his mother's pregnant white female friend. He claimed he could not conduct a courtship from that starting point because he would not be taken seriously. 'They'll laugh me right out of town', he declared. The way to be taken seriously, as a man, was to arrive in his own car with a number of his cousins to back him up in the event of opposition from his girlfriend's relatives.

The young people generally keep certain of their affairs secret from the adults. These affairs may include not only their own pursuit of courtship, but each other's. Thus, in order to lend support to his suit, David's sibling-cousins went with him to LaMarr. In similar cases, girls will accompany one another from town to town, both to lend support in courtship and to help maintain the secrecy of that courtship. A girl who travels alone to another town for no obvious reason, and who does not give any plausible reason for wanting to travel will be strongly suspected of 'chasin some boy'. Three girls travelling to that town for no apparent reason may say they're just going for a look or to visit or just for a change of surroundings. The adults may suspect that one or another of them is pursuing a boy, but they will not be able to pick which one with certainty when all three deny any such interest. It is this kind of behaviour that leads adults to explain the young people's travelling habits by saying, 'They just jump into any car that's goin. They're cracked. They just like ridin around in cars.'

The young people as a group in Nyungar society have affairs which are quite separate from the affairs of their various families. They engage in disputes and recreational interests which cross kinship boundaries and create boundaries among themselves in ways that do not necessarily correspond with the kinship boundaries between family communities. These alignments and estrangements among the young people will prompt or inhibit the travel of individual adolescents. They are unlikely to inform the adults of their reasons for wishing to travel, or not unless it concerns such innocuous interests as the formation of an amateur sport team. The adults more usually find out about the adolescents' secret affairs well after the event, and sometimes from one of the younger children who has overheard the older ones talking.

As well as the maintenance of kin relationships then, the conduct of affairs and business also takes people up and down the line or around the run. The nature of these affairs and items of business depends on the individual's age, gender and social relationships within the family community.

Authority relations through the run and line

The dispersal of the family community throughout the towns of the run or line is to some extent ensured by the pattern of authority relationships made possible by this pattern of dispersal.

The foundation of authority in the Nyungar system derives from a mother's authority over her children, expressed in the Nyungar maxims: 'a mother is boss for her children', and, 'your aunty is the next best thing to your mother.' If a woman rears her children according to what is termed 'Nyungar way', she will hold her children in a web of indebtedness when they grow up. In adulthood, they will acknowledge her authority to advise them, and in certain situations to command their obedience. In the absence of the mother, a person's maternal aunt can hold this authority. Just as cousins who are reared-up together become like siblings, the aunts who reared them cooperatively become like mothers to them. It is the task of these women, the senior women of the family, to work to gain stability of lifestyle for their descendants and support in times of need which, for Nyungars, is difficult to obtain outside the family community.

These women together form an action set, that is, a set of people who are distinguished from all others by their commitment to a social purpose contained within an order of activity (Sansom 1980, 35). That purpose is child-rearing, and the order of activity is anything which the women define as related to the rearing-up of children. Given this broad definition, it is not difficult for a woman to control such varied and vital aspects of social life as the organisation of households, the distribution of goods and privileges, and even to arrive at a course of action aimed at resolving the personal problems of an individual family member.

The undisputed heads of the family are the women of the third ascending generation—a sister-cousin set of long standing. But not all the women who are part of that sister-cousin set achieve a position of ascendancy. Years of careful work and single-minded devotion to child-rearing goes into a woman's eventual career as a part of that small respected group of women of authority. Those who do not make it are those who have a history of drinking, or leaving their children too often, or regularly failing to give help to individual family members, or being inconsistent in their behaviour toward the family. The inconsistent person is sometimes friendly and open-handed, but can also be inexplicably hostile and off-hand in fulfilling her kin obligations. None of these women will become one of the respected women of the family. Their own children will, as they mature, show a consistent preference for the support, advice and authority of their aunts over that of their mothers.

By the time their children have grown up, the women who have been devoted to the family community have had a long, hard life of service. As they put it, they have had to 'battle the whole way'. They will not think kindly of their sisters who have taken an easier road by leaving their children to be cared for by their relations, or who may from time to time have declared that they could not help their needy sisters, or could not afford it, had no room, or who, when they did give help gave it with bad grace, making the petitioner clearly aware of the debt incurred. In later life, when they are in a position to take on the highest authority in Nyungar society, the responsible women may need to undermine the interests and authority of their less responsible sisters in order to take that authority. They will not hesitate to do this, even to the point of publicly disgracing their irresponsible sisters.

These women who acquire authority will systematically back or promote the authority of those of their daughters they consider to be worthy, useful and above all dependable in the performance of their duty to the children and to each other. These younger women, part of another sister-cousin set, form the subset of the total action set which controls the ongoing business of the family.

As a case in point, I again turn to the McNishes. In each of the towns of the line lives one of the senior women of the McNish family community. Mary lives in Perth. Originally she came south because her son required medical treatment which at that time was unavailable in Bayshore where she then lived. After she obtained the rental lease on a State Housing Commission house she was joined in Perth by five of her nieces. Four of these were then girls in their teens and they lived with their aunt prior to marrying and obtaining rented houses of their own. These women, now grown, still live in Perth. None of Mary's own adult daughters live in the capital, though they visit regularly.

Mary's sister Elsie lives in Bayshore. Also in that town live their sister Rose, Rose's adult daughter Venis, Dorie who is one of Mary and Elsie's sister-cousins, two of Elsie's adult sons and all the dependant children of these people.

In DeLand lives Granny Elizabeth McNish, the oldest member of this family community. Also in DeLand live three of Granny Elizabeth's adult daughters—Ernestine, Marcia, and Augusta—two of Augusta's adult daughters and all the dependant children of these people.

The senior women are Mary, Elsie and Granny. They are the senior women partly through age and partly through the disqualification of others. Mary is the only woman of the third ascending generation of the family living in Perth. Elsie is the oldest in Bayshore, but also, her sister Rose and her sister-cousin Dorie are both drinkers and so are disqualified from holding authority. Granny is the oldest woman of the family in DeLand. Augusta drinks, and Marcia shows no inclination to hold authority over anyone but her own children. There is some conflict between Ernestine and Elizabeth which will be discussed later on.

In part, it is by the process described above that Mary, Elsie and their mother have become the senior women of their family community. The groups that have gathered around them form the kin networks of each of the towns of primary residence along the line. The reasons each of these individuals give for choosing to live in one town rather than another are highly variable.

Residence choices
In general, the family members at Perth can state their reasons more definitely than the family members at either Bayshore or DeLand. The Perth McNishes, when asked why they live in Perth rather than Bayshore or DeLand, cite the milder climate and the better housing and schools. Also, they say that the social workers in Perth are more kindly disposed to their problems than those in the country towns. However, there may be other reasons why they choose to live in the capital. Three of Mary's nieces are married to men from southern family communities. By living in Perth, these women can remain within their own family community and their husbands have easy access to their family communities, some of whom also live in Perth. A fourth niece lives in Perth because her husband is permanently hospitalised there and the fifth came south to live near her sister.

None of these women would have come south to Perth on her own. It required the establishment of a respectable woman of their mothers' sister-cousin set in Perth to make it possible for the younger women to follow. Now, one reason Mary does not live in Bayshore is because all these younger women and their families look to her for advice, for help in time of need, and as the authority on which to model their own responsibilities to one another and to each other's children.

The family at Bayshore give less well defined reasons for living where they do than the family at Perth. The generalisation the Bayshore McNishes make in regard to themselves is, 'We're just country bumpkins, that's all it is. We just can't stand that city life for too long a time.' But they do have the option of going to DeLand, which is another country town after all. When this is put to them, the Bayshore McNishes say that, apart from their own family there, the DeLand Aborigines 'got very funny ways. You never know how to take em. A lot of em are real bushies, you can't hardly understand what they say.'

As with the Perth McNishes, however, there appear to be other reasons which keep them in Bayshore, primarily the marriages of the younger women to men from Bayshore. Although the Nyungars 'tend to fall on the mothers' side', as they put it, it seems it is still important to the men who marry into the family to maintain contact with their own family communities. Similarly, the women at DeLand have married men from that town.

Other possible explanations of the choice to live in one town or another may lie in the relationships between the senior women and their daughters and nieces. As an example, let us look at the relationships between Granny Elizabeth and her daughters Elsie and Ernestine.

The potential for conflict in authority relations

Ernestine lives in DeLand. In Nyungar reckoning she is in all respects a dependable and respectable woman who has 'battled' to make a home for her children. In this she is no different from her mother or her older sisters Elsie and Mary. But she is not the senior woman of her family at DeLand because this role relationship within the family community is held by her mother. The evidence of this is to be found in the behaviour of the family at DeLand toward these two women and also in Granny's treatment of Ernestine in contrast to Elsie.

Apart from Ernestine's own children, the young women and their children go to visit Granny rather than Ernestine. Ernestine goes to visit them far more often than the reverse. In settling various disputes between family members, the young women say, 'better ask Granny'. Ernestine would be quite capable of fairly judging any such matters, but she is not called upon to do so. Her opinion is highly regarded, but hers is not the deciding voice.

Granny Elizabeth can be a very generous woman, both with regard to her affections and the resources at her disposal. She displays this generosity to various of her children and grandchildren but she often withholds it from Ernestine. Elsie, for example, always stays with her mother when she comes to DeLand. Ernestine's comment on one of these occasions was to say loudly and with emphasis, 'Yeah, you can go there'. Elsie once told Ernestine of what a nice afternoon nap she had just had 'on Mummy's bed'. 'Oh that's a lovely big bed of Mummy's,' she said. Ernestine responded, 'I never even sat on that bed, so I wouldn't know.' In these and other ways,

Ernestine makes it clear that she considers herself to receive poorer treatment from her mother in comparison with her sister.

Despite this, the person Granny Elizabeth habitually goes to for help when she has trouble of her own is her daughter Ernestine. At these times, Ernestine displays none of the bitterness she shows on other occasions and gives her mother whatever help she can. It is from this evidence that I draw the conclusion that Ernestine is the second most senior woman at DeLand. All the epithets applied to her by the rest of the family are the same as those applied to Granny, Mary and Elsie. She is said to be 'a very good type of person', 'always ready to help', and 'always the same'. It is also said that she is a very fair minded person, but that she is not to be crossed. A senior woman cannot be crossed. Either she will exercise her authority directly and subject the miscreant to public sanction, or her adult children will wordlessly apply such a sanction.

Elsie, as I have noted, gets on very well with her mother and is one of the beneficiaries of Elizabeth's generosity. Elsie is very fond of her mother and visits her as often as she can. She goes with her niece Venis, who goes to visit her two sisters in DeLand. These two women expend much time and money and interrupt their children's schooling in order to visit the family at DeLand. Why don't they move to DeLand?

In Bayshore the family looks to Elsie the way the family at DeLand looks to Elizabeth. Venis and Elsie cooperate closely and Elsie relies on Venis the way Granny Elizabeth relies on Ernestine. The family talk about Venis in the same terms as they talk about Ernestine. This pattern is repeated in Perth between Mary and her niece Alicia, who is one of Elsie's daughters. In each town, then, there is a senior woman in the third ascending generation or above, and one younger woman in the generation succeeding her on whom the older woman relies as her junior partner, so to speak, in the task of managing the problems presented to her by members of the local kin network.

If Elsie went to DeLand she would not be a senior woman. She might not even be the junior partner, as that position is held by Ernestine. Conflict between them would arise, or so the evidence of their interactions would indicate. The same is true of the relationship between Mary and Elsie. Here too, there is an undercurrent of competition between the two women.

The friction between Granny Elizabeth and Ernestine is not present in the relationships between their counterparts in Bayshore and DeLand. Both these other sets of role relationships are between aunt and niece rather than mother and daughter. This may explain the friction between these two particular women.

Authority of mothers and aunts

Mothers are characteristically very hard on their own children. The saying 'a mother is boss for her children' is acted upon in daily life. Nyungar mothers seek by means of scolding and corporal punishment to establish absolute authority over their children. 'You can't let em boss you', or, 'You can't let em put it over you', they may say. They may criticise one another for being too indulgent with their children, saying, 'That little one, she's your boss. You oughta be her boss.'

Aunts are more indulgent. The aunty–niece relationship could never be called a joking relationship, but women generally present a fonder, less punitive face to their nieces and nephews than to their own children. This seems to carry on into adulthood to a degree, resulting in a relationship less characterised by authority and obedience than by comradeship and cooperation.

Conclusion

By maintaining separate networks of authority relationships in different towns the senior women of the McNish family can avoid conflict among themselves which would threaten the unity of the family community. By maintaining residence in three towns, more women have the opportunity to aspire to positions of authority within the family community than would be possible were the family community to reside in one town.

Despite their aspirations to positions of authority, the McNish senior women do not wish to establish their own separate family communities. This is evidenced by the continued practice of travelling up and down the line. In the course of travelling the children who accompany their mothers, aunts and grandmothers come to know their kin. The senior women and their daughters welcome into their homes the children of kin from other towns and work to establish strong, warm relationships between these children and their own children. Eventually, these children will go on to establish a particular attachment for one set of sibling-cousins in one of the towns of the line. It is through the practice of regular, frequent travel that the unity of the family community and the continuity of Nyungar social organisation are maintained over the distances of time and space which separate the members of the community from one another.

Notes

1. No figures exist on the size of the total Nyungar population. However the 1981 census shows that there are over 20,000 Aboriginal people living in the southwest, which alone amounts to over eighty per cent of Western Australia's Aboriginal population. Census figures of course do not reveal the group identification of Aboriginal people. But according to the verbal reports of social workers and anthropologists who have worked throughout this area, nearly all of these Aborigines identify themselves as Nyungar.

2. Recorded on 3 February 1981, sitting in the car 'havin a yarn' on the main street of town. The speakers are two sisters, both grandmothers—one a Bayshore resident, the other visiting from Perth.

3. This system of distributing the responsibility for a child provides, as one of its functions, the means of safeguarding the welfare of children. Should the mother fail in her duty toward her child for whatever reason or in any way, it is the duty of her own mother to step in and take responsibility for the child. It is the duty of the mother's sisters to 'watch out' for the child and send word promptly to their mother should they judge the child to be in danger owing to the mother's failure toward her child. The child may be removed from the mother's care by the grandmother and placed by her with any of the child's maternal aunts, or kept by the grandmother.

4. Among the Nyungars, any child is welcome, legitimate or not, and whether or not the parents live together. Birth control is rare. In the McNish all one family of more than 300 individuals, I was able to find only one woman who certainly used a birth control method and one who probably did. No woman had ever had an abortion and no-one knew of any Nyungar woman who had obtained one. Interference with a woman's natural capacity to bear children was regarded as very odd and abortion was simply disgusting.

References

Berndt, R. M.
1980 Aborigines of the South-west. In R.M. Berndt and C.H. Berndt (eds), *Aborigines of the West*, University of Western Australia Press, Nedlands.

Biskup, P.
1973 *Not Slaves, Not Citizens: The Aboriginal Problem in Western Australia 1898–1954*, University of Queensland Press, St Lucia.

Bott, E.
1957 *Family and Social Network*, Tavistock Publications, London.

Haebich, A.
1982 On the Inside: Moore River Native Settlement in the 1930's. In B. Gammage and A. Markus (eds), *All that Dirt: Aborigines in 1938*, History Project Inc, Research School of Social Sciences, Canberra.

Howard, M.C.
1980 Aboriginal Society in Southwestern Australia. In R.M. Berndt and C.H. Berndt (eds), *Aborigines of the West*, University of Western Australia Press, Nedlands.

1981 *Aboriginal Politics in South-Western Australia*, University of Western Australia Press, Nedlands.

MacIver, R.M.
1948 *Society: A Textbook of Sociology*, Rinehart, New York.

Rowley, C.D.
1970 *The Destruction of Aboriginal Society*, Australian National University Press, Canberra.

Sansom, B.L.
1980 *The Camp at Wallaby Cross*, Australian Institute of Aboriginal Studies, Canberra.

Tindale, N.B.
1940 Distribution of Australian Aboriginal Tribes, *Translations of the Royal Society of South Australia* 64, 140–231.

9. Basil Sansom   A grammar of exchange

The modality for exchange, which Aborigines promote in the fringe camps of Darwin and in camps of that city's hinterland, is no new creation. It belonged to the hunter-gatherer forebears of the fringe dwellers of today. Handed down through generations, the modality is a heritage preserved intact. Hence I deal with cultural continuities in a world of material change. Furthermore, the Aborigines I know are well acquainted with whitefella notions that govern the use of cash, promote the work ethic and turn labour into a creature of the market. I have taped long conversations in which speakers take turns to produce a recitative of comparison, dealing point by point with differences between whitefella practice and their own. Well supported by argument, the conclusion to one such conversation was issued thus: 'You see Basil, you jus work for wages. You always jus workin for wages. We fella got that money blackfella style.'

I cite this fragment of text to make two points. The first is that the speaker, in awareness of difference, knows blackfella style as a lived-in, experienced and—above all—alternative reality. The alternative reality persists because Aborigines resist the colonisation of their world by the ideas that ordinarily attach to general purpose money. Their resistance to the monetisation of mind is an aspect of what Rowley (1972) identifies as 'the Aboriginal intransigence'—a general refusal on the part of a tiny indigenous minority to succumb to assimilation into the ways of the settler majority who now constitute the mainstream in Australia. This leads me to my second point.

Refusing assimilation of being to mainstream ways, Aborigines have turned things round by assimilating money to their modality for exchange. Once cash enters a Darwin fringe camp, the dollar remains an Australian dollar only to the extent that it is still backed by the Reserve Bank and so retains its potential to be re-entered into the general, outside economy where it will return to its market function. While in Aboriginal possession, the dollar is a thing both transformed and ambivalent. It is transformed because, if entered into transactions between Aborigine and Aborigine, it will no longer function in market terms as a generalised medium of exchange but will instead take on character as an amount subject to valuation in acts of help, helping and helping out. When this happens, dollar amounts lose their capacity to function as prices. All at once, the conventions of regular economising are left behind. Just how and why will only become clear when my discussion is complete. However, I can note at this stage that the dollar secreted somewhere in Aboriginal clothing has double valence because the holder can either commit it to internal dealings where its measure will be 'help' or otherwise reconsign the cash to its origins via the local supermarket, garage or pub. Moving between two worlds, Aborigines experience the double use of cash from day to day. And this is both to reassert and to explain their pointed awareness of the differences between two coexistent and rival philosophies, the one a philosophy of money in Simmel's sense (1900), the other a philosophy of voluntaristic social action in which giving and receiving is conceptualised as the rendering of services by one person to another.

Before getting down to details, it is only fitting that I should prepare readers for the radical nature of the departure required in order to make sense of the opposition between Aboriginal and Western philosophies. When Bohannan (1959)—in a well known, often reprinted and much cited essay—dealt with the yielding of the Tiv of West Africa to monetisation, he modelled the transformation as the outcome of a confrontation between two economies. During the traditional era, the Tiv economy was pre-capitalist and multicentric, its multicentricity a result of the maintenance of separate spheres of exchange guarded one from another by limited possibilities for the conversion of value between sphere and sphere. With the introduction of cash, the Tiv economy rapidly lost its multicentric dimensions. The conversion possibilities inherent in cash soon saw to that. And Bohannan joins company with Simmel (1900), Weber (1964), Nalson (1965) and others in attributing undoing force to cash itself once the idea of general purpose money has been communicated among those who enter into deals and dealings. In this vein, Bohannan (1959, 502) writes, 'Money is one of the most shatteringly simplifying ideas of all time, and like any new and compelling idea, it creates its own revolution.' Similarly taken by the power of cash, Rowley speculates that the most retiring and remote of Aborigines may be expected one day to succumb to its compulsions: 'In time the attractions of cash and what it can buy may well reduce even these people to the conformity of "one-dimensional" economic man. For cash poisons the generous mind by opening up possibilities of endless acquisition, not only of goods but of power' (Rowley 1986, 134–35). If, as I allege, Aborigines can as a people stave off the lucregenic revolution and as individuals each remain immune to lucretoxin, then it seems that their case must indeed be special.

Special or not, I find that the best way to deal with the Aboriginal case is to stop talking economics. This is no more than to take the advice of Robbins Burling (1962, 819) who writes that 'unless the anthropologist uses concepts of economics, cost, value, demand, supply, and so on in a much broader context than is the custom of the economist, over a range of meaning far wider than that which is priced, he had better stop talking about economics.' I find that economically defined concepts of cost, value, demand and the rest cannot be stretched to comprehend conceptions of giving and receiving in the world of discourse that is an Aboriginal encampment. And the resilience of Aboriginal notions and formulations leads me to the finding which is the beginning and end of my analysis. The story of culture contact in Australia has not entailed opposition between two economies. Instead, there has been and still is contraposition of a different order. Aborigines counter the Western philosophy of money with their voluntaristic philosophy of action. The two philosophies are worthy contenders one against the other because both have the capacity to pervade human activities although each one is grounded in premises of its own. A major index of contrast in pervasive capacity is that while a money price can in a money economy be put on any gain or loss, Aboriginal people can assign value to all significant human acts by construing them in terms rendered up by a grammar of service. On the analyst's part, a grammar of service is propounded by establishing ratios between elementary terms in the manner of Kenneth Burke (1969) who has essayed the definitive *Grammar of Motives*. In the Aboriginal case, the primary terms are: actor, patient, witness, purpose, act, means, scene and style. The grammar of service exchange will be made clear once I have deployed a clutch of these terms to establish the major ratios which Aborigines employ to bring prime terms into meaningful relation with one another, thereby endowing acts of exchange with meaning.

Goodbye to price: economics and limited utility

Moving with Aborigines, I learned how to value most of the acts and things they valued in the terms they used. Price was another matter. In the ways things worked, it seemed that prices belonged not to a generalised system of exchange but to the particular transactions in which they vested. The reason why Big Maxie could get ol Luke to use his expensive 4WD Toyota to travel 200 miles down the track by offering a measly $20.00 for incentive, was less a function of market forces, more a product of two intersecting biographies. If one knew enough of Big Maxie and ol Luke, the power of Big Maxie's few dollars made a kind of sense. Those dollars vested in a transaction that brought the past history of a relationship to the present and also implicated the future which was contained in a declaration of the social significance and human urgency of Big Maxie's southward mission. With $20.00 now in hand, ol Luke joined in Big Maxie's purpose. They set out with reason, knowingly foredoomed to run out of petrol on the way home. They would then rely on the essential cameraderie of the road which, in the remoter regions of Australia, impels travellers to help fellow motorists who fall into trouble. The bitumen is graced by frequent acts of generalised reciprocity to make it an authentic ribbon of the goodwill whose token is the headlight-flash of greeting. It is, by the way, easier to accommodate the cameraderie of the road to Aboriginal conceptions than it is to take the vocabulary of the supermarket back into an encampment.

Where transactions between Aboriginal countrymen are massively conditioned by the current state of the relationship between the money economy and the internal Aboriginal system for exchange, straightforward economic notions do, however, have some small measure of utility. Because money is money, the matter can be simply put.

The major factor that mediates the relationship between inside and outside dealings is the temporal determination of the money supply. Regular variations in the supply of money create overall conditions for being. Aborigines define the conditioning circumstances existentially as two contrasting moods and states which pertain to camps and to the mob which each camp contains. There are 'good times' (of plenty and ease) and 'those miler times' of dearth and meanness when everyone 'gets hard'. Furthermore, good times and miler times alternate with short term periodicities that are calendrical and long term periodicities that are an expression of seasons.

People receive wages or welfare benefits on a fortnightly basis and every second Thursday is universally established as an Australian pay-day. A 'miler week' is a Thursday-to-Thursday stretch marked by its commencing Thursday's 'notta a pay-day notta pension-day' status. Miler week contrasts consistently with 'pension week' and sometimes with a week of both pensions and wages.

In the monsoon country of the Australian north, the year has two segments—the wet and the dry. The dry is a time of work and wages on the cattle stations, in the estuarine fisheries and on the buffalo-shooting ranges which extend through the country of black soil plains. The wet is a time of inundation and lay-off when industries bog down. All weeks of the dry are good when compared with the weeks of the payless stretch from September to April. During the wet, itself 'altogether that miler time', each pensionless miler week is doubly mean—a bad week in a bad season. And the index of times that are really bad is an increment of 'noise' which is the measure of fractiousness and contention. Hard times quickly translate into problems of social control.

Good time–miler time alternations are regularities imposed to define the scene in northern Australia whose Aboriginal countrymen bring these structural alternations to a logic for discounting debts. Put simply, if A lends B $100.00 during the dry season and then waits to retrieve the debt during the subsequent wet, A will ordinarily have to accept a much-reduced sum as total repayment for the loan. After intense negotiations, A may manage to get $40.00 or even $50.00 for the original outlay of the $100.00 sum. And A will have to agree that the debt is now altogether 'clear'. If uncontent with a discounted sum, A's only recourse will be to postpone collection and wait for a better time. If A's claim were entered in December, this would mean waiting for the June recovery. The question then is: Can A afford to wait through miler times for June?

Very broadly, the extent to which debts will be discounted (note, I refer to extent, not rate), is determined by the current state of the money supply within the local grouping to which a debtor belongs. Nor is generalised seasonal or calendrical determination absolute. A particular camping mob can experience its own miler time of dearth in a season of plenty. With regard to particular debts, the extent of discounting is agonistically determined by the debtor's capacity to rally the cash to pay in the face of a creditor's power of insistence. With regard to the aggregate of regional debts, the wet is generally associated with spectacular discounting, while the dry is more a time for the recovery of loans at evens or thereabouts. Everyone knows that wet season repayments are generally paid over at a discount described not as a fraction of the original payment but indeterminately as 'lotta dollar'. While there is acknowledgement of the overall probability of gross discounting, nobody speaks of a going rate or a fair rate, a good rate or a bad one. There is active resistance to aggregate thinking which would endow cash with a life of its own after grouping transactions together as like acts, commensurate with one another and therefore properly made subject to arithmetic. It is with wry regret that I find myself unable to develop the notion of 'negative interest' as a concept analogous to the 'negative growth' of ailing economies in the West.

The general point I am making is this: conceptualisation in economic terms can bring one halfway to an understanding of overall circumstances determined by the relationship between welfare capitalism and the wage and welfare dependency of Aborigines. However, until I have fully developed an analysis of service exchange, there are features of A's dry and wet season dealings with B which can now only be raised as questions to be addressed anon:

1. Why ever lend in the dry season rather than save one's cash for the rainy days to come?
2. Why is there no 'positive interest'? Why cannot a lender supply $50.00 in December and hope by next June to recoup a usurious 100 per cent increment on the investment?

3. Why do people resist aggregate thinking in relation to cash and exclude 'going rate' formulations given that they know well enough how to calculate interest, as evidenced on those rare occasions when they have money in a savings bank at ten per cent or whatever?

I took leave to interpret good time–bad time alternations wholly in etic terms. For countrymen, these alternations are put beyond the power of human volition to correct.

> Apter [after] that rodeo, apter all that muster, we got miler time. You jus caan help it. You know Basil, you fella bin have that Christmas. Longa this place: longa this place you gotta say that Christmas really that miler day!

The conception of the onset of good times and the bad is one in which Aborigines allow that a condition is dominated by the ratio of patient to scene. Whole mobs are subject or opened to conditions which no mob member has moved to establish and which no mob member can work to change. I can neither find in notes or transcriptions nor can I recall an occasion on which one of the countrymen charged whitefellas with the imposition of seasonal alternations even though the season of pay-off is to me self-evidently the invention of employers and thus a social rather than a natural fact. In the world of mobs and camps, however, the patient:scene ratio is invoked to endow good time–bad time alternations with the humanly unsubjectivised facticity of causation that belongs also to the work of the Dreaming Powers which once created and now sustain the firmament. Proponents of direct action would find it difficult to persuade countrymen that by joining in combinations (whether lawful or otherwise) they might work against government or the collectivity of their sporadic employers to alter these experienced givens of subsistence. Put in terms of a famous opposition, countrymen see miler time–good time alternations as facts not of culture but of nature, thereby defining themselves as subjected patients and so object to the rhythms of a peculiar temporal governance. The patient:scene ratio pertains to conditions beyond human capacity to alter. Broadly defined for all as givens, these frame all structures for social action.

That Ada's private haul

In a camp down at that Estuary, that Ada has just retrieved a loan of a 'whole lotta dollar' from ol Martie. There were three witnesses to her dealings with Martie and so five people know the inner details of the moment of extractive negotiation. The rest of us knew what was going on—we had made a two-car expedition out of Darwin to get this 'lotta dollar'.

That Ada next comes out of the business huddle and shows forth the money as a wad. She announces, 'We all clear now; I bin get that money, you lookim.' We look. Ol Martie signifies assent: 'All clear now, youfella witness for that.' We indicate agreement and our witnessing has its routine form. Both the clearing of debt and entry into debt are generally registered thus. Close witnesses know about amounts, other witnesses know about the fact of debt on a 'lotta money' and 'lil bit money' basis unless for some reason the parties decide they need to register actual amounts more widely.

Ada pays off the two 'driving men' who transported the party of extraction. Again her transactions are witnessed; and the drivers hand over some of their receipts to the strong-arm passengers who came along to intimidate and have a ride. As it happens, I am one of the drivers.

That Ada now does something else. Stepping forward she calls out 'Lookmi, lookmi.' We respond. Then she says,

> I bin get my haul. Driving men bin gettim pay. This lotta dollar, all this lot free. Every dollar longa this lot free. Doan anybody gonna askim mefella for no more dollar. I'm tellin you, this very private money now. Really private. Me fella, I'm keeping this money. This free. Money for kid longa different place. Money for tucker for all them kid. This very private money now.

This reported moment contains three artefacts of the modality for exchange. There are:
1. the witnessed transaction;
2. the privatised holding; and
3. vectored cash, which is to say money dedicated to purpose.

Later that day as the light fades, the two vehicles are driven back home and enter the Darwin encampment. We debouch. At once, Ada rallies the homebodies most of whom are, in any case, walking or looking toward us as they make moves to 'check up longa that trip' and 'find out what bin happenin'. That Ada steps forward cryptically to announce that the mission was successful. She got her 'lotta dollar'. However, she spends a lot more time doing the rounds to make tight-fisted demonstrations. She tells everyone that her haul is thoroughly purposed, unassailable and private cash. Nobody challenges her by entering a claim against the haul. The episode ends when Ada issues a last and general challenge: 'Well you lot, you gonna leavim me?' There is no demurral and so that Ada relaxes into satisfaction. She adjusts her dress after stowing the haul away in a place that is private indeed.

The point to remark is that Ada has made her cash 'free' and 'private', establishing her right to be 'left' unbadgered with due consideration as to jurisdiction and constituency. The people of the home encampment are not mere countrymen—that is known Aborigines of Darwin and its hinterland. They are all in some degree countrymen who are 'close-up' to that Ada. Not a few are 'close-up lations' too. According to degrees of closeness (established by prior transactions, reasserted by new ones, and undone by acts of denial) people of a single mob share with relative intensity in one another's dealings and in each other's futures. The test of close-up intensity of relationship is, in the end, the extent of one's ability to cause a close-up countryman to render service. In this, close-up relationship is a lien and, most often, a compound lien rather than a single order of personal obligation. That Ada made her money 'free' and made herself a person to be 'left' (alone) in the very theatre of intensive give-and-take.

It is to be noted that 'close-up' identity, 'love' and the 'knowing' of persons are all terms that serve in propositions formulated to posit relationships between giving and receiving, on the one hand, and states of intersubjective being on the other. When the driving men got back that day, each was targeted. Young Leon (close-up to me) wanted some bit of my driving man's reward. I said 'No.' Recently he had been a drain. The trouble was that I had been paying up to get him out of trouble. So what he had cost me had not gone to satisfying his positive desires. Such acts of 'bailing' people 'out' of trouble merit later discussion because they have a kind of negative positivity that could render them forgettable. Though decisive, they are positive interventions dedicated to the end that nothing will happen.

I responded to Leon's requests by telling him he was 'bludging' and by listing my recent contributions to his welfare. An audience of youngfellas stood by and my cash holdings were in some peril—if I was easy with Leon, there would be a flood of applications that only the sight of an empty wallet would stem. In the end, Leon went away 'growling' his displeasure. He told the world that the anthropologist was 'this fella who doan lovin mefella any more'. His final remark of bitter dismissal was that 'Maybe soon mefella I'm jus not gonna know this Basil too much anymore.' It was some time before we two made up. In the interim, Leon would not even 'lookmi'. He wholly denied me his regard.

Helping and helping out

I now want to substantiate the nature of a difference—the difference between 'just helpin' and the helping that is 'helping out'.

Paulie Smithson and I were close. We served one another turn and turn about for quite a time. It happens that Paulie Smithson was a 'dancing man' of renown much attuned to ceremony and so master of what Stanner (1966) calls the 'High Culture' of the north. He was also a good translator, commanding English that also was 'quite high really'. He served me as a commentator; in return, I gave him what I could. At first, he defined our relationship as one of help for help. Then came the night that I helped that Paulie out.

I was decamping when that Paulie fell prostrate in front of my departing truck. As I learned later, he had come up from the pub. He was bleeding from a massive scalp-wound and crying out for succour. I rallied assistance to get him into my vehicle. The trip to the hospital was an episode of blood, vomit, voided urine and a driver's experience of the distracting embrace of a patient determined to express appreciation for his rescuer. We arrived at the hospital where a doctor declared that Paulie needed to be put under in order to be stitched up. A good dancer is always lithesome and muscular and Paulie resisted. He had a great fear of 'that jection needle'. Finally, he consigned himself to me. 'You Basil', he said, 'mefella I always bin lovin you, you stay longa mefella and I'll go.' I consented to stay and Paulie accepted the local anaesthetic. Then I held his hands while the doctor repaired the laceration. He brought two great flaps of skin together with clips and then did a fair job with thread and a needle of another sort. Paulie then refused admission to hospital. After time spent in a recovery cubicle, he became possessed by the state of the truck's front cab. He kept on saying, 'Lookim mess, just lookim mess.'

When we got back to camp, Paulie was rather weak and he tended to reel about. It was late, but he completed the waking-up initiated by our approaching headlights to rally the campers to him. He wanted gratuitously to tell how I had really that day 'bin helping out'. To my embarrassment, he kept on declaring, 'This fella really bin lovin me.'

This is not an essay on the anthropologist as hero. That Paulie's wound was spectacular but, day by day, in lives punctuated by acts of violence, people deal offhandedly with 'damage' of this sort. In the run of happenstance, on this occasion of wounding it had fallen to my turn to help out. Further, that Paulie did 'right thing' by volunteering his obligation to his rescuer. He announced thereby that we two are linked in special and particular association that comes of 'bailing' or of 'helpin'' someone out. All this happened a decade ago but let me add that Paulie and I still subsist in a relationship grounded in the memory of that time of my helping out.

Heroes and signal service

When Kenneth Burke discusses heroes in the West (Burke 1969, 42), he argues that, for Westerners, the truly heroic act transforms a scene, which is to say a collective condition for being. Burke's prototypic heroes are active kings who win battles or saints whose charisma is attested by miracles or the communication of inspiration. By their acts or words, Western heroes change the worlds which they inhabit. In Aboriginal conspectus, things are otherwise. What I call heroism is defined as a saving act of rescue. As such, heroic acts pertain essentially to those who have been saved. It is thus the saved who owe accolades to the saver. A communal recognition of the significance of the heroic act is coupled with a collective insistence on the fact that the onus for rewarding a hero belongs to those and only those who benefited from the saving action. There is thus a division between those who were saved and those witness to the saving.

If I today made demands on Paulie Smithson and were he to deny me, I could rally witnesses to the fact that once and signally I had helped him out. I would recruit someone to tell 'that stitches story'. In face of such concerted pressure, the probability is that Paulie would be constrained to accede to my requests. In my badgering of him, I could thus still make an old act live. However, I do much injustice to the real Paulie Smithson. When I go back to Darwin, he of his own volition always offers me the world—insofar as he can dispose of it. What do I want done? Just name it and he's gone to try to do it. Furthermore, Paulie always tells everyone the umpteen stitches story as soon as I hove in sight. With young Leon it is otherwise. When I turn up, it is others who insistently remind him of how in his life's progress he became indebted to that Basil. With justification drawn from the past, people pressure him into my service.

In Aboriginal society, service value is referred to need. The significance of $10.00 entered into a transaction is determined by the measure of a recipient's distress. Thus the $10.00 I lend you to buy fish and chips is not the same as the $10.00 I yield up to make up the last bit of a $100.00 fine which, when paid, will save you from serving thirty days in jail. The first-mentioned amount is 'money for lil bit tucker'. The other $10.00 is 'money for bailing out'. There are then two acts to compare: 'helping for tucker', and 'helping for police business'.

If I help you for police business 'then you gotta say you gotta givin me whole lot'. There is a considerable entailment. The first $10.00 is given over as an act of routine exchange (just helping). The second constitutes an act of signal service (really helping out/bailing out). In the end, the measure of every transaction is its quality as help. It should be clear that the two $10.00 sums are wholly incommensurate. Giving $10.00 to help or bail someone out is as much an act of help and helping as taking a wounded person to hospital. Both are acts of signal service.

Referred to need, service value sets the terms for defining those 'situations of ultimate reference within which and in the light of which men transact their socially significant selves' (Gilsenan 1976, 200). Situations of ultimate reference recognised by countrymen can be formally classified by referring them to four orders of threat or loss. These are:

1. The loss of proper association with powers where the issue is spiritual survival. (The desecration of sacred objects or the breaking of taboo would pose threat of this order.)
2. Threat to the body, danger to life itself where the issue is physical survival and the cause of trouble is sickness or the ensorcellment that leads people to 'get accident'.
3. The threat to life and limb which belongs to fighting and to vendetta.
4. Finally, threat of degradation manifest in loss of worth and achieved position, the threat of being wholly 'rubbished' within the ambit of some particular group.

Payments or acts dedicated to helping a person out of any trouble that belongs to one or other of these four orders is to be counted as signal service—a saving act of rescue that, in principle, transforms the relationship between heroic rescuer and saved victim for as long as they both shall live.

Uncertainty, pretension and performance

The social field in which Aborigines move is characterised by structural indeterminacy. Individuals concerned with futures move in a world where decision making is conditioned by uncertainty rather than by risk.

The countrymen see themselves as battlers, 'all the time fightin for something'. The object in personal struggle is to gain and retain social position, and any achieved position is continually under threat. Aboriginal biographies are thus often stories of ups and downs, of marriages made and lost, of paternity denied, of missed chances; in sum, biography is given as a story of good time–bad time successions.

Structural indeterminacy begins with the nature of kinship, which in the Australian north is 'performative kinship'. I not only have to explain performative kinship but have also to account for the lack of emphasis on the indeterminacy of social relationships in the literature on Aboriginal society.

Performative kinship is a label applied by Esther Goody (1982) to Inuit. She notes that for certain Inuit groups, recognition of social paternity is contingent on the active rearing of a child by a putative father. For Inuit, then, a *pater* is a man who has made consistent and significant contributions to the socialisation of a child. When paternity is made contingent on performances, time enters to admit the development of two notions. These are: fathering by degrees; and a fathering succession. These ideas are contained in Aboriginal English as when one poses the questions: 'How much that ol Tommy bin rearing up youfella?'; and 'Whichfella altogether you reckon you gotta callim Dad?' Now consider this answer to the second question: 'Ol Luke, mefella always callim Dad. Got that ol Martie bin rearin mefella longa Minkelbury. That Toby Nelson, thatta father-for-nothing.' Here the speaker gives credit to two rearers and consigns his genitor to nugatory fatherhood. And from a practised genitor without socially acknowledged offspring: 'Really you gotta say I got kid everywhere. That little Jamie longa station, Nancy, Tim, Pig-eye-one—you know? But I bin missim all them kid—nothing.' The man who said this is a multiple father-for-nothing. Over months of association with him, I discovered that he had entered into twenty-three separate marriages during a career of extensive movement between cattle stations and along the droving trails.

In a world of the frequent reassignment of children to hearth-holds, 'unmothering' also occurs but to an extent that does not match the negation of fatherhood. Even those mothers who yield their children to be reared-up by other women have usually at least brought their babies to the weaning stage before so doing. Given this contribution to rearing-up, they cannot wholly be counted as mothers-for-nothing. The desultory mother who breast-fed a child and then consigned that child to others is accorded a weaker appellation that is still a phrase implying dereliction: she is 'notta mother really', that is, not in the full sense a dedicated rearer-up.

There is another way in which the business of rearing-up can be shared round to proliferate relationships between guardian figures and the children they helped 'grow up'. Children can elect to stay with aunties or other kinswomen they favour for periods of a year or so. When this occurs, the rearing-up relationship is established without undoing or denigrating the tie between mother and child. Again, a mother may ask a kinswoman to 'look after' one or more of her children for a time on the understanding that this is an act of temporary fostering. The mother of any child left too long in the care of others slides toward the state of being 'notta mother really'. She can regain full motherhood only by retrieving 'that kid' and showing motherly dedication to it for a period of months or years.

Mothering and fathering by degree has a general consequence. Some children have four to eight putative fathers and/or a set of female relations, all of whom reared them for 'times'. Who counts presently as nominated father or mother is roundly determined by operation of the principle of situational selection.

In the camp at Wallaby Cross in the camp section dominated by ol Luke (who is a Mullak Mullak by tribal affiliation), Young Petey—aged eighteen—calls ol Luke 'Dad' and denies four other fathers. Two years later, the anthropologist collects a genealogy from Young Petey who is now at Blue Grass Station. We find that Petey has not only switched fathers but, following his Blue Grass father's lines, Young Petey has shifted tribal allegiance from Mullak Mullak to Warai. Anyway, the Warai are entering a claim for land and Petey's newly asserted allegiance is a birthright that could allow him to share in royalty payments if the claim for land is won.

While shifts in child placement result in multiple filiation, frequent divorce and the business of on-and-off marriage further enhance the indeterminacy of kinship as a lived-in order. When I return to Darwin, I have always to find out who now is married to whom and who among those previously married has reverted either to 'youngfella' or 'young girl' status and so is 'running round' in unattachment. In this world, notable Darby and Joan marriages stand out as remarkable for a durability that has been maintained against the odds.

In the conduct of relationships, credit is given for any time-bracketed contribution to a child's rearing and a rearing-up relationship between guardian and child is thus constituted with reference to performances. But marriages also are sustained only by and through adequate performance. The prime rule is that a couple who pretend to marriage in a camp must continue to turn their own rations into tucker. The domestic group (a hearth-hold) is defined as an essentially self-supporting unit. Couples who fail to continue in self-supporting commensality (I use the word, though invocation of a table is problematic), find that their marriages are denied them. Fellow campers will not tolerate marital pretensions if a hearth-hold cannot be regarded as free or materially independent in the matter of basic procurement of food. Couples who 'got no real kitchen anymore' can subsist only by begging, bludging and snatching from others. This is not on. Penurious couples are denied their marriages, the man and the woman each separately finding a place as a subordinate in the domestic group of some close-up countryman. Such partings can create marriages conducted on-and-off, for having found some source of income, the separated couple may rejoin to reassert both hearth-hold and their marriage. Where couples part because they thus have to, children often go with a mother to join her relations or they may be placed with yet other kin. Either way, divorce, whether forced or unforced, initiates further rearing-up relationships that join accepting hearth-holders to those displaced children admitted into kitchen-centred dependency. It should thus be clear that marriage is a socially accorded state, continuously to be sustained by performative acts and subject to communal undoing. In the light of all this, the word 'state' better describes the marital condition than does the concept of status.

In this performative world, I do not think that there is anything to match our consciousness of status as perduring social position. Rather, there are claims to current position in sets of relationships and claims to identity entered on grounds of affiliation to groups which are themselves labile, or to broad categories of kinship in which membership can also be negotiable.

For the individual adult, marriage is a performative condition. The rearing of kids is a capacity that comes of being able to render service by participating signally in the socialisation of a child in the domestic group in which one currently subsists. Further, prime credits for contributions to rearing-up redound to the hearth-holders who are 'boss for that place'—usually the presiding couple who maintain their hearth-right as they daily show forth their ability to get rations both to feed themselves and 'feed up all that kid'.

I have discussed aspects of performative kinship in detail elsewhere (Sansom 1980; Sansom and Baines 1983). In comparative perspective, Esther Goody (1982) regards performative kinship as a rarity of social organisation. It is the north Australian mode. Its spectacular features receive less than due emphasis in the literature because most contributors evince interest in what they call kinship structures, kinship systems and social organisation where these umbrella terms shelter everything that pertains to kinship save the conduct of relationships of kinship between persons— Ada, ol Luke, Leon and Paulie Smithson.

Beyond kinship, all positions and relationships among countrymen are referred to the performances, spans of experience and general inputs that qualify pretensions to a social state. One then gains both recognition for performance past and worth accorded with reference to one's current pattern of provisioning, giving and taking. Developed notions of service exchange subserve the estimation of a person's current standing. There are reckonings in which people are accorded their due by interested others. The things to be reckoned are expressed in the idiom and through the grammar of service exchange.

I now return to that Ada and her haul to bring concepts of exchange to the trends of social action that characterise work done to gain and sustain position in a world where uncertainty conquers risk, and rationality dictates that all participants are gamblers and so should hedge their bets.

The gift of service

When that Ada (aged forty-three) went down the track to get her haul she had just reverted to a young girl's state after divorcing Big Jack. She and Big Jack had struggled to sustain their marriage through a miler time that lasted for weeks of desperate borrowing. Ostensibly, they had used up all the credit that either could command. Fellow campers at Wallaby Cross would no longer countenance their pretensions to marriage. Ada and Big Jack parted. Then Ada suddenly discovered that far away ol Martie owed her 'that whole lot'. She convinced us that there really was a debt to collect and so the two-car expedition was mounted.

Calculatingly, we went down the track early on a pay-day Thursday. Ol Martie's mob would be in funds. Our extractive mission was muscled. Ol Martie quickly rallied helpers to make up a fund to redeem his acknowledged debt to Ada. I have no idea of the original amount, no idea of how ol Martie could generate the power to rally a cash amount that would satisfy Ada (save that he is boss for his encampment), no real inkling of just how much Ada retrieved. By its bulk it was a lot. Further, I do not know the circumstances of contraction of the original debt. We all knew, that Ada had once lived for over a year with ol Martie's mob. But there is something else.

During those weeks when that Ada and Big Jack had struggled to keep their marriage together, that Ada was a wife who kept the fact of her credit with ol Martie secret. The fact of the debt relationship was made public only after Big Jack had gone away from Darwin to find a place elsewhere. That Ada could have prolonged her marriage. She chose not to. Instead, she defined her ol Martie credit as a hedging investment—something to take up if the marriage proved unviable.

That Ada privatised the residue of her haul with grave intent. She was off to that 'nother place' in which she intended to retrieve three children from their foster-guardians and be a mother to them again. She would enter that other camp well funded. Later I learned that she made a marriage there, taking her children into it. Her marriage to Big Jack had been childless—by which I mean the pair had no children under their care during their association. After going away, that Ada gave three children of her own bearing a new father, for each of them an additional rearer-up.

Service value
There are three registers for the recognition and calculation of the import of service.
1. The first of these registers pertains to acts described in Aboriginal English as 'jus helpin'. Just helping I gloss as routine service. It is unmarked give-and-take of the *quid pro quo* variety. One has to accept that the patient:scene ratio dictates that the debts that come of routine service are subject to discounting with reference to miler time–good time alternations.
2. There are acts of signal service ('helping out' and 'bailing out') that establish the relationship between rescuing hero and the victim who once was saved. Such acts are celebrated in recounted story. They provide the rescuer with a lien on the surviving victim. Its meaning is a negotiable asset, never quite used up no matter how many times a one-time rescuer has invoked the story of the heroic intervention. I have distinguished between orders of signal service. Those that save life and being are irredeemable. Such liens find their quittance only when one of the parties to the relationship dies.
3. The third major order of service, I call dedication. Here I group two kinds of time-tried relationship together. Rearing-up is one of these. One gives and gives again over time to a child who can only be called on to repay in adulthood. Between adult and adult there can also be dedication. This is a mutual favouring that persists between two persons and outlives vicissitude. It is expressed as, 'That ol Tommy always, always helpin mefella.' This means that, by and large (but not really always) that Tommy expresses his regard, favour, attention, preference and support in regard to me. Then, 'You gotta say, that Tommy really lovin mefella.'

By dealing with patient and scene, I have dealt explicitly only with one ratio that belongs to the grammar of service exchange. I now introduce a second. This is the ratio between actor and patient. It is entailed in the derivation both of dedication and signal service. The person who needs to be bailed out is situationally reduced into a passive state by sickness, overwhelming challenge or whatever. Such a person requires a rescuer if a saving act is to be performed. Children, by definition, are patients. The actors who give them succour and rear them up deserve regard. In old age, rearers-up should be supported by those whom they helped to rear. Always helping a chosen other signals an affinity of spirit, a commitment that transcends the *quid pro quo* and puts value on a relationship for its own sake. Such constancies of mutual involvement accrete other relationships to them to become axes of constancies in an inconstant world. In the face of commitment, the unequal relationship between actor and patient dissolves into 'love'. Ol Luke will always help, serve and work for that ol Petey because Petey is that Petey—after all, 'Them twofella bin running together for years n years.' So, a transcendent value but a value which, nonetheless, is referred to a history of services consistently contained in the give-and-take of a relationship that is all but perpetual. Further to parade the Aboriginal glosses on such relationships, I would have to deal with religion. Those evident affinities between persons which cause them to favour one another above and beyond the call of rational recompense are realities which Aborigines refer to the Dreaming—to the sharing of totem and the sharing of spiritual concerns that endow persons with like will.

Conclusion

There are some loose ends to tie up. Accept that it is difficult to conceal personal accruals in an encampment. There will always be people around one who are strife. If defined as a person who has substance in excess of current needs (a surplus), one becomes a target for importuning. The cry is 'Help me out. Maybe I gonna losim this marriage.' In the face of bludging insistence, the person in command of surplus tends to help (selected) others until their own store of wealth is gone. In the long term (and given uncertainty) the witnessed acts of helping are investments. The rub is that no investment is subject to any guaranteed time-valence with regard to its collection. By incurring multiple debts, one creates a generalised but unspecific potential to be able to collect. 'Lotta fella bin owin me whole lot' is the correctly vague but, nonetheless, accurate reckoning. I have now explained why people do not save for rainy months to come. Instead they put cash out to create a generalised though indeterminate potential for recovery.

There is an answer of another order to the question about the absence of 'positive interest'. The person who lends during a miler time of scarcity to collect in a time of plenty will be celebrated. Put at the centre of jolly consumption, the bad time lender becomes the most indulged, most favoured, most complimented focus of attention in a time of general consumption. What we might call interest is paid in the coin of adulation and studied indulgence.

As to why there are no going rates, I think that I have already said enough. Where everyone's realisations are uncertain, the amount in a reclaimed debt is a function of the circumstanced liquidity of a debtor balanced against a creditor's powers of extraction.

The last issue I address is that of vectored cash. Ada dedicated her holding to 'all them kid' who lived in another place. In contentious discourse about the destiny of funds, morality is invoked. Would you claim money for beer when I have nominated this sum as the price of a child's dinner? In front of witnesses, just try to press your claim. Cash holdings then can be ticketed and so taken to human volition as money for help in some specified regard.

I know that this chapter is only indicative. Because service exchange pervades Aboriginal dealings, it would require a volume to analyse the subtleties of a system based on the proposition that giving is to be construed as help. Yet I hope I have written enough to merit a conclusion.

When countrymen enter money into their modality for exchange it is made over into the stuff of help, helping and helping out. To effect the transformation, Aborigines rely on an achievement which the ghost of Talcott Parsons must envy. They assimilate cash to a developed philosophy of social action which has voluntarism at its core, the reconciliation of human needs for its dynamic and the substantiation of persons as its end.

References

Bohannan, P.
1959 The Impact of Money on an African Subsistence Economy, *The Journal of Economic History* 19(4), 491–503.

Burke, K.
1969 *A Grammar of Motives*, University of California, Berkeley and Los Angeles.

Burling, R.
1962 Maximization Theories and the Study of Economic Anthropology, *American Anthropologist* 64(4), 802–20.

Gilsenan, M.
1976 Lying, Honour and Contradiction. In B. Kapferer (ed), *Transaction and Meaning: Directions in the Anthropology of Exchange and Symbolic Behavior*, Institute for the Study of Human Issues, Philadelphia.

Goody, E.N.
1982 *Parenthood and Social Reproduction*, Cambridge University Press, Cambridge.

Nalson, J.
1965 *Usury: From Tribal Brotherhood to Universal Otherhood*, Chicago University Press, Chicago.

Rowley, C.D.
1972 *Outcasts in White Australia*, Penguin, Harmondsworth.

1986 *Recovery: The Politics of Aboriginal Reform*, Penguin, Ringwood.

Sansom, B.
1980 *The Camp at Wallaby Cross*, Australian Institute of Aboriginal Studies, Canberra.

Sansom, B. and P. Baines
1983 Aboriginal Child Placement in the Urban Context. In *Collected Papers*, Symposium 4: Aboriginal Law and Tradition in Australian Society—Problems of Conflict, Co-existence and Adaptation, The Australian Law Reform Commission, Sydney.

Simmel, G.
1900 *Philosophie des Geldes*, Duncker and Humblot, Leipzig.

Stanner, W.E.H.
1966 *On Aboriginal Religion*, Oceania Monograph No 11, University of Sydney, Sydney.

Weber, M.
1964 *The Theory of Social and Economic Organisation*, The Free Press, Glencoe.

10. Gaynor Macdonald   A Wiradjuri fight story[1]

In the old days there always used to be fights up at the gates. I asked some of my companions, two sisters, which fights they remembered:

> Up at the gates? There used to be gates right up there in the corner, there used to be gates—are the gates still there? Yes...up at the gates, at the gates, that's where they had the fightin ring—and underneath the railway bridge.
> If they had a row in the night, young fellas over the girls and the like...
> Now Johnny Slater one time...there was Gavin Thompson, yes, and Bundy Hughes. They was gonna...ah...they was chucking off at him and he was gonna fight them, til you see, my father, he said, now, 'Git him in the mornin, Johnny!'
> And of course, all of the Thompsons on one side and the Collins and the Slaters on this side.
> 'Now!' he said, 'They're gonna have fightin. I don't want no barrackin,' Billy...Billy Brody said.
> Now there's Johnny Slater there, and they're all talkin there, some of em saying, do this and do that. Anyhow...
> Out comes...Bundy!
> 'Now, no interference!' he [Billy] said. 'I'm the referee—no-one else gets in.'
> So there's Thompsons on that side and all the Slaters and Collins on this side. And, of course, they started!
> Only two or three minutes and Bundy was down. He knocked him! And he was prancin around! 'Righto!' he said—he was jumping around like this see!
> 'Righto, Gavin—it's your turn now. Git ere or I'll knock you down where you standin.'
> Oh! an he was prancin! Rarin to go then, he was, rarin to go.
> And Paula, that when Paula started then: 'Go on, Johnny, give it to him,' and Billy said, 'Paula, that'll do now.' It woulda end up in a big brawl, see.
> Anyhow, two or three rounds and down went Gavin. Knocked a Thompson!
> 'Oh! No more!'
> That was it then. He downed em. They left it like that.
> 'No more then,' someone said.[2]

The two sisters who told this story were born in 1923 and 1928. They are members of the Wiradjuri (Wiradjeri) tribe of central New South Wales (see Beckett, Chapter 7).[3] The fight they describe happened about thirty years ago but their memories of it were very vivid: we laughed and paused and exclaimed as if the events were all being heard for the first time, as indeed, in its particular dramatisation, it was. The principal story teller, the older sister, acted out the story in such a way that those who had been there seemed to relive the experience. Both a fight and a fight story are great dramas, with all the ingredients dramas should contain. The story is representative of the way such fights were conducted—and still are.

In common with many Aboriginal people in southeast Australia, Wiradjuri people refer to themselves as Kooris. They are great story tellers. Many hours have been whiled away telling stories of the past and present, most of them about real characters and events in time and space which, in the telling, take on an intransitive and cyclical quality, a timelessness and an enduring significance. Most stories carry basic messages, highlight concerns, and reveal features of Koori life and values which have persisted over time. In this sense, the story is like a myth. Stories are not told to inform or illuminate but, rather, to illustrate and to emphasise. They are told among people who have the capacity to understand all the nuances because they are themselves part of the story world. Stories can be told over and over without losing their intrinsic quality of conveying messages with which people can identify.

Sansom (1982, 120–22, based on the work of Pat Baines) describes how Aborigines in 'settled' Western Australia have developed a new form of story telling that has transformed a set of traditional myths, which highlighted the taking of country into ownership, into modern stories based on history rather than myth. In these stories named ancestors move across the landscape and establish or reassert familial ownership of territory. These land–people stories have much in common with the story I discuss here, which is concerned with fighting among Kooris but may also be described as a modern form of myth: an historical tale which concerns one's own people and which highlights the enduring dynamics of social relations and social processes.

Fights have a symbolic significance of which Kooris are well aware. In the fight, as in the fight story, there is a transformation of the basic themes which can be discerned in social relations generally. The fight becomes the anecdotal expression of life, the ordering of reality into one symbolic event which expresses the various tensions, oppositions, contradictions and values with which people live day by day. These are relived in the stories which thus take on their timeless quality.

The fight, as a vehicle of value transmission and a confirmative expression of social structure, has had an important part to play in maintaining Wiradjuri meanings over time. Whilst by outward appearances Kooris in central New South Wales may seem to have lost touch with their traditional social patterns, they reveal in the fight (as in various other social activities), traits and values which have always given, and continue to give them their distinctive Wiradjuri world view, which has much in common with that of other Aboriginal people throughout Australia. This fighting story illustrates some of the themes in Wiradjuri life that have endured over time. It demonstrates the tenacity of values and modes of relating, despite the various changes to which Wiradjuri people have had to adjust over the past two centuries. I discuss it scene by scene to explore some of the messages it contains, for the informed listener, about the Koori world.

Act I Setting the scene

The setting
> Up at the gates? There used to be gates right up there in the corner, there used to be gates—are the gates still there? Yes...up at the gates, at the gates, that's where they had the fightin ring—and underneath the railway bridge.

A 'good fight', as opposed to 'fooling round' or 'fightin dirty', would take place in an area symbolically set aside from daily living. In the past this would be up at the back gates of the Aboriginal station, known as the mission, or in a clearing by the railway bridge just along from the mission. There are still favoured spots today—near particular street lights, in a natural or created clearing such as a carpark. This is somewhere where the fighters can 'have a fair go'.

The occasion
> If they had a row in the night, young fellas over the girls and the like...

The social order has been disturbed: there has been rowing, a quarrel while the boys were drinking. Over what, the story teller is not quite sure, but the general reasons for fights will do as explanation: 'rowin over girls an that'. Arguments over women in the case of men, or over men and children in the case of women, are popular explanations as to what triggers off a fight. One woman explained how fights could start between men or between a man and his wife:

> Well, in this time now, once he gets a few across his chest [having had a few drinks], he starts thinkin see—he gets jealous of his cook or takes a look at his cook, well—starts a fight.

Another woman claimed that most fights started with 'women's mouths—they'll always start a big brawl—carryin on about their kids, that's what does it.'

The young fellows were drinking. However, this is not the reason for the fight itself as the story teller later explains:

> Them days, see, they wouldna have it on when they drunk. They wouldna. They'd have a fight, but the next morning, they'd go up to the bridge or up to the gates and they'd fight it out: 'I'll see you in the morning!'

Fights cannot be understood only in terms of their stated causes—fights over women, money or possessions have their origins in the social whole of which Kooris are a part. Any attribution of motives can only be approximate. The motives for wanting to fight the night before may be very different from those constructed by the time morning comes and the circumstances and the audience have changed. There can be many variations between what a person says they are fighting about and what they are thinking, and what others say and think.

The protagonists

> Now Johnny Slater one time...there was Gavin Thompson, yes, and Bundy Hughes.

The hero of the story is introduced and then his 'victims'. The causes of the fight are not mentioned: the fighters themselves sum up in their very existence, the issues at hand. The social identity of the fighters and the forces and structures which go toward their composition as social identities are immediately apprehended by the audience. The causes are inseparable from the protagonists.

The fighters are remembered well. They are well known to each other and to everyone listening to the story. Their names evoke messages about family allegiances and thus political and economic relationships as well. The Thompson and Hughes kin networks[4] are generally considered close, as are the Slater and Collins networks, but the two networks are not as close to each other. 'Close' refers to social distancing rather than genealogical reckoning. In fact, the fighters themselves are not genealogically close,[5] although they refer to each other as cousins.

A 'fair fight' is a fist fight which takes place in accordance with accepted Koori standards of fighting. A fight becomes 'dirty' when it contravenes the rules, as when weapons are introduced. A fair fight takes place only between people who know each other well, and in all such fights that I have recorded the fighters are counted as related. A fight is set in a context of mutual interaction and communication: strangers do not fight. Disputes with strangers are very difficult to settle because there is no relationship, no communication, no guarantee that the rules are shared and valued. Acknowledgement of shared experience means that interaction will take place within an accepted framework.

Knowing the composition of the fighting dyad tells the listener or audience whether it is going to be a 'good' fight (worth trooping up to the gates to watch), whether it will be exciting (highlighting a particularly competitive social dynamic), whether it will be fair and whether it will result in any shifts in intra-societal dynamics.

Johnny is the story teller's nephew and the main actor so far as she is concerned. Her own allegiences come out clearly in the story as it unwinds. He is the son of her elder sister and the same age group as herself (mid twenties at the time of the fight), as are Gavin and Bundy. The listener is expected to be able to share in all the nuances of these relationships and they are not explained. Names symbolise oppositions which are obliquely referred to and may only express themselves from time to time in activities such as fights.

Establishing the ground rules

> They was gonna...ah...they was chucking off at him and he was gonna fight them...til you see, my father, he said, now, 'Git him in the mornin, Johnny!'

Limits have to be set on whatever is potentially limitless or uncontrollable. Order has to be imposed on disorder. The older man, the story teller's father, intervenes. He is a respected member of the community and other members will accept his authority. He appeals to the recognised values concerning fights: they should not take place when people are drunk or in the heat of the moment—for in both cases events could easily get out of hand.

Later, after the main story had been told, parts of it were dwelt on and laughed over as the memories flooded back. The story teller herself is now the central character as she unfolds the events. She adds:

> Yes...Johnny called them out next morning. Our father, he went up there the next morning and said,'Git up out of that bed, John!' 'Aah! Dad, Dad...' he goes.'You just git out,' he said, 'or I'll punch you on the mouth,' he says. 'You git up! You're gonna fight them two this morning up there at the gates,' he said. 'They were callin you all dirty, filthy names and they wanted to fight you last night. You was drunk and they was drunk. Up the gates! Go on pull em out there!'

In the morning the fight takes on the characteristics of the honourable duel rather than a drunken brawl. Feelings are not left to simmer from the night before—they are to be confronted in the fight. Any resentments brought about by the quarrel, as well as angry words, can then be expressed ritualistically and set aside. They are not talked out of the fight by the older man. In fact, next morning, Johnny had to be talked into it until he was 'prancin around then, waitin to get up to the gates'.

The audience

> And of course, all of the Thompsons on one side and the Collins and the Slaters on this side.

It was at this point that the story teller rose from her chair and started to act out the rest of the fight as she spoke. She was the Thompsons on one side, moving then to become the Collins (of which she is one) and the Slaters. She does not mention the rest of the audience, the spectators, until later adding, 'Oh there was a mob watchin...Gawd! There was a mob all right! All the mission!' It is taken for granted that a fight between a Thompson, a Hughes, and a Slater would interest everyone on the mission. Two significant kin networks are to battle it out through their members.

A fight is an event in which all the community may participate. One man remembers how he used to wake in the early mornings in his youth, hardly waiting for his shoes, to run over to the gates 'frost n all'. At the gates the clustering of spectators declares interest in the fighters by an informal spatial positioning with regard to one side or another. This reveals the direction and extent of people's involvement in social processes—the association of people with like mind and like allegiances, and the desire to be near one's own should the fight become a 'big brawl', which to Kooris means that other dyads will get worked up and start interfering or fighting themselves.

The referee

> 'Now!' he said, 'They're gonna have fightin. I don't want no barrackin,' Billy...Billy Brodie said.

The referee is self-appointed, but as no-one challenges his role it is presumed acceptable. Billy is older than the fighters (who are in their mid twenties) but not old enough to be considered 'one of the old people' (in the sense of a community leader or decision maker). At least some of the latter may be presumed to be present but they take no active part except insofar as their presence as witnesses lends legitimacy to the proceedings (see Sansom 1980). Billy is closely related to Johnny, but also traces links to both Gavin and Bundy.

The referee announces the fight and lets everyone know there is to be a referee in charge of the event. There will be no barracking, no jeering, calling out or stirring up the fighters. This is a fight between the antagonists only and will not be allowed to turn into a free-for-all. It is an ordered, controlled activity, conducted within well established boundaries.

Act II The action

The build up
> Now there's Johnny Slater there...and they're all talkin there, some of em saying, do this and do that. Anyhow...

The referee's caution is based on his awareness of the mood of the audience: the excitement of the fight is there—advice, encouragement and 'psyching up'—and all the ingredients of trouble. It is largely up to him to keep things in hand, to keep it a fair fight which will turn into a memorable story rather than a shameful event to be suppressed.

The fight starts
> Out comes...Bundy!
> 'Now, no interference,' he [Billy] said. 'I'm the referee—no-one else gets in.'

Billy reiterates his role and his right to determine the course of events. He will restrict involvement to the fighting dyad and will not permit indiscriminate brawling or 'double banking' (allowing two people to fight against one).

Lining up
> So there's Thompsons on that side and all the Slaters and Collins on this side. And, of course, they started!

The story teller lets us into the real drama—the meaning of the fight for the social order as a whole. For her, the protagonists are representative of their kin groups. The fight has polarised community members on the basis of their primary allegiances. They group themselves accordingly on each side of the fighting ground. They remain spectators, not fighters, but still have an input to the fight dynamic because of their spatial arrangement. They are also under the direction of the referee and it is his task to keep them as spectators.

How they fared
> Only two or three minutes and Bundy was down. He knocked him! And he was prancin around! 'Righto!' he said—he was jumping around like this see!

> 'Righto, Gavin—it's your turn now. Git ere or I'll knock you down where you standin.'
> Oh! an he was prancin! Rarin to go then, he was, rarin to go.

Johnny is the star of this tale. It is, after all, a fight story unlikely to be told by a Thompson or a Hughes. Had they done so, particular meanings in the telling would have altered accordingly. The experience of the fight would be different from their point of view. In this case, the story teller wishes to notch up a point for her people. Bundy doesn't last long. Johnny makes easy work of him and starts showing off, gearing himself up to what is expected to be a greater challenge and making sure he maximises the psychological advantage gained by downing Bundy. That there is a qualitative difference for the story teller between Johnny's fight with Bundy and that with Gavin can be detected in her second reference to the audience alignment: this time the Hughes are not significant but the Slater supporters take on a greater role through mention of the Collins mob, their close relatives. This fight with a Thompson is going to be of significance for the Collins mob.

Involvement and restraint

> And Paula, that when Paula started then: 'Go on, Johnny, give it to him,' and Billy said, 'Paula, that'll do now.' It woulda end up in a big brawl, see.

Paula is Johnny's sister and Billy's wife. She is getting too carried away with the action and it is her husband who restrains her. The story teller reminds us that barracking and interference can escalate tensions and disturb the delicate emotional balance that the spatial location of the fight, the observance of ground rules and presence of the referee are designed to maintain. The fight takes place in the clear light of day.

Consequences

> Anyhow, two or three rounds and down went Gavin. Knocked a Thompson!

It took Johnny longer to get the better of Gavin but, although the story teller faithfully records this, she cannot help a reference to her own rueful delight at his having knocked a Thompson. As she is a Collins herself, the Thompsons represent the opposition and she makes it quite clear in her words and presentation that she is glad they have been got the better of. The fight is perceived as a tussle for the right to impose views of self in social relationships. She is claiming the right of Johnny and, by extension, herself to determine his own status or positioning in the social order. Whilst there is an informally recognised pecking order in terms of influence in the community, each Koori asserts him or herself when need be to ensure that others do not think they can get away with pushing people around. One Koori girl expressed in her readiness to fight with the words, 'I wouldn't let no-one stand over me.' Johnny has been subjected to insults which are an attempt to impose a definition and social position on him. It is this that he has to repudiate. His willingness to fight is enough, but that he has also knocked a member of the more influential network is a bonus.

Ending the fight

'Oh! No more!'
That was it then. He downed em. They left it like that.
'No more then,' someone said.

The knocking of a Thompson heralds a quick end to the fight before further damage is done to the reputation of this family. Later the story teller explained, 'Oh, they're alright, we're related to them all anyway, but they try and stand over—well, I don't have to tell you.' In this comment she recognises and verbalises the divisions which are apparent in the fight itself. An informed listener would not need to have them explained: the story already says all that needs to be said. The fight has not terminated social relations, nor was this the intention.

Meaning and messages in Wiradjuri fights

To understand a fight situation one has to understand a whole complex of social, economic and political relationships in their historical context. A fight should not simply be attributed to too much alcohol (for often it is absent altogether), to violence characteristic of those of low socio-economic status (as in a culture of poverty thesis), or to the ravages of colonisation (eg Wilson 1982). The meanings which are shared by all those involved in the fight drama help to locate this particular activity within an overall social framework. A particular disagreement may spark off a fight but meanings extend far beyond the episodic encounter. Fights do reveal conflicts and tensions within the Wiradjuri world but they do not represent its breakdown. Taylor's (1971) discussion of shared meanings shows that a society can contain, and may even require, a great deal of diversity and conflict without disturbing its essential balance. The minimum requirement is that people share meanings to the extent that their life together is intelligible and these meanings not only unite them over and above their differences but some relationships will, in fact, be defined in terms of such differences. Meanings about the significance of actions, celebrations and feelings can go along with divisiveness because they imply that people understand each other—not, however, that they agree with each other (Taylor 1971, 28).

Fighting does not threaten Koori meanings: it is an integral part of certain meanings, acting to reinforce social values and perceptions, creating and re-creating meaning. There are means by which people articulate their social reality which are understood by others within a social group. People selectively internalise symbols which are meaningful to them. They become means of expression and resolution, of coping with the requirements and contradictions of everyday existence, and of bonding people in a shared experience. They are ways by which people state who and what they are. Thus a fight is about the negotiation of identity which is an essential part of self–other relationships (Brittan 1973, 97). However the meanings of a situation are not necessarily clear to everyone. They are induced by observers or actors through the ways in which they experience the action. Kooris are aware, for instance, that their perceptions of the significance of fights—and other Koori activities—differ from many of those held by non-Aboriginal Australians. The two groupings should not be expected to share meanings: they have distinctively different historical experiences from which these emerge and to which they refer.

Certain ground rules are applied in a fight context that become evident when one has watched several fights, including those which get dirty in the sense that they do not adhere to these norms. These rules are reflections of values upheld in the society generally, and are shared by participants as a framework within which interaction takes place (see Taylor 1971, 27). They reflect the emphasis Kooris place on social and physical equality and the right of individuals to stand up for themselves and to brook no interference from others (Macdonald 1986). Autonomy, and thus equality, can only be maintained if one is willing to stand up for oneself (cf Evans-Pritchard 1940, 184). People vigorously protect their right to do their own thing, to be, as Bell (1983, 7) heard a four-year-old child at Warrabri say, 'boss for meself'. People must take responsibility for themselves, they should not tolerate stand-over tactics.

It is in the audience, as much as in the fighters, that the real significance and drama of the fight are to be found. Without the audience there is no fight—only a brawl, a flogging or mucking around. The audience acts, first, as an agent of control and spectators will act to ensure the fight does not get out of hand. They may restrain other onlookers from getting involved, prevent the fighters from introducing weapons and ensure that the referees do their job, and stop the fights if one of the antagonists says they have had enough. Second, the presence of an audience legitimates the activity: spectators are assenting witnesses, even if they are not formally watching are in the vicinity and close enough to know what is going on (see also Sansom 1980, 105).

There is a third important feature involved in making a fight public: it becomes an event 'owned' by the public, the audience (Sansom 1980, 106). As witnesses, the members of the audience take on a responsibility for the fight and certain of its consequences, and acquire knowledge from the fight which will be necessary in subsequent community interaction. The fighters, in consenting to fight publicly, are requesting public support for that right, or otherwise.

If, for instance, the fight is between two men, one of whom has accused the other of advances toward his wife, the accused may wish to defend his honour by standing up to the challenge to fight, and the accuser may wish to make a statement about his rights. There may be people in the audience who know of and have condoned the extra-marital relationship. If so, the accuser is letting them know that he is someone to be reckoned with—he is challenging them as well. In future, those who are a party to the liaison will need to be much more careful, or may choose not to go on sanctioning the relationship. Alternatively, they may urge the woman to decide which relationship she wants and stop making trouble. There will be a subtle realignment within the community. People will act differently, if only in exercising more caution or discretion. The fight is thus an exercise in communication. It informs community members of the current state of play regarding certain others and allows them to devise appropriate responses on the basis of what they have witnessed (or heard about).

Fighters may also select an audience which will place them at a social and psychological advantage. For instance, they may sit on a grievance for a long time before choosing the time and place to challenge or confront someone. This may be when they have a sufficient number of kin around or when they are back in their own home territory rather than visiting elsewhere. To have a supportive audience can affect not only the fight itself but also community reactions afterwards.

Who wins the fight in physical terms (such as who is downed or bloodied first) is not always of significance. It may make a difference to the accuser who, by winning, would strengthen his case and his claim to recognition, but the manner in which the fight is conducted also carries a prestige value. Someone who does not make a good show for themselves—is half-hearted or starts to fight dirty—will not win support. Someone may put up a good fight against an opponent recognised as being stronger and more skilful. Although technically the loser, they will still be admired for their pluck.

On returning to the community after an absence, people will normally be filled in on any recent fights, deaths, accidents and so on. This is an important means of being let in on the shifts which have occurred, of making sure one is aware of any realignments. Such news is often given in the form of event stories, the significance of which are clear to listeners who belong. There may seem to be little interest in the causes of fights, but this is because community members can be assumed to understand the dynamics operating in certain relationships at any point in time. Only the unusual needs additional explanation.

In the fight story above, Johnny's message to Gavin is probably simply to get off his back. Johnny was fighting people who more normally call the tune. His dad insisted he fight them and not allow them to get away with defining him as they chose. It is the father who may have most to lose or gain in the fight. Whilst he has respect within the community, he is not at the fore of the pecking order. The fight does not change the pecking order but does act to place constraints on those who are 'first up'. This is not so much because it threatens further violence but because the fight signifies an individual's and/or a kin network's preparedness to act independently of, or in spite of, the recognised definers. Gavin's family network is a significant force in the community; for example, it has influence when decisions have to be made which affect people as a whole. This fight does not make much difference to the structural alignments in the community. It establishes or confirms where people stand in relation to each other at this point in time. In doing so it also contains a message about the limits and extent of the power of any group or individual over others.

After the fight, 'They had to shake hands and told them to make friends...and they sorta made friends.' Not only the fight but also the antagonism and the recognition of community divisions are publicly acknowledged and brought to a formal end. Life goes on in the usual way that signifies people's commitment to each other rather than their lack of difference or their agreement. The next fight could well be between a Thompson and a Hughes or between a Collins and a Slater, but the same basic oppositions will form and dissolve and the same basic values and relative positions be upheld.

There are many ways in which a fight can be interpreted or given meaning depending upon the participants, the observers and commentators, and the issues involved. The total of these meanings tends to ensure the continuity of the system: they are not revolutionary in intent or consequence. Such fights do, however, point to a society in which life is continually being negotiated or reconstructed, in which people and positions are not taken for granted.

Conflict, tensions and controls

It is normal for contradictions and ambiguities in a social order both to exist and to be given expression in overt form. A fight is not just a social commentary separate from the actions it addresses (contra Geertz 1973, 448) but an integral part of the social system and essential to its working. The fight symbolises and expresses oppositions which emerge from the ways in which social relations and values are structured. It enables the resultant tensions to be lived with but does not necessitate their resolution, which may imply revolutionary change to the social order. The tensions, not the oppositions, are resolved: the oppositions can be lived with a little longer.

Bateson (1973, 83–84) saw intense and total involvement as a frequent means of releasing the tensions that habitually build up in relationships. Tensions induce entropy. People cannot act unless outlets are provided, otherwise such tensions may escalate and threaten the social order. In a large-scale society there is usually room to opt out, to socially or physically remove oneself and engage in an alternative lifestyle. Kooris move around within their 'beats' (Beckett, Chapter 7) for many reasons—one of which is diffusing tensions—but opting out is not always possible or desirable, and some conflicts will wait around for one's return: they need to be confronted. Rituals have long been recognised as one major means of expressing contradictions and conflicts (Turner 1964, 1974). Fights are another.

Howard (1978, 82–83) has argued for a break from the functionalist approach, which stresses consensus and equilibrium, to one which recognises a 'complex web of interaction, of alliance and competition' among Aborigines. The two are not irreconcilable and together they make for a more dynamic approach.

A conformity view of society cannot encompass conflicts or divergent perspectives (Sider 1980). Kooris are socialised into consistency rather than conformity. They want people to be predictable, to be consistent with the perceptions that others hold of them so that they then know how to act. They operate on the assumption that people can develop natural talents but that they are not changeable. Whether someone is described as a good bloke, silly in the head or dangerous, the designation means that others will know how to relate to them, including how to stir them up or quieten them down. Fights take place in the context of known relationships. Strangers are unknown and unpredictable.

Fights are thus a means of maintaining balance in social relations and are not an index of disturbance. The causes are structural and the disagreements which are referred to by community members are triggers or apparent causes. Disagreements—

someone trying stand-over tactics, trying to take someone's woman off him, usurping the rights of a woman over her children, and so on—will continually arise. Fights do not necessarily settle or solve anything, but in expressing the tensions, workable relations can proceed once more—or at least until the next time. People revive their capacity to act.

In his introduction to the stories of Paddy Roe, Muecke (1983, viii–xi) argues that story telling itself is a means of solving social problems, 'in the sense of integrating and normalising disruptive social events by absorbing them in narrative structures'. He adds, 'this is not to say that the problems disappear entirely and forever'. The ability to tell the story does provide 'some sort of comfort or therapy'. A fight acts in much the same way. It involves people, expresses tensions and liberates people for action.

Any sort of conflict is involving, and avoiding conflict means not getting involved in the first place (see Romanucci-Ross 1973, 93). Kooris accept certain levels and expressions of conflict as an expected dynamic in social relationships. They also recognise that unsanctioned involvement exacerbates conflict. People do get involved for various reasons, including the mounting excitement they experience as spectators, their concern for kin or, as in the case of non-Kooris such as the police, a concern to maintain order as defined by an external value system. People who are not defined as principal antagonists are counselled to stay out of a dispute. If a fight does get out of hand, drawing in people who interfered in some way, one might hear that 'so and so should have minded their own business', or, 'Ah well, they're asking for trouble, sticking their neck out like that, they got what was coming to them.'

Kooris place a high value on personal responsibility for one's own actions: one has the right not to take up another's case, including that of a close relative. At the same time, they value sharing and support among kin. There is an inevitable source of contradiction in this perspective. However, by ensuring a certain amount of freedom or autonomy, even from the demands of kin relationships, many conflicts can be averted, defused or have less occasion to arise in the first place. People emphasise their differences and differentiation is assertive: it brings about a sense of self vis-a-vis others. Kooris will resist categorisation without consent ('Don't you lump me in with that lot') or domineering, stand-over attitudes in others. They like to make a statement about where they stand. Paradoxically, the emphasis on autonomy does not create divisiveness but ensures that consistency in social relations is re-established.

The high value Kooris place on egalitarianism may lead from time to time to competitive and tension-provoking situations because there are in fact differentials of authority and status. Nevertheless, egalitarianism is not a fiction: it is a means of ensuring that individuals maintain the right to define their own place in the world and are not stood-over by others. The values put on egalitarianism and autonomy are brought into action to ensure that a person or group will not mobilise others and assume power. However, there are countervailing forces as well: people do in practice mobilise groups. Nevertheless, these values provide for strategic action and freedom of choice. Allegiances can be formed, dissolved and manipulated to a greater extent if one retains independence. The right to withdraw is always an option.

In the absence or irrelevance of externally imposed controls, social order has to be continually re-negotiated. Fighting is one of the ways in which re-negotiation (or continuing negotiation) occurs. An attempt to damage a person's reputation in a small society has to be challenged: as it increases someone's shame and potentially leads to social death (Baroja 1965, 85). The value placed on personal reputation leads to fighting, sparked by insults or public insinuations. The value placed on autonomy and responsibility for one's own actions limits the consequences of conflict as it condemns interference. The value placed on sociality and responsibility to certain others, such as kin, demands adherence to certain codes. The myriad relationships in which people are involved give rise to a dynamic in which negotiation continually takes place.

Physical confrontation in a fight also minimises the dangers of self-disclosure in a society in which shame is socially debilitating and threatens autonomy (see Brittan 1973, 123). A fight allows for the avoidance of what may be more threatening forms of communication; people do not have to reveal their pain, weakness, shame, wrongdoing, or loss. To talk out an issue may bring raw wounds into the open. The physical pain of fighting is a small cost compared with having to confront the contradictions, ambiguities and inconsistencies of life, and the accusation that one has acted in bad faith. By expressing these, the fight enables them to persist without creating irreversible divisiveness either within social relations or within oneself. As an avoidance technique it is not an opting out, but a means of being able to re-negotiate the process necessary for social relations to continue, and continue to be valued. Fighting between individuals, or between symbolised factions, does not threaten the social order unless the fight is conducted outside of the social norms—in which case it becomes 'dirty fighting', for example with weapons or without an audience.

The fight also allows for a degree of social closure: one does not have to admit openly to the existence of opposing factions in the society. Whilst these are well recognised, stories and gossip can focus on two fighters who were talking up too big when they were drunk one night. The presence of the audience also makes a social statement distinct from that of the fighters themselves. The event must be shared to take on meaning and in the sharing is the structuring of a corporate community awareness which transcends the oppositions in the fight. In the fight, the whole mission comes together, and the audience both constrains the fighters and liberates them.

Conflict can be a way of celebrating differences which are valued. It does not imply that people are not associated. Kooris can fight because they are close and two fighters are likely to turn on anyone who intervenes and who thus appears to interfere in their relationship. The fight does not rupture the association. However, people may take care to disassociate themselves from a quarrel between a member of their kin circle and another so as not to have the issue rebound on to them or the family in general. Thus, not only should one mind one's own business, one should also ensure that others mind theirs. Interference, gossip, accusations and the like are intrusions—although, at the same time, they are inevitable because they provide the information necessary for assessing or negotiating relationships. Kooris, and other Aborigines, place a high value on knowing each other and their environment generally. This knowingness is not intended to eliminate problems or conflicts but to make them understandable and manageable.

Fighting liberates people, if momentarily, from the oppressive aspects of their lack of power vis-a-vis others in the community, from discipline, from conformity, from the need to be sociable, from the restraints of clothing (removing or loosening shirts, for instance), and from the ever-present dominating influence of Europeans. The fight becomes a release from all that is held to be oppressive and constraining, physically and emotionally. It is one of those moments of 'dangerous confrontation' which 'frequently bring an air of festival, of exhilaration, of release from ordinary restrictions' (Tilley 1978, 182). Their fighting prowess has paid dividends in various ways both within and beyond the Wiradjuri world as a means of standing up for themselves and expressing who they are: the sport of boxing was once one of the only arenas in which Kooris were treated as relative equals by whites. Some of these myriad messages are echoed in the words of a ten-year-old Koori boy who was explaining the difference between Kooris and whites:

> Kooris are better cos they're black, strong, muscly and tough. Kooris were the first ones in the world, I mean Australia, so they're tougher and should be the boss. They fight more cos they're the best fighters in the whole world and good at sports too.

Fighting in the traditional Wiradjuri world

Fighting is not only a significant part of contemporary symbolic meaning-expression: it was also significant prior to the influence of Europeans. Having said that social stability is reflected in continuity, it is interesting to observe the similarity between fighting today and in the recent past, and Aboriginal fighting recorded in New South Wales in the nineteenth century. The same patterns, often the same rules, and the same values are upheld. Fights were staged in particular locations, had an audience, and were fought out as duels even when many were fighting at the same time (Smyth 1878, 292; Rudder 1899, 264). There was usually little or no bloodshed and fights ended with one of the fighting parties, close relatives or people from a neutral tribe calling for a halt (McDougall 1901; Smyth 1878, 292–93). Although Flanagan (1888, 40) recorded that 'the hostility of the tribes to each other seems to be almost unremitting', he nevertheless added:

> As very few incentives to inveterate warfare are to be found amongst them...they seem to have come to a mutual understanding that their struggles, however frequent, shall be as harmless as possible.

Struilby (in Graham 1863, 134–39) records such a battle between about 600 Wiradjuri of the Lachlan and Macquarie River areas. The battle, which ended with a fierce duel between the two groups' leaders, 'lasted about five hours and there were only six killed and some fifteen wounded'.

There are differences in the way Wiradjuri people fight today. Their codes are modelled on those of boxing. They fight with fists in fair fighting, and not the spears and clubs of the past. New weapons, such as knives and broken bottles, are resorted to in dirty fighting, resulting in different types of injury. Perhaps most significant is the restriction placed on fighting in public—and on the consequent supervision and control of fighting—under Australian law (see Langton, Chapter 11). Wiradjuri people are now encapsulated in Australian society and are not always able to determine or exercise sanctions and constraints in their preferred ways.

The fight story as myth

The thirty-year-old story with which this chapter began is about a single historical event, but there were many events like it. It carries meanings which are enduring and which give it its symbolic quality. The characters are named because the oppositions they represent are still relevant, as are the values expressed. In time, the surnames may cease to convey messages and new fight stories will have new names. This gives the story its myth-as-history significance, as Sansom (1982) maintains of the Nyungar stories of Western Australia (and see Sutton, Chapter 13). One of the characteristics of myths is that they define basic social oppositions and define the position of people vis-a-vis others (see Berndt and Berndt 1970, 117). Wiradjuri people today use their history stories to symbolise and express the relationships once encapsulated in myth. The Wiradjuri also draw on history to depict their social relations in the face of European expansion and the inability of traditional forms of social life to continue unchanged (see also Sansom 1982, 121). The stories are part of what Sansom (1982, 122) refers to as 'emergent, vital and traditionally untraditional cultural expression'.

Muecke (1983, ix) maintains that events 'cannot be transmitted in any raw state, they have to be normalised by some discourse such as narrative'. Although this fight story may seem sparsely told, as such it is deceptive: it is rich in meaning for those who are part of that community. It was told as re-enacted drama, not necessarily to be informative. As it was being told, the story teller acted out parts of the story, becoming one or other of the participants in turn, using facial expressions, gestures, and voice tone to bring the whole event to life. As she moved from one sequence of action to another there were pauses, or shifts in her posture, to indicate a change in mood or build up to a climax. The listener was being brought into the event and failure to understand the meanings and nuances would have registered them as an outsider, one on whom the story would be lost. Annotation is unnecessary although variations in the stories are plentiful. These are also characteristic of myth. Only the uninitiated (in a broad sense) do not understand its messages.

The messages of the fight story are also discerned in various Wiradjuri myths, in which conflict, unresolved more often than not, is an ever-present theme. These myths, perhaps the best known of which are those of the Eaglehawk and Crow, are full of dramatic conflict, oppositions and contradictions, many of which are not resolved but leave off with the infliction of punishment on wrongdoers. Like stories, they do not ask the questions posed by historians or by those who do not belong to the world of which they are a part.

Conclusion

Kooris state in their preparedness to fight that they will not concede the right of others to define their place in the world. They have not, for instance, been prepared to enter the wider Australian society on the bottom rung—the only one offered—as this is inconsistent with their own world view, in which they will not bow down to each other. The fight recognises and highlights contradictions and tensions. Its inconclusiveness symbolises the wider predicament, that of living in such a world and having to come to terms with it without succumbing to its more destructive aspects.

Prior to the arrival of Europeans, and to some extent while Kooris were spatially confined in camps and reserves, Kooris did not have to define themselves as they do now. Other forms of symbolic expression are being developed in the contemporary world, such as political action, poetry, dance, art forms and drama. These carry meanings similar to the fight but are set on a larger stage as Kooris themselves become part of a world wider than the camps and reserves to which they were confined in the past. They are constantly exploring new means of stating what and who they are in a world in which they have been deprived of traditional modes of cultural expression. The history and relations depicted in the newer symbolic forms convey messages which draw Kooris together from disparate groups as they articulate the shared experience of contact history. The fight story above, as a sharing of a more local experience, is significant to all Kooris in that they understand such fighting, but its particular messages about relations in the particular community to which it belongs will be lost. Other stories may come to take its place and lessen the significance of fighting itself in the process, just as these stories took over when particular social constellations could not be continued and the myths that expressed them lost their significance.

Kooris do not fight because they are drunk, poor or aggressive. They fight because they have something to say, something to protect and something to change in a world in which fierce independence, individuality and factionalism go hand-in-hand with social concern, loyalty and cooperation.

Notes

1. The information upon which this paper is based was gathered during field work conducted among Wiradjuri people between 1981 and 1985. I would like to thank Ruth Tonkins, Daphnie McGuinness and Agnes Coe for their cooperation and assistance. I am particularly indebted to Dr John von Sturmer for his guidance in putting this paper together and for extensive comments on earlier drafts.

2. Ellipses indicate pauses.

3. Wiradjuri country covers over 80,000 square kilometres of central New South Wales, stretching east–west from Bathurst to Hay, and north–south from Dubbo to Albury.

4. I have used the expression kin network to refer to the egocentrically defined kindred which forms part of a significant social universe at any particular time for a Koori.

Wiradjuri people do not have a concept of lineage, nor is the composition of a kin network fixed or dependent upon residence. The network is unbounded and non-discrete.

5. Bundy would trace his relationship to Gavin as one of MFZHBS or WFZS, and to Johnny as BWB. Gavin would trace his to Johnny as being either MZSWZS or WFZSDB.

References

Baroja, J.C.
1965 *Honour and Shame: A Historical Account of Several Conflicts*. (Translated from Spanish by R. Johnson.) In J.G. Peristiany (ed), *Honour and Shame: The Values of Mediterranean Society*, Weidenfeld and Nicolson, London.

Bateson, G.
1973 *Steps to an Ecology of Mind: Collected Essays in Anthropology, Psychiatry, Evolution and Epistemology*, Paladin, London.

Bell, D.
1983 *Daughters of the Dreaming*, McPhee Gribble, Melbourne.

Berndt, R.M. and C.H. Berndt
1970 *Man, Land and Myth in North Australia: The Gunwinggu People*, Ure Smith, Sydney.

Brittan, A.
1973 *Meanings and Situations*, Routledge and Kegan Paul, London.

Evans-Pritchard, E.E.
1940 *The Nuer: A Description of the Modes of Livelihood and Political Institutions of a Nilotic People*, Clarendon Press, Oxford.

Flanagan, R.J.
1888 *The Aborigines of Australia*, Edward F. Flanagan and George Robertson and Co., Sydney. (Series of papers first published in the Sydney Empire.)

Geertz, C.
1973 Deep Play: Notes on the Balinese Cockfight. In *The Interpretation of Cultures: Selected Essays*, Basic Books, New York.

Graham, J. (ed)
1863 *Lawrence Struilby: Or, Observations and Experiences During Twenty-Five Years of Bush Life in Australia*, Longman, Green, Longman, Roberts and Green, London.

Howard, M.C.
1978 Aboriginal 'Leadership' in the Southwest of Western Australia. In Michael C. Howard (ed), *'Whitefella Business': Aborigines in Australian Politics*, Institute for the Study of Human Issues, Philadelphia.

Macdonald, G.M.
1986 *The Koori Way: The Dynamics of Cultural Distinctiveness in Settled Australia*, PhD thesis, University of Sydney.

McDougall, A.C.
1901 Manners, Customs, and Legends of the Combangree Tribe, *Science of Man* 22 April 1901.

Muecke, S.
1983 Introduction. In S. Muecke (ed), *Paddy*

Roe, *Gularabulu: Stories from the West Kimberley*, Fremantle Arts Centre Press, Fremantle.

Romanucci-Ross, L.
1973 *Conflict, Violence and Morality in a Mexican Village*, National Press Books, Palo Alto, California.

Rudder, E.F.
1899 An Aboriginal Battle in Queensland, *Science of Man* 21 January 1899; 21 February 1899, 8–9; 21 March 1899, 36.

Sansom, B.
1980 *The Camp at Wallaby Cross: Aboriginal Fringe Dwellers in Darwin*, Australian Institute of Aboriginal Studies, Canberra.

1982 The Aboriginal Commonality. In R.M. Berndt (ed), *Aboriginal Sites, Rights and Resource Development*, Academy of Social Sciences in Australia, University of Western Australia Press, Nedlands.

Sider, G.M.
1980 The Ties that Bind: Culture and Agriculture, Property and Propriety in the Newfoundland Fishing Village, *Social History* 5(1), 1–39.

Smyth, R.B.
1878 *The Aborigines of Victoria with Notes Relating the Habits of the Natives of Other Parts of Australia and Tasmania*, Vol.II, John Ferres, Government Printer, London.

Taylor, C.
1971 Interpretation and the Sciences of Man, *The Review of Metaphysics* 25(1), 3–51.

Tilley, C.
1978 *From Mobilization to Revolution*, Addison Wesley Publishing Co., Reading, Massachusetts.

Turner, V.
1964 Symbols in Ndembu Ritual. In M. Gluckman (ed), *Closed Systems and Open Minds: The Limits of Naivety in Social Anthropology*, Oliver and Bond, Edinburgh.

1974 *Dramas, Fields and Metaphors: Symbolic Action in Human Society*, Cornell University Press, Ithaca.

Wilson, P.R.
1982 *Black Death, White Hands*, George Allen and Unwin, Sydney.

11. Marcia Langton   Medicine Square

The Aboriginal people of Australia suffer the highest recorded imprisonment rate in the world, and it has long been recognised that dispossession, racism and cultural misunderstanding are the most significant contributors to the disproportionate rates of arrest, conviction and penalty for Aboriginal people (Clifford 1981; Tobin 1976; Eggleston 1976). Little information is available on the types of offences for which Aborigines are imprisoned, but the figures available indicate that drunkenness and alcohol-related offences are the highest in incidence of charges and imprisonment for Aborigines. As well as being locked up overnight for drunkenness or until bail is paid, Aborigines prefer to serve prison sentences in default of fines imposed for other offences. Across three states, it seems that charge and imprisonment rates for Aborigines are highest for the following three categories of offences in descending order: disorderliness (which includes swearing and fighting); breaking and entering; and unlawful use of motor vehicles.

In New South Wales, between 1973 and 1976, Aborigines were over-represented in prisons at seventeen to twenty-two times the rate for non-Aborigines. Proportionately more Aborigines than non-Aborigines in prison had juvenile convictions, and had undergone juvenile corrective measures, had been committed to juvenile institutions, had past adult convictions, had experienced more fines and imprisonment in the past, and more had records of repeated imprisonment. One third had three or more prior imprisonment episodes compared with twenty-three per cent for non-Aborigines (New South Wales Department of Corrective Services 1974).

Precisely how racism, cultural misunderstanding and other factors operate to cause the highest recorded imprisonment rate in the world has not been thoroughly examined to date. Explanations such as the 'vicious circle of poverty' and 'high tolerance of deviancy' are most commonly proposed but without any sound evidence such as case studies, survey material or ethnographic data.

In New South Wales in 1978 and 1980 'unseemly words' and fighting (under the terms of the former Summary Offences Act and the Offences in Public Places Act) were the most common behaviours to constitute the grounds for a police charge. In this chapter, I examine swearing and fighting, both among Aboriginal people and between Aborigines and others, to show how Aboriginal customary law is expressed in this behaviour, how the rules operate, and how culturally meaningful it is for Aboriginal people to employ these social devices, which are, I argue, ritualised codes.

I intend to focus on swearing and fighting in contemporary Aboriginal society, particularly in northwest New South Wales as reported in government documents, in order to provide an explanation of the behaviour in the cultural terms of Aboriginal society, and as it is interpreted and treated by non-Aboriginal society, especially by the police and courts. My aim is to demonstrate that swearing and fighting in contemporary Aboriginal society constitute dispute processing and social ordering devices derived from traditional Aboriginal cultural patterns, as Macdonald implies in the Wiradjuri case (Chapter 10). The behaviour in question is not deviance and anarchy, as some would have it, but appropriate rule-governed behaviour adapted from earlier indigenous patterns to enable meaningful existence in the new political, legal and social situations imposed by the dominant Australian regime.

Since pre-invasion times, Aboriginal people have used swearing and fighting as means of conflict resolution. Some anthropologists have reported these forms of behaviour, but their accounts are constrained by prudery or by attention to what they have seen as the significant areas of inquiry—social structure, land tenure patterns, and so on. These ethnographic reports, however, do provide clues to a phenomenon which in contemporary times has vexed police, the judiciary and governments. Unfortunately it seems that ethnographers have felt it necessary to delete much of what may be called obscene language from their reporting, and thus in the traditional literature detailed dialogues of swearing leading to fighting are unavailable. In the frequent quarrels which arose over acquisition of wives, and the abuse which was flung by one antagonist at another, it seems unlikely, given the lack of prudery in Aboriginal society, that these verbal duels would have been devoid of at least some insult.

The status of the various items of ethnographic evidence referred to below varies. One finds that while one anthropologist searches for causes of conflict in marriage negotiations, for example Hiatt (1965); others such as Warner (1958) and Stanner (1968) describe the ritual of fighting for its own sake, emphasising reciprocity and retribution. Meggitt (1962) and Taylor (1983), by examining indigenous law ways, have classified swearing and fighting within larger schema. Berndt's analysis of Arnhem Land love songs (1976) allows a broader conceptualisation of fighting as 'natural' human behaviour through the symbolism of the songs.

Fighting and feuding

Swearing and fighting have been organised forms of social interaction in the traditional Aboriginal societies, and ethnographers have widely reported oral abuse as a form of punishment and fighting as a form of retribution. In what follows I review some of their accounts.

Apparently, few other matters led to the level of dispute that marriage negotiations caused. Hiatt (1965, 103) states that 'disputes over property were rare and usually trivial'. People were expected to act generously, and gain at the expense of others was not approved. People offered hospitality as a matter of course and never quarrelled over land. Even trading relations rarely led to conflict. Neither did Hiatt record any instance of theft. In relation to adultery, he concludes that, given the small number of disputes which he recorded, many married people 'either ignored the affairs of their partners or did not discover them'. Sorcery did not account for much fighting, although as Hiatt (1965, 119) explains, the Gidjingali blamed sorcery for all serious illnesses and for all deaths that were not the result of physical violence. Sickness, injury, and death often provoked retaliation from the sufferer or someone acting on their behalf. When a person fell seriously ill, their close kin appealed publicly to the sorcerer but allegations rarely led to fights unless the patient succumbed, and not always then.

Fighting within a patrilineal group may have been less likely than between patrilineal groups of the same land owning unit, because of closer kinship links. A certain precedence was given to the uterine link for defensive purposes and was probably a result of the competition for wives among certain agnates. Indeed, men whose loyalties were divided, instead of taking sides, often attacked the woman about whom the antagonists were fighting: 'In this way they not only showed publicly how angry they were at being placed in an invidious position but threatened to bring the conflict to an end by removing its object' (Hiatt 1965, 139). Inter-community fights occasionally flared up, and killings resulted. However, as Hiatt points out, these often proceeded in much the same way as intra-community fights. Clashes of interest did not normally lead to permanent breaches between individuals and groups, because 'although opportunism over women gave rise to conflicts, it also limited them by creating cross-cutting genealogical ties' (Hiatt 1965, 127).

Warner's ethnographic study of the Murngin (1958) presents a detailed examination of six different varieties of what he termed 'warfare' among this group. Each variety is named and has a distinct pattern of behaviour: *nirimaoi yolna*, a fight within the camp; *narrup* or *djawarit*, secret killing; *maringo*, a nocturnal attack in which an entire camp is surrounded; *milwerangle*, a general fight between two or more groups; *gaingar*, a pitched battle; and *makarata*, a peace-making ceremony and ordeal (Warner 1958, 155). Warner investigated some of the rules of fighting. He found that the duty of relatives to avenge was clear; but all was not anarchy in these fights, for if a close relative was accidentally hit with a club or spear during a fight, the person responsible should hit himself on the head and apologise. Here, as elsewhere, the underlying principle is reciprocity—the idea is to inflict an injury on the responsible person similar to the one the injured party suffered (Warner 1958, 148).

Warner (1958, 150–53) also found swearing played a crucial role in inciting fights:

> The use of obscenity and profanity against a man results in a camp fight. Profanity usually reflects not only on the man but on his clan and carries an incestuous connotation.

Warner (1958, 74–75) records the role of swearing in the final coming to account of runaway marriages, or elopements. Where a man had run off with the wife or promised wife of another man:

> no man's clan would desert him in such a situation to the point of allowing him to be killed or attacked by the injured man's group. Ordinarily, such a situation ends in a 'growling' match, in which the two sides stand armed behind the two opponents, the lover allowing the injured husband to have the better of the cursing. Sometimes such a runaway marriage leads to permanent union.

Of everyday swearing within the family, Warner (1958, 87) explains that there is no sanction on children swearing at or in front of their mothers.

Warner (1958, 165) reports that women's fights were frequent. They were usually occasioned by a young woman 'seducing' another woman's husband. Women may take sides with their sisters, or co-wives attack their husband's sweetheart, in which case the latter would call upon her relatives for help. The weapons were usually ironwood digging sticks, or a man's club, if one were to hand.

No more eloquent description of the ritualised nature of Aboriginal feuding and fighting can be found than Stanner's short description in *The Boyer Lectures 1968: After the Dreaming*. I quote at length from it to indicate how kinship, marriage and other features of the social order combine to produce a system of conflict resolution which relies on individual autonomy of action and choice making in a web of social links, rather than on any formal judicial institution:

> In other days I was an eye-witness of many fights in which more than a hundred men came to an appointed field. There would be a warming-up period given over to threat-signals and other ritualized gestures of hostility but once the true fighting started it might go on fiercely for hours. ...Their lives together certainly had a full share of conflict, of violent affrays between individuals, and of collective blood-letting. But in some ways they were more skilful than we are in limiting the free play of man's combative propensity.

If we judge by their settled customs they admitted to themselves that people simply *are* aggressive and that it was no bad solution to allow what could not be avoided, and to ritualize—and thus be able to control, approve and enjoy—as much as possible of what has to be allowed.

The impression I received in watching their large-scale fights was that an invisible flag of prudence waved over the battlefield. There was a tacit agreement to call a truce or an end when a few men on each side had been grievously wounded or at the worst killed. Each life in a small group was a great treasure.

This is not to say there were never occasions on which whole groups were put to the spear, or that there was no lasting bad blood between groups at enmity. ...The conquest of land was a great rarity. And the war of extermination, with one group bent remorselessly on the complete destruction of the other, as far as I have discovered, was so rare as to be all but unknown. There were few or no 'total' enemies. It was much more commonly the case that groups which fell out contained a proportion of people who were closely tied by kinship, marriage, friendship, trade, or some other precious bond.

In such cases, a man could stand aside—honourably, and with social approval—or play only a token part if he had to oppose and might injure people who were precious to him. The ties that bound overrode the conflicts that divided. Prudential and countervailing forces of these kinds were with many conventions and canons governing the actual conduct of conflict. For example, in the great public fights which, as I have said, were ritualized affairs, it would have been bad form to use a heavy killing spear against an opponent armed only with a light duelling spear...

There was a distinct canon of equality at arms, a norm of sufficient—but just sufficient—retaliation, and a scale of equivalent injury. One could see them working in the case of a man who, knowing that a mortal wound would not be given, would offer his body to the spear of another man he had wronged; or in two men, both with a grievance, each clasping the other with an arm, and using the free arm with equal opportunity to gouge the other's back with a knife; or in two unreconciled women, giving each other whack for whack with clubs, but in strict rotation.

Swearing in the processing of disputes

Aboriginal social life and organisation are reflected in language in a number of other ways. Special styles, such as respectful and avoidance styles for communication directly or indirectly with affines, 'secret' languages which male novices learn for communication within the sanctified surrounds of the initiation ceremony, and hand sign languages for use by women under speech taboos during mourning, were once common throughout Aboriginal Australia.

As Haviland (1979, 209) notes, 'when Aboriginal Australians theorise and talk about languages, they concentrate on its social aspects'. He argues that,

> Language does not exist and utterances do not occur in a social vacuum. Speech between two people both expresses and helps to maintain the relationship between them.

Haviland refers to the existence of discrete registers, such as the obscene register between a *gami* and *gaminhdharr*, as symptoms of the different sorts of interaction that occasion speech in the community. While not actually providing examples of spontaneous obscenity, he does define the continuum from familiar to polite vocabulary:

1. everyday words that can themselves be used in speech with tabooed relatives;
2. sensitive everyday words that, for one reason or another, require brother-in-law replacements; and
3. words whose referents simply cannot be labelled at all in polite brother-in-law speech.

These last are often called 'swearing words' and are used in extremely rude curses in the everyday language.

Thomson (1935, 471), the first ethnographer to report on the joking relationship and organised obscenity in Australia, gives examples of spontaneous 'swearing' behaviour in North Queensland. A series of expressions in the Wik Munkan language, relating chiefly to parts of the body, show a gradation from merely jocular references to the hands, face, and legs, to obscene references to the pudenda that constitute the grossest insults in the language. Taunting, used to express ridicule, contempt or defiance, was not employed jocularly among adults. There were, however, frequently-used swear words which conveyed minor shock or surprise, such as when one stubbed one's toe, or missed spearing a fish. These expressions included tabooed names of those long dead; an exclamation of disgust particularly aimed at a part of the body, such as the forearm, which had failed to carry out an intended task, attributing the failure to 'bad luck', or the equivalent of the English terms, 'oh, mother' or 'oh, father'. Thomson (1935, 468–69) adds:

> The expressions...are frequently heard and are in everyday use, but in three years spent among these natives I never knew them to depart from their traditional behaviour and to use foul or obscene expressions under stress of pain, fear, or surprise, although these are freely used under other circumstances.

Thomson records how ritual well being induced by jocular swearing, obligatory between certain relatives of the same moiety, reached its maximum on ceremonial occasions, when social sentiments were stressed, as on the *narti kintja*, the taboo ground, during the preparations for the ceremonies of the *Okajnta* (hero cult and initiation). Any departure from the customary norm of behaviour, however, even if inadvertently committed, was a ritual offence and was followed by ritual purification even in mundane, everyday circumstances, usually by washing the mouth out with water, or passing a fire stick or lamp across in front of the mouth.

Thomson (1935, 469) proposes that swearing and obscenity play an important part in social life, and that swearing is of two main types:

1. *Kul kentanak* ('for the purpose of arousing anger')—unorganised swearing and obscenity used by both sexes during quarrels, and to goad an enemy to fight. This category includes 'all the worst expressions in the language: deadly insults that it would be intolerable for any native to receive in public'.[1]
2. Organised, licensed, obligatory and public swearing and obscenity between people standing in certain kin relationships. It contrasts with prohibitions *(kintja)* between a man and his wife's mother, wife's father and wife's brothers, and is supposed to 'make everybody happy'. Obscenity referring to the pudenda is permitted between grand-kin usually of the same sex; and certain relatives are permitted 'to snatch playfully at one another's genitalia, and even to handle those organs in public'. References to the anus and excrement are permissible or obligatory generally between distant relatives of categories between whom licence of a restricted kind is permitted, but the use of sexual obscenities or behaviour is prohibited.

Obscenities, like explosives, can be used for peaceful as well as aggressive purposes (though of course they must always be handled with care). Their potentialities for promoting and preserving amity have been perhaps most notably explored by white Australian sub-cultures, where powerfully-charged words are combined with facility to produce expressions of endearment (eg 'you fucking old cunt'). But obscenities have a comparable dual purpose in traditional black Australian cultures, where they function not only as insults between antagonists about to engage in armed combat but also as good-natured banter in the context of formally-defined joking relationships. Whether these two cases exemplify a general tendency is a question for further investigation. It may turn out that the amity-generating capacity of sexual obscenities depends upon universally pleasureable elements in sexuality itself and is thus a potentiality everywhere present though not necessarily everywhere exploited.

However, there is at least one major difference between swearing behaviour in Aboriginal societies and swearing in Western societies—for instance, there is no public sanction on swearing by women in Aboriginal Australia. Thomson provides several examples, and the clear implication is that no sanction is applied to women except in the avoidance relationships.

I would suggest that swearing, especially with reference to sexuality, is an important *leitmotif* of Aboriginal life, and adds an excitement or piquancy to relationships which could become boring and onerous in the close and constant contact of everyday life. In the intimate social setting of Aboriginal communities everybody is expected at least publicly to act out social roles determined by kinship status, whether actual or putative, in a dutiful, mindful and sometimes cautious manner. This explanation is attested to by Aboriginal explanations of swearing, such as that the use of obscenity between appropriate kinds of kin is aimed to 'make everybody happy'. On the other hand, the function of obscenity to goad another to fight is explicit in the above descriptions of Aboriginal swearing. People are not happy with each other all the time in any society, and reports on Aboriginal societies attest to frequent disputes (eg Warner 1958; Hiatt 1965). Swearing, while it may serve a sanctioned purpose of creating harmony between particular kinds of kin, also provides individuals with linguistic registers which they may manipulate to achieve particular social ends. Contrary to Thomson, this type of swearing—that is, swearing aimed at inciting a fight—is an organised social activity, dependent both on the existing social norms of swearing and on individual calculations of how to manipulate these norms to cause insult beyond the acceptable standard. It is organised within the dynamics of dispute processing, which are governed by kin and marriage norms.

In situations of conflict, the linguistic arsenal which individuals may bring to bear to exacerbate anger and ill-feeling or to de-escalate a dispute is considerable—and it seems clear from the literature that swearing constitutes not only a social device for harmony but also a code for inciting dispute.

A list of rules of right conduct is provided by Taylor (1983) for the people of the Edward River area in northern Queensland. Two English phrases are used to describe their codes of behaviour: 'old custom' and 'Murri law'. (Murri is the term used to denote Aboriginal people in Queensland.) In reconstructing pre-settlement law derived from consultants' accounts and from his own observations of disputing behaviour which occurred during his field work, Taylor has augmented his descriptions of contemporary Aboriginal life on a government settlement in Queensland with the work of Sharp (1934). Taylor's account shows just how enduring Aboriginal traditions are and how strong is cultural continuity. Interestingly, according to one of the rules the invasion of personal jurisdiction in kindred, tract and ritual matters is not to be tolerated, and personal integrity should be defended (cf Macdonald, Chapter 10).

At Edward River, rules of right conduct were self-enforcing or self-regulating in that conformity to a rule governing a focal activity carried with it rewards that went far beyond the satisfactions inherent in its immediate enactment. Alternatively, failure to follow the rule was attended by conspicuous ill-success in the business of life. Supernatural sanctions and gossip were also powerful enforcers of the social order. Sharp (1934, 430) notes the strongly conservative influence women exercised 'with their gossip, power over public opinion and studied ability to shame or excite their men into following conventional lines of behaviour'. Human retribution typically occurred in situations where an individual 'perceived her/himself to have been wronged by some other individual. ...When a person was wronged, it was that individual's responsibility to identify the wrong action and then to organise redressive measures out of his or her own resources.' Taylor (1983) observes the degree to which violence and the threat of violence was an integral part of the redressive system. There were three possible outcomes when individuals felt they had been wronged by others. They could signal that a dispute situation existed and seek to have the matter resolved publicly; undertake private redressive measures in secret; or do nothing, that is, elect to suffer the wrong in silence.

Again, insult was a normal prelude to fighting. Taylor describes two main forms of insult. The first involved the use of the personal name of a recently deceased person within the hearing of the mourning relatives. The action was regarded as an insult to the memory of the deceased, and a source of grief to the relatives, and would precipitate an immediate fight. Taylor records that he never came across a single case of a breach of the convention, other than by Europeans. The second kind of insult entailed swearing at and taunting opponents in a dispute, as a prelude to physical violence. It was hearing verbal abuse directed toward a close relative, especially a sister, mother or mother's brother, which was likely to make a man feel shame and anger, and provoke him to join in the dispute because of the insults. This swearing was a means of mobilising support when a quarrel was about to 'erupt into violence' (Taylor 1983).

Although anthropological reconstructions of this kind leave me in some doubt as to their accuracy, it cannot be doubted that the observation and reporting of actual disputes in Taylor's work retains at least some of the ebb and flow of the conflict situations. He has identified the generalised form of conflicts in the following way:

1. declaration;
2. rejoinder;
3. argument;
4. insult and physical combat;
5. separation; and
6. reconciliation.

However, not all disputes inevitably followed the whole sequence.

Rejoinder and argument, called by the Edward River people 'fighting with tongues', was followed by insult and physical combat in the following way. Physical conflict was usually preceded by a phase of 'studied insult and intense swearing' on the part of each disputant and their supporters, in order to goad the other side into making the first move. Scurrilous and personal insults were accompanied by hoots, jeers and violent displays of spear clashing, or the pounding of fighting sticks on shields or the ground by the men. Women would sing insulting songs and perform a kind of dance designed to shame their opponents, in which they slapped their sides with their elbows, drummed their feet on the ground and often concluded by turning their backs on their adversaries, bending over and exposing their posteriors.

Swearing and fighting in contemporary Aboriginal society

> Fighting...establishes what is true. It is public legitimation. ...Law based on community norms is effective only to the extent that such norms are shared. ...The Wiradjuri have moral and jural leadership in their elders and these elders are the symbols of community norms which sanction what is publicly acceptable behaviour. They are a symbolic source of legitimacy. Wiradjuri social organisation is a political entity and its legal system is maintained in part through fighting behaviour. Fighting is law in action. It is not a reflection of anarchy (Macdonald 1982, 15–16).

There is clearly an historical precedent for contemporary swearing and fighting in traditional Aboriginal society. The way in which social organisation and language use organised these conflict resolution methods in traditional societies can be seen to survive in contemporary society, operating to the same effect, although dispossession of land and near-genocide have occurred in the meantime. Indeed, accounts from police and criminologists of swearing and fighting involving Aborigines are powerfully suggestive, however unwittingly, of the cultural basis of the behaviour of conflict resolution.

The intention of such language depends on the social relationship between the interlocutors and not on any quality of the words as such. Lexicon and meaning are manipulated and exploited to achieve a social end, whether joking and endearing, or insulting and disrupting, or any state between these two ends of the emotional continuum. The ways in which such social ends may be achieved are ritualised, especially between certain classes of kin or in socially recognised formulae. This is not to deny that the same words used to joke or startle in some contexts can be used also in ordinary conversation without causing any disruption whatever, except in the case of epithets which imply absolutely prohibited behaviour. The words themselves can range in meaning from sacred through mundane to profane, depending on the intention of the speaker and his or her interpretation of the social surroundings.

The aspects of these dispute processing devices which have survived in 'settled' Australia in Aboriginal communities of mixed descent are common themes in Aboriginal societies: the right of the individual to demand public redress for grievances; the abundant opportunities for conflict in small communities where definitions of public and private space allow a great deal of information on marriage matters and such to be widely known and discussed; the ties of kinship which ensure shifting allegiances according to context; the polysemy of lexicon and the complexity of the language situation.

Macdonald (1982) has perceived among the contemporary Wiradjuri the continuity of traditional Wiradjuri fighting behaviour, as well as the changes which it has undergone during colonisation. She refers to swearing as 'oath' in the tradition of Hoebel's (1954) 'oath and ordeal', and recites the new factors in Wiradjuri fighting in the multicultural context of black–white relations: the use of alcohol, gambling, and football alongside the traditional features of aggression, warming up for the fight, ritualised behaviour, drama, prestige, joking and sex (see also Chapter 10).

Fighting in contemporary Aboriginal communities differs only in surface detail from the traditional forms outlined above. The rules of fighting, although (like weapons) slightly different from area to area, may be generalised in the following way:

1. The aggrieved calls a fight by swearing and accusing.
2. The event must occur in a public place.
3. No-one but particular kin and close friends may interfere.
4. Kin must call off the fight if it goes too far.
5. Individuals tend not to become extremely violent (unless extremely intoxicated) and finish the fight with threats and boasts about what they could have done.

The exercise of these rules by Aboriginal disputants is not as straightforward as it may seem however. In the occupied and urbanised south, legal and social prohibition on Aboriginal gatherings outside the tiny residential reserves, as well as cold winters, leave only the hotels and public parks which Aboriginal people (often to the exclusion of non-Aborigines) frequent. Hotels and public parks become then the arenas of the Aboriginal legal process. As these are both places which fall under the ambit of legislation and are regularly patrolled by police, the risk of arrest is high. Aboriginal disputing procedures are used in these contexts against the police, and indeed against any whites who insult Aborigines or cause them harm. The usual order of events in Aboriginal disputing is then disrupted after repeated interventions, causing conflict between Aborigines and non-Aborigines which tends to be ritualised. A conflict of this kind might proceed as follows:

1. An Aboriginal dispute proceeds according to the rules in a public place, designated so by Aboriginal conceptions of their own spaces in white-dominated areas.

2. At some stage, police intervene in these Aboriginal swearing and fighting ordeals.

3. When Aborigines are approached, spoken to or touched by police, they use their traditional swearing and threatening codes as forms of insult and declarations of offence and accusation.

4. In some cases, Aborigines threaten violence and sometimes carry out the threatened violence toward the police and police property or other public property.

5. The police usually arrest Aborigines for 'unseemly words', 'assault' and a range of other charges under various Acts.

The police are not merely interacting with, arresting and imprisoning individual 'troublemakers' but are interacting with a social process which is invisible to them. They are intervening at various stages in the process of conflict resolution between two individuals or between two groups, treating a legal process of one society as an illegal process in their own society. A case of this interactive process has been documented by McCorquodale (1982, 228–90) following a 'near-riot situation' between Aborigines and the police in Taree, a mid north coast town in New South Wales.

The Taree affray

Between ten in the evening and two in the morning, one Friday night in August 1979, about 150 Aboriginal men, women and children gathered in the main park at Taree. A group of police, including the inspector in charge of the division, requested the group to disperse peacefully and return to their homes, but the crowd ignored the requests and moved to the Manning River US Sailing Club, where a melee broke out between groups of Aborigines, police, and patrons of the club. As a result three Aboriginal women and fourteen Aboriginal men were charged with unlawful assembly, assaulting police, resisting arrest, hindering police in the execution of their duty, causing damage to police vehicles, assaulting civilians, damaging civilians' vehicles, and damage to property.

Less than two months later, on a Saturday evening in October 1979, a large number of Aboriginal children, aged from about eight to nineteen years, gathered at the Taree Show Grounds during the Annual Show. The children are reported to have chased, abused and assaulted a number of non-Aboriginal children. As a result, an Aboriginal girl of fourteen and two Aboriginal boys appeared on five charges.

A police investigation concluded that the August 'unlawful assembly' resulted from an incident on the previous Friday evening when it was alleged that a young Aborigine had been assaulted by an unemployed white male in the Queen Elizabeth Park near the Sailing Club. The man pleaded guilty to the charge, and was fined $75.00. At the trial the man gave evidence that his wife and her female friend had come into the club complaining that four or five Aborigines had abused her and grabbed her on the breast and private parts. The defendant came out of the club with two or three others, and remonstrated with the Aboriginal youth and an Aboriginal girl, who were among twenty or thirty Aborigines along the river bank. The youth allegedly replied with a string of obscenities, whereupon the defendant was alleged to have punched him.

The following Friday the local police sergeant noticed a group of forty to fifty Aboriginal people in the park. McCorquodale (1982) reports:

> He went to their apparent leader in order to defuse a potentially volatile situation. The leader (aged 33) let loose a string of epithets, but in the course of almost two hours of negotiations, during which both Aboriginal and police numbers markedly increased, he made two significant observations. The first, in his own words, was: '...You...let our kids get bashed up. Tonight we are going to take it into our own hands. We'll get the white bastards'. The second was a retort to the Sergeant's protest that

no report had been made to police of any assault on Aboriginal children and that, in the absence of such a report, the police could take no action. It was couched thus '...We're only black. You wouldn't touch the white...anyway. We'll fix them ourselves. We don't need you white bastards to do that...'. As the Aborigines moved en masse in the direction of the Sailing Club they were chanting, obscenely, about the police and the law. Police investigations revealed that the white defendants, and others involved in the initial assault, had heard of an imminent brawl and had kept away from the area on the night of the ensuing brawl.

The form of dispute processing suggested above is amply demonstrated in the Taree case. The ritual code of swearing (and in one case obscene physical gestures) and accusations, precede the actual fights and gestures of violence toward white persons and institutions. Indeed, even young Aboriginal children involved in the Taree incidents seem to have mastered the code. Aboriginal definitions and use of public places are evident in their use of Queen Elizabeth Park as the primary arena for the initial stages of the dispute processing. However, the magistrate's response demonstrated the ethnocentrism of official attitudes and ignorance of the motivations and customs of Aboriginal people. The subsequent court records show how cultural perceptions of swearing and fighting differ, and how Aboriginal cultural behaviour is persistently treated in terms of the behaviour of the dominant society.

Swearing as a mode of discourse

Swearing, I have argued, has operated in Aboriginal societies as a mode of discourse, based in particular forms of social organisation and concomitant community norms, operating principles, strategies and values. It constitutes, as much as any habitualised lexical code does, a linguistic strategem, a device employed in particular kinds of social operations, especially fighting. We have seen that while there are many other ways in which swearing may be used, and many forms of fighting, there is one particular complex of actions—a social code—which involves both swearing and fighting performed in order to achieve public redress for grievances. A particular form of swearing is a prelude to this kind of fighting.

The coeval strategems of swearing and fighting are demonstrated in the case provided below of Aboriginal women negotiating social goals. The following conversation is an example of the way in which Aboriginal women use dialogue and a range of language strategies toward achieving particular social ends. The power of gossip among women is evident as they re-cast past incidents to influence others to adopt their particular point of view, to cast moral judgements in order to alert others to an impending dispute, and to actually incite disputes and fights over alleged breaches of the Aboriginal legal order. The conversation is edited from actual dialogue and the characters and incidents have been concealed, but it is in my experience typical.

> 'Who was at the pub last night?'
> 'Dunno. Me and Jimmy went to the [establishment's name] because Uncle George had a big win on the TAB. The relations would have skinned him if we went to the pub. He wanted to shout us a few.'
> 'They reckon the kooris don't go there now cos that Gubba [white person] banned Sharine after that fight.'
> 'A few sneak in there. Talk about sneak. That cunt Brian was in there with that little bitch Paula, and his wife is *buribara* [pregnant].'
> 'Paula [surname]?'
> 'Yeah. I'll tell Pat's [Brian's wife's] aunty. She'll drop that little bitch.'
> 'Here comes Roger. Look out.'
> 'Don't worry about that moll.'

This is a conversation of a type that occurs between Aboriginal women in New South Wales. The dialogue is performed in a special kind of language reserved for dealing with privileged information. The social situations in which these conversations occur are those which might arise in any urban setting, from small rural town to city. An understanding of the goals and strategies conveyed or disguised by the verbal exchanges requires not just access to the privileged and personal information which the interlocutors possess and are willing to divulge to each other, but also competence in the norms of communication required in these privileged conversations. The range of competence includes the cultural assumptions about what kind of behaviour is appropriate or inappropriate, right or wrong; the subtle range of levels which imply allegation, threat, sense of personal insult, degree of personal involvement in an issue, and so on; the ability to interpret the indigenous humour and especially the thin line between aggressive exaggeration and humourous exaggeration, always a risky business, even for the insiders. Most important is the ability to interpret the difference between mere posturing and real threat of imminent violent attack or threat of intended attack. This, of course, depends upon knowing whether or not a breach of the Aboriginal moral or legal order has been committed and/or if the allegation of such a breach is well founded and backed up by ability to avenge the misdeed.

In this situation, Paula has committed a grave breach of acceptable behaviour; not only has she been seen publicly with a married man, but the man's wife is pregnant. She has been noticed in this compromising situation by the second conversant who makes it clear to the first that she will ensure that Brian's wife's kinfolk are informed. Paula will be ostracised by kin and friends of Brian's wife, and if she does not desist from this behaviour, she may be the victim of a punitive and violent attack by the wife's close female kin.

When this matter of Paula's breach of the rules of proper behaviour was brought to the second conversant's attention, it was important for her to communicate an uncompromising stand on it. For women, this is important because they would wish to have reciprocal support if they were in a similar situation, and because such incidents provide opportunities for them to 'flex their muscles' in the socio-political affairs of the community and to be seen to be behaving as responsible and active members of a small, beleaguered society.

How English swear words are used by Aboriginal people is also illustrated in the following summaries of cases, which have been taken from police report sheets of charges laid during 1978 for unseemly words under the Summary Offences Act 1970 and the Offences in Public Places Act 1980. The summaries were published in a report by the New South Wales Anti-Discrimination Board (1982) and indicate just how police intervene in what the report refers to as 'trivial' offences requiring more discretion by police. It can be seen that some of the cases are ones of internal dispute settlement in which the police have interfered on the grounds that a 'reasonable person' would be alarmed and affronted, while others are clearly cases of Aborigines abusing police for a number of reasons—for entering reserve areas and for invading privacy, for their intention to arrest Aboriginal people with or without justification and for their interference in private conflicts, among other reasons.

Summary Offences Act 1970

Case 1

The offender was alleged to have said 'Shut ya cunt' when asked to make room for 2 ambulance men to pass to treat the offender's friend who had been injured in a brawl in a hotel. The police stated that while the words were not said in a loud tone, the men and women drinking in the bar would have had no difficulty in hearing them. No evidence was led that they had in fact heard them. The offender was charged under section 9 of the SOA and pleaded guilty. He was convicted and fined $50, in default 10 days imprisonment with hard labour, and was allowed 2 months to pay. (At the time, the period for 'cutting out' fines was $5 per day imprisonment.)

Case 2
The police facts alleged that they heard a commotion outside a hotel and saw the female offender walk towards them, followed by two other women. After they were about 40 yards from the hotel the offender picked up a stick about 4' long from the gutter, faced the other two women and called in a loud, clear voice: 'You two had my fucken husband and I'm gonna knock your fucken head off with this stick'. She was charged under section 9 of the SOA. She pleaded guilty, was convicted and fined $30, in default 6 days imprisonment with hard labour, and allowed one month to pay.

Case 3
The police approached the offender in his own backyard on an Aboriginal settlement in relation to allegations that he had earlier been driving a car in a manner dangerous to the public. After some questioning, he was alleged to have said: 'I don't know where I was sitting in the fucken cunt of a car'. He was charged under section 9 of the SOA. He pleaded guilty and was convicted and fined $50, in default 10 days imprisonment with hard labour, and allowed one month to pay.

Offences in Public Places Act 1980

Case 1
Two police officers on a routine patrol entered a public bar and allegedly heard the offender say in a loud tone of voice: 'Here are those fucking coppers again to lock up us black fellows'. There were no other customers in the bar at the time and no staff. The offender pleaded not guilty. She was convicted, fined $100, in default 4 days hard labour, with 3 months to pay.

Case 2
The offender allegedly called out in the main street: 'You can get fucked you bastards, and you coppers can get fucked too'. The offender pleaded guilty. She was convicted and fined $50, in default 48 hours imprisonment with hard labour, with 1 month to pay.

Case 3
The offender was approached by police officers in a private residence on an Aboriginal settlement after his de facto wife complained about his throwing articles of furniture from the house. On being approached, it was alleged that he said: 'You cunts can do as you like, you won't prove anything'. He pleaded guilty. He was convicted, fined $100, in default 4 days with hard labour, with one month to pay.

Case 4
Two offenders were arrested for fighting in the rear yard of a hotel. They were both convicted, fined $100, in default 4 days.

Case 5

The police alleged that the offender, in a public street near the bowling club at 10.55 p.m., said: 'I wouldn't come home with you, you rotten drunken cunt. Fuck off'. She pleaded guilty. She was convicted, fined $60, in default 3 days with hard labour, with 1 month to pay.

Case 6

The two offenders were in the police station on another matter, when one defendant allegedly said: 'Ah you white cunt, you fuck dogs' while facing a police officer. The other defendant then allegedly turned and said, 'Yea, you fuck dogs'. Both offenders then escaped when approached by the officer, and were arrested 2 days later at the scene of a brawl. They pleaded guilty. Both were convicted, fined $100, in default 4 days with hard labour, with 1 month to pay. Both were subsequently jailed for non-payment of the fine.

In summary, of the cases under the Summary Offences Act 1970 for charges laid in 1978, Cases 2 and 3 constituted matters of internal dispute processing, while Case 1 was an instance of Aborigines turning this ritualised form of insult against the police. Of the charges laid in 1980 under the Offences in Public Places Act 1980, Cases 3, 4 and 5 were clearly matters of internal dispute processing while Cases 1, 2 and 6 are instances of insult directed solely at police.

Swearing for sedition

Indigenous swearing and fighting codes are used against the white population and against the police and courts. White society, regarded as lawless, and its legal system, regarded as illegitimate, become the accused in these incidents of black–white dispute settlement, although there is no possibility that restitution or consensus can be achieved by these methods. Obscene chanting by large groups and physical threats leading to violence are reported in those areas of high Aboriginal and police concentration, and where racism is an entrenched form of social interaction. The swearing and fighting which Aboriginal people aim at individuals and institutions of dominant society are forms of protest against discrimination, deprivation, dispossession and brutality.

Without power, resources, or equal access to institutions of the state, Aborigines have turned the institution of the court to their own ends. While it continues to incarcerate them, they use it as a forum for their insults and accusations. A further protest is the almost universal refusal by Aborigines to pay fines imposed by the court.

Thus, in the neo-colonial context of conflict, Aborigines have adapted a traditional cultural form to the purpose of sedition, however ineffective. The way in which Aboriginal swearing and fighting socially order the internal Aboriginal world under extremely adverse conditions, and provide a form of resistance to an oppressive dominant society, attests to the positive adaptive capability of contemporary Aboriginal cultures.

For Aboriginal people, swearing and fighting are still familiar features of life. There are well known rules, or at least, the individuals involved manipulate the action according to certain well known and approved formulae. In daily discourse, swearing is subject to social rules, so that individuals who choose swearing as one of a number of discourse strategies will know that they may swear jokingly to certain people and in certain contexts, and yet by swearing aggressively to others will know that the likelihood of precipitating a fight is high. Thus, fighting also proceeds according to rules and is usually precipitated deliberately by public accusation and insult involving aggressive swearing. But this dynamic style of dispute processing, while effective within the Aboriginal domain and space, has implications beyond the maintenance of the Aboriginal legal order. Once disputes reach the stage of open declaration and loud, public insult and accusation in the traditional Aboriginal style of achieving public redress for grievances, it is not difficult to see what might happen if police are in the area, or if non-Aborigines, finding this behaviour offensive (or at least using this excuse), call the police. The women would be charged with the offence of using unseemly words under the terms of the Offences in Public Places Act 1980.

Thus I am suggesting that the dynamic relationship of Aboriginal swearing and fighting with the dominant legal system has a number of consequences. First, swearing and fighting are deemed illegal by Australian law and Aboriginal participants are subject to alarmingly high arrest rates, fines and imprisonment. Second, while swearing and fighting are usually aimed primarily at resolving conflicts between Aboriginal people, they are also used as tactics of sedition against white society. Third, such use of these dispute processing mechanisms as a response to the legal institutions—police, courts and the system itself—exacerbates rather than alleviates racial conflict.

The police are not simply arresting and detaining individual 'troublemakers', but intervene in an indigenous social process aimed at conflict resolution. These police intrusions have a two-fold effect. First, they become the subject of social action in the course of the dispute processing mechanism. Second, they aggravate a tense, and sometimes violent, situation causing more personal insult to the interlocutors as well as other actors. These others may feel called upon to act out the Aboriginal social procedures which call to public redress such behaviour as insult, injury or interference on the part of those without right or authority. Many Aboriginal people feel that the police have no right or authority, from the Aboriginal point of view, to interfere in Aboriginal problems. Furthermore, the Australian legal system is perceived as illegitimate and oppressive by many Aboriginal people who feel that its actions against them can and should be challenged. Such challenges are framed in Aboriginal social and linguistic codes used in daily discourse for calling to public redress offences to their dignity or person.

In part, Aboriginal people enjoy irony and caricature in their 'unseemly words'. The nature of irony, caricature and the grotesque, as discussed by Thomson in relation to the arts and literature, gives some indication of the liberating effect Aboriginal seditious humour has for its exponents. Aboriginal people can overcome fear of police brutality at the time of confrontation, laugh at their oppressors and exercise their own legal method by using swear words which portray the police and their legal culture as grotesque. Thomson (1972, 55–56) puts it this way:

> We might ask ourselves...what are the psychological factors involved in what I have described as the classic response to the grotesque: the experience of horror (or disgust, or anger) and amusement (or glee, or delight) at the same time, the laugh which dies in the throat and becomes a grimace or which is tinged with wild hysteria or embarrassment?... Delight in seeing taboos flouted, a sense of momentary release from inhibitions, intellectual pleasure at seeing the joke, at perceiving the comic element, all are present.

The supreme stroke of wit in this Aboriginal strategy occurs in the courtroom as the police, for the prosecution, read out the alleged offences of 'unseemly words' directed by Aboriginal people at them. Aboriginal people use the courtroom as their political audience in a game of irony. Muecke (1970, 29) suggests that the secret of success in irony lies in the unawareness of the victim:

> The victim of irony does not need to be, though he often is, arrogantly, wilfully blind; he need only reveal by word or action that he does not even remotely suspect that things may not be what he ingenuously supposes them to be. ...Other things being equal, the greater the victim's blindness, the more striking the irony. It goes without saying that the ironic observer must be aware of the victim's unawareness as well as the real situation.

Conclusion: two laws or one

I have tried to show that swearing and fighting are dispute processing mechanisms and that they constitute cultural codes for the actors. They are forms of cultural knowledge allowing for strategic interaction aimed at achieving a particular outcome—redress between aggrieved Aboriginal persons and those whom they accuse as responsible for the grievance, which is usually insult or adultery. In traditional times, the behaviour may have constituted conscious knowledge, labelled and acknowledged as aspects of law maintenance. In recent times, as a result of cultural repression and the illegality of these cultural forms under the Australian regime, they have tended to become tacit forms of cultural knowledge, depending on the extent of repression and contact with white society which Aboriginal groups have experienced.

The swear words, although apparently English words, are polysemous, relying for much of their cultural content on traditional Aboriginal ways of looking at the world. The fighting behaviour proceeds according to Aboriginal rules, and particularly according to the Aboriginal principle of reciprocity.

Swearing and fighting among Aboriginal people in 'settled' Australia are two aspects of evolving indigenous law, but are misperceived by the Anglo-Australian legal system and its enforcers as drunken anarchy and anti-social misbehaviour. The penalties for Aboriginal people acting out tacit cultural and legal rules are high. The extraordinary arrest and imprisonment rates for swearing and fighting are major contributors to the overall arrest and imprisonment rates of Aborigines nationally—the highest recorded in the world.

That there are two systems of law operating in most areas of remote Aboriginal Australia is no longer doubted. The Australian Law Reform Commission (ALRC) has been reporting on its terms of reference relating to recognition of Aboriginal customary law since 1981. The Commissioner recommends (Crawford 1983) that it is possible to suggest that special measures for the recognition of Aboriginal customary law will not be racially discriminatory, or involve a denial of equality before the law or of equal protection, if these measures are reasonable responses to the special needs of those Aboriginal people affected by them; are generally accepted by those people; and do not deprive those individual Aborigines of basic human rights or of access to the general legal system and its institutions.[2]

The question of the 'repugnancy' of traditional punishments, especially traditional killing, has been a major consideration of the ALRC. But the repugnancy of swearing and fighting, in that they might constitute 'cruel' and 'degrading' treatment, infringe the human rights of Aborigines, or should be disqualified from recognition, should not be a foregone conclusion. The Commission has recognised that, while traditional killing seems no longer to exist and in any case is excluded from recognition by Articles 6 and 7 of the International Covenant on Civil and Political Rights, the context of such traditional sanctions as thigh spearing and the effect of existing Australian law allow for legal reform solutions other than outright suppression.

Indeed this seems to be the case already in some parts of Australia. Police tolerate Aboriginal swearing and fighting behaviour and accept the areas designated by tradition or circumstance as Aboriginal areas or arenas for law maintenance, as long as severe intoxication, or the possibility of the conflicts escalating into larger events do not threaten the 'peace and good order' of the township. One such case is a small town in the central coast area of Western Australia where a large proportion of the population is Aboriginal. The Aboriginal people of this town have two designated areas for conflict resolution by means of swearing and fighting. One is the cattle saleyard out of town to which the disputants and witnesses drive in their vehicles and which they illuminate at night with car headlights. The other in the town area is called Medicine Square.

> They call it Medicine Square, you know, like Madison Square Gardens. That's where you go to get your medicine. The police tell you, 'Alright, go down to Medicine Square or the Saleyards or we'll arrest you'. And there'll be twenty cars down there, not just two. They park around it in a circle and shine their car headlights on it so the two fellas can see what they're doing (personal communication).

Such venues for dispute processing are common in areas of large Aboriginal populations, but not all are tolerated to the extent that Medicine Square seems to be tolerated by the police in that area.

A policy of tolerance toward Aboriginal swearing and fighting by law enforcement authorities seems unlikely however. Whatever the considered views of the ALRC, the dominant society would not accept such a measure which would be seen to discriminate against the white population, however absurdly the existing legislation operates for either group. Secondly, the argument would be advanced that Aboriginal swearing and fighting of the dispute processing type would have to be distinguished from other types, for example, actual drunken or otherwise motivated lawlessness, whether judged by Aboriginal or white Australian standards. Certainly, Aboriginal communities would not want a situation in which 'anything goes', or in which there would be no restrictions on, or penalties for, disruption of the peace or unjustified assault and violence.

Even without a formal policy of tolerance toward these law maintenance devices of Aboriginal society, several other reformative legal measures are possible. One such measure would be to enable a customary law defence of swearing and fighting charges in the courts, to distinguish such behaviour from 'offensive' behaviour in Australian legal terms, admit its status as custom in such incidents, for example, excessive violence, to be imposed, thus reducing the excessive penalties such as fines and imprisonment. The Australian Law Reform Commission may wish to investigate the problems outlined here with a view to appropriate forms of recognition.

In the absence of interest in these problems from the ALRC, Aboriginal legal services may choose to defend cases under the Offences in Public Places Act 1980 or under equivalent legislation in other States as customary law cases. By so doing, Aboriginal legal services would raise the problem effectively as one requiring the attention of the legal fraternity as a case of potential and necessary law reform.

Yet another solution would be for cases of the kind discussed here to be referred to Aboriginal community justice mechanisms which may be established following the final recommendations of the ALRC. Complaints from Aboriginal people on the conduct of dispute settling procedures could be dealt with in such structures without compromising accepted standards of justice under the Australian legal system. Clear cases of simple assault and other delicts arising from Aboriginal community justice mechanisms could then be referred to the Australian courts.

It may be too much to expect that police and magistrates will be prompted to appreciate contemporary Aboriginal culture by the approach taken in this chapter, but it is hoped that legislators and judicial interpreters in the upper levels of the Australian court system will take a more informed view of the swearing and fighting deemed illegal under Australian law and yet legal and appropriate under Aboriginal law and custom. That legislators and the judiciary should be aware of the cultural patterns underlying this behaviour is particularly warranted in view of the alarming arrest and imprisonment rates which Aborigines suffer on account of police implementation of the relevant legislation and the frequent and blatant racial discrimination of the police in carrying out the terms of legislation. Clearly, there is an urgent need to bring a sense of a larger rationality to the conflict of Aboriginal dispute processing styles with the dominant Australian legal system. The possibilities for this suggested by the discussion papers of the ALRC seem the most likely to succeed in reducing the Aboriginal arrest and imprisonment rate. In this respect anthropological inquiry may help to refine the specific kinds of knowledge required by legislators and Aboriginal people to establish legal structures and guidelines to deal properly with this situation.

Notes

1. However Hiatt (1965, 112) observes that among the Gidjingali, 'insult was usually a feature of conflict rather than a cause.' The exception among the Gidjingali, as reported by Hiatt, was if a man heard someone swear at his sister or classificatory sister: 'A father might say to his jealous son-in-law: "Stop swearing at your wife. Sooner or later her brother will hear you. Then he will spear her because you have speared him through the ear with your words. I ask you not to swear at her in his presence"'.

2. The act of faith which has permitted so many government officials and social scientists to assume that 'part-Aborigines' lack a distinctive culture (see Langton 1981), has resulted in such sparse inquiry into Aboriginal societies in urban or rural areas, that the ALRC has until recently ignored the possibility that there might be indigenous law ways in Aboriginal areas in 'settled' Australia (Rowley 1970).

References

Berndt, R.M.
1976 *Love Songs of Arnhem Land*, University of Chicago Press, Chicago.

Clifford, W.
1981 *An Approach to Aboriginal Criminology*, Australian Institute of Criminology, Canberra.

Crawford, J.
1983 International Law and the Recognition of Aboriginal Law, paper presented at the Conference on Aborigines and International Law, Centre for Continuing Education, Australian National University, Canberra.

Eggleston, E.M.
1976 *Fear, Favour and Affection: Aborigines and the Criminal Law in Victoria, South Australia and Western Australia*, Australian National University Press, Canberra.

Haviland, J.
1979 How to Talk to Your Brother-in-Law in Guugu Yimidhirr. In T. Shopen (ed), *Language and Their Speakers*, Winthrop, Cambridge, Massachusetts.

Hiatt, L.R.
1965 *Kinship and Conflict: A Study of an Aboriginal Community in Northern Arnhem Land*. Australian National University Press, Canberra.
1978 Obscenity, unpublished manuscript.

Hoebel, E.A.
1954 *The Law of Primitive Man: A Study in Comparative Legal Dynamics*, Harvard University Press, Cambridge, Massachusetts.

Langton, M.
1981 Urbanizing Aborigines: The Social

Scientists' Great Deception, *Social Alternatives* 2(2), 16–22.

Macdonald, G.
1982 Fighting: Communication, Controls and Cognitive Ordering among the Wiradjuri of Inland New South Wales, paper presented at the Department of Anthropology, Sydney University.

McCorquodale, J.
1982 Aborigines and the Police: Unlawful Assembly, Affray and the Incidents at Taree, *Australian Journal of Social Issues* 17(4), 288–94.

Meggitt, M.J.
1962 *Desert People: A Study of the Walbiri of Central Australia*, University of Chicago Press, Chicago.

Muecke, D.C.
1970 *Irony*, Methuen and Co., London.

New South Wales Anti-Discrimination Board
1982 *A Study of Street Offences by Aborigines: A Report of the Anti-Discrimination Board in Accordance with Section 119 of the Anti-Discrimination Act 1977*, New South Wales Anti-Discrimination Board, Sydney.

New South Wales Department of Corrective Services
1974 *1974 Census of Prisoners: Aborigines in Prison*, Publication No 11, Research and Statistics Division, New South Wales Department of Corrective Services, Sydney.

Rowley, C.D.
1970 *The Destruction of Aboriginal Society*, Australian National University Press, Canberra.

Sharp, L.
1934 The Social Organization of the Yir-Yoront Tribe, Cape York Peninsula, *Oceania* 4, 404–31.

Stanner, W.E.H.
1968 *The Boyer Lectures 1968: After the Dreaming*, Australian Broadcasting Commission, Sydney.

Taylor, J.
1983 Law and Order and Social Control, unpublished paper held at the Australian Institute of Aboriginal Studies Library, Canberra.

Thomson, D.F.
1935 The Joking Relationship and Organised Obscenity in North Queensland, *American Anthropologist* 37, 460–90.

Thomson, P.
1972 *The Grotesque*, Methuen, London.

Tobin, P.
1976 A Meeting of Nations: Aborigines and the Police, unpublished paper.

Warner, W.L.
1958 *A Black Civilization: A Study of an Australian Aboriginal Tribe*, Harper Books, New York.

12. Patricia Baines   A litany for land

Until recently the southwest Aboriginal people, who usually speak of themselves as Nyungars, have been considered to be a people who have lost their Aboriginal spiritual heritage or whose knowledge of things of the spirit is a diluted (or worse still, made-up and inauthentic) tradition. This chapter is premised on the understanding that all people continually generate and maintain meaning. A loss of meaning and knowledge was not presumed when I first sat down with Nyungar people. Rather I simply asked them to share with me and teach me how they made sense of their existence. I have sought to show here how Nyungar people read country and see themselves in relation to their ancestors and to the land, in the context of the attempt to prevent the desecration of a small brook on the edge of the city of Perth in Western Australia.

The first part of this chapter sets out to reveal not only what Nyungar people feel about a particular area of country, but also to show the underlying premises upon which these feelings are based. The second part is about the forty days and nights which a small company of Nyungar people spent on Heirisson Island. This sojourn is viewed here as an attempt to express Nyungar values and meaning in a form which would be comprehensible to others. It was an act of revelation of the central value of Nyungar life, presented through a translation of Nyungar spiritual beliefs into a morality play. In it, Nyungar people sought to make biblical images and Christian theological concepts mediate culturally diverse ways of seeing the land. The third part of the chapter describes the Nyungar metacommentary on the failure to achieve sufficient white comprehension to permit a transcultural dialogue.

A Trinity of being

The Bennett Brook flows from north to south, joining the Swan River at a bend known by white people as Devil's Elbow which is situated between the outer Perth suburbs of Bassendean and Guildford. For Nyungar people however, the confluence is noted as being beside Success Hill which was once a registered Aboriginal reserve. The confluence, Success Hill and all the springs in the immediate area are associated with the presence of a *Wakal* (water snake), which is said to have formed the river bed in the original creative era of the Dreaming, but is still present in the area moving along the watercourse or underground. The west side of Bennett Brook is an area which is known variously by Nyungar people either as Lockridge or Hammersley's property. It was an area of multiple Nyungar stopping places—for prior to urban development Nyungar people camped on Success Hill on Hammersley's property and on the adjacent Eden Hill (also at one time an Aboriginal reserve).

In the present day the area has been overtaken by housing development, and rather than being on the fringe of the urban area is gradually being encircled and engulfed. The paddocks and paperbark swamp that remain with the brook flowing through them are all that is left of a much larger area that a large number of different Nyungar kin groups still hold dear. One kin group returned to live on the Lockridge land in the 1970s. At first they simply camped there. Later they were given some mining camp huts. The first route chosen for the gas pipeline traversed the fields on the east side of the Bennett Brook (also associated with camping places and soaks) and headed in a southwest direction for a crossing of the brook close to the confluence with the Swan River.

A subjectified land

To look at the land through Nyungar eyes is to perceive personhood in all life-forms. Old trees are parents and seedlings are children. Birds and animals, particularly when one of them behaves in an unusual manner or is distinguished in some way (by uncommon size or colouring), may be a deceased ancestor. The land is seen as a huge body—most often it is recognised as the body of one's mother. To put a trench through the ground is to scarify the mother's back or dig into her guts. This recognition of all living things as subjects, that is, as sentient and cognisant beings or persons, is one of the crucial premises of the Nyungar commentary on and reaction to white excavation, clearing or 'landscaping' of the land. From a Nyungar perspective, the essential relationship of generation and regeneration is seen to be shared in by all living things. The lives of animals and plants participate in the same life processes as people.

In the same way that Nyungar families are aware of the presence of other people around them organised in families, they perceive other forms of life as organised in terms of kinship. The place where the green frog or the sergeant ant, the kangaroo or a particular plant lives is, for that being, a home. Walking along the Bennett Brook one day with Robert Bropho, we came to some ant hills. He pointed out that this was 'bull ant and sergeant ant area all through here'. Asked the significance of his comment, he continued,

> He goes along on the side of us Aboriginal people, along with the association of the land, they move alongside of us. This is home of the green frogs, kangaroos...living in harmony with us. Rain, sun, everything sharing.

It is this perception of sharing the life-world with other forms of expressions of life, that belong to the country in the same way as people belong to a place, which is basic to Nyungar thinking about acts of desecration. Nyungar people see the ecological consequence of any intervention as the endangering or destruction—the murdering—of personalised forms.

If duration is added to this ongoing, moment by moment relationship of living things in a particular area, then to the acknowledgement of consciousness and intelligence in other living things is added memory. 'The stinkweeds have grown in remembrance of the people who walked through here,' Robert Bropho said. Another old man, in discussing the regenerative potential of native trees, spoke of 'the willing of the trees'. The landscape is, then, a company of embodiments of kin. The trees which gave shelter and shade to past lives stand now as the living representations of these old people. The tree is respected for its particularity as tree. It is also and at the same time an icon, for tree is the sign of immanent ancestral presences by virtue of having shared in the life and times of the old people. Instead of human lives being set off against the landscape, here locations within the landscape are integral to the interpretation of human acts.

It was a Nyungar woman who claimed me as like a sister—'your spirit and my spirit they run together,' she would say—who first drove with me around the perimeter of the small piece of land under discussion. Now 'crippled up', she was no longer able to walk across the land.

> There's two trees and an old brick house...wattle trees not allowed to be touched because they belongs to a Nyungar, a Nyungar man and lady who died...trees just growing nice and green...used to be a brick house there...find coins and old metals what Nyungars used to keep...there's an old chimney, old Jamadji (Nor'West Aborigines) camp near. Old Mrs Bropho telling, always talk about trees and old brick house...not allowed to touch the bridge too...one soak I know where the olive tree, you can't touch it...[there's] a water snake, what they call a water snake, it don't harm you, if you don't harm it...real cold, blue water, beautiful...Granny Dick and Granny Molly Kickett got a soak and got a *Wumballa* (water snake) in there too. They shouldn't move anything from there because it was like a gift for her. Her old mother made that soak.

She pointed to the tree under which she and her man had made a camp. Above all, Lizzie wanted to locate trees and springs for me, but she insisted that really I should speak to her mother-in-law Granny Bella Bropho, who knew all about it. She nevertheless shared what had been told to her by her man's people on how to behave on the land in the present, and also the stories of her own kin who had dug for water on Success Hill.

When I went to see Granny Bella she had said that she was too old now to walk across the land. Nevertheless from her own hearth on the rise she pointed out the places of significance. There was the place her old uncle used to stop, the old mud hut with its lilac tree and Daisy Bates's camping place. In a sweep of the arm and a turn of the head, she gathered the past company into the present moment. She said her second oldest son, Robert Bropho, should walk over the land with us once we had permission to do so. Some time later when a report regarding the proposed link road was being put together (the preferred routes both crossed the remaining area of land from east to west), Granny Bella sent for me. On this occasion she took me into her room in one of the mining camp huts and we talked alone. Granny's room was sparsely furnished. There were no photos, no sporting trophies, no flowers. That is, there were none of the inner domestic signs of spirit which I had grown used to in places where small children were being reared-up. Their absence signalled not her impoverishment, but the uncertain and temporary nature of her domicile. This was where she was camping, not stopping. Her treasured vehicles of meaning and evidences of spiritual verities were carefully wrapped up and put away inside her suitcase.

Despite the fact that she had lived for years at a time here and called this home, she had over the years I had known her, reiterated that they would be putting the road through at any time. So Granny lived in a tension which extended across seasons that she would once again be made to leave the place she called home. Her life history had been patterned by forced exodus. She had been put in a children's home, sent from there to a 'government native settlement' down south at Carollup. When that one had been closed by the government, she had been put on a train and conveyed to the one in the northern wheatbelt at Mogumber. Memories of coercion and compliance mingled with stories of those moments when she had escaped compulsion. Other families had been rounded up at daybreak without warning and taken to the government settlement in trucks, she remembered. Her family was not on the list, as her husband had a labouring job at the time. She had nevertheless expressed her conviction on a number of occasions that they could suddenly be forced to move again.

Granny Bella's first account of the area had been marked by a setting of the *Wakal* alongside and among the other old people (Nyungar and white), who had lived on the land. The Bennett Brook and the Lockridge land were thus conjoined in a matrix of spiritual propinquities.

Although Granny Bella had been placed in a children's home by her uncle, she had come back to the land again and again. Her life had, despite repeated acts of forced removal, been marked by a series of returns to the area around the Bennett Brook. Her life history had thus succeeded in encompassing coercion and external determination by her own acts of volition. She had given birth to several of her children in the area. Now the births and lives of her descendants, the 'little grannies', her children's children and their children, had been set in meaningful conjunction to the place, for they had been reared-up here.

Granny Bella had glossed the paddocks around her as camping and stopping places. Her son, Robert, whom she had delegated as the person to walk the proposed route of the gas pipeline with us, cast another matrix of meaning over the area. He began by setting the few paddocks of remaining land within the years of services rendered by the Nyungar families to the white land owners. It was a recitation of labouring and laundering, hard work recompensed with exactly recalled financial rewards. The Nyungar people were thus set within the landscape as 'good old workmen'. If the tasks had been menial it was, nevertheless, from the sweat of Nyungar bodies that the white man had grown rich.

The meticulous remembrance of work histories and the praises received for services faithfully rendered, was a genre of recital which I had heard many times before from middle-aged and old Nyungar people. These curricula vitae of Nyungar families were not only evidence and denial of the negative stereotypes of Aborigines as lazy and loath to work (in a time when agricultural labouring jobs have virtually dried up). It was also a profound assertion of ongoing contact with the land. The forced removals from the country they knew, the dispossession of their lands, had been countered by labouring on the self-same land.

We had approached the brook from the east side, starting out near the place where Barker's Bridge crosses the Swan River. We came across a ploughed paddock and, now close to the brook, were moving through squelching mud. Closer to the brook, Robert began to recall the people who lived on the land. Pointing upstream toward the centre of the paperbark swamp, he spoke of the line of trees that Nyungar people believe was once a fish trap: 'Sticks been broken and put in a line and those sticks being in the water so long have started to shoot. We believe that that was Aboriginal peoples in the early days, those trees soaking there.' At a place, which is now a patchwork of autumn growth and liquification of earth, he spoke of the old

Nyungar woman, Ngilgie, who had made her camp there and had slept under a blanket of dogs. Then, indicating the direction of the proposed path of the gas pipeline across the land, he said, referring to the *Wakal*: 'Like a spear gonna run straight into that old fella sleeping over there.' As we walked toward the *Wakal*'s cave and home, in the area of the confluence of the Bennett Brook and Swan River beside Success Hill, he continued to speak of the presence in that place:

> Jack Moore seen that *Wakal*. A fortnight from then he died...that *Wakal* has been passed on from generation to generation as far as we can remember back...two Chinamen used to have a garden there and that *Wakal* tipped that boat over...the history of our background is here.

It was Granny Bella who, along with a recital of all the Nyungar families who had once camped on the Hammersley's property, had insisted I should go and talk to Old Girl Alice. Old Girl Alice, who had been born on the land, had laughed aloud at my request in the listening presence of other Aboriginal people. Yet once they had distanced themselves from our conversation, she spoke in an altered tone. At the time I did not understand that I had asked a woman who was held in dubious regard by others to find words which validated her own being and essential meaning. For Old Girl Alice's words were not usually taken seriously. Nonetheless, on the day she chose to speak about the place of her birth, those who observed our conversation from out of earshot were able to testify to her sobriety.

The intimacy of Old Girl Alice's association with the *Wakal* was testimony of her birthright. Born of and at the place, she could, after showing proper respect by sprinkling sand into the water, swim alongside the *Wakal*. This same familiarity was also attributed to another Nyungar man, Bob Mead, born at the turn of the century on Success Hill. He had been sent into the river as a boy when he was sick. Granny Bella said of the Nyungar man, Des Parfitt, who was also born on the land and whose afterbirth was put into the water there, that he could swim there because they were his *Wakal* and he belonged to the place. Other individuals who had come to live there but were not born beside the brook, showed more circumspection. They would avoid the area around the *Wakal*'s cave, instructing the children to swim further down.

Old Girl Alice's memories of the Lockridge land comprised stories of childhood and girlhood. They were accounts about the ways she was instructed to behave toward the spirits of the place, counterpoised by a child's acts of daring. Although Old Girl Alice had been taught the prescriptive performance for relating to the *Wakal*, her relationship with the spirit of her birthplace was one of childlike familiarity. But Old Girl Alice's relationship with her birthplace was forcibly terminated.

> We all got shipped along the big truck one morning. Before we got out of bed and they came down there [to Hammersley's property] and picked us all up, put us in the big truck to Mogumber. ...Beautiful Indian lilies used to grow wild there, like gladiolas, oh beautiful. ...We were in bed and they shipped us away. 'Oh wake up, wake up everyone.' You could see camps here and there. Big truck waiting to load us on. I ended up there [at Moore River Native Settlement] and they decided to adopt me out.

The integrity of Nyungar land associations seems to be belied by the visual testimony of the alterations perpetuated to the land. The Bennett Brook runs through farmland. Housing developments have come to encompass it. Many of the places where Nyungar people used to camp have been ploughed up, or bulldozed. The brook and the small swamp with its paperbarks, bullrushes and arum lilies, have nonetheless survived. Even the Bennett Brook has experienced the pressures of land development for Nyungar people recite incidents of pollution and point out its altered contour. Yet looking at the flowing water, Nyungar people still speak of the 'goodness' of the place. The point is that Nyungar people who have lived on the land and recall the landscape of the 1920s, 1930s and 1940s, still regard the place as spiritually intact, uncompromised, if now constrained and threatened. The *Wakal* has not been killed, has not departed from the place in anger, despite the altered landscape of the surrounding area.

The camp on Heirisson Island

> The failure of history is none other than the tragedy of the lack of agreement between what exists as human and personal on the one hand, and on the other all objectification, which is always extra-personal, non-human, anti-personal and anti-human (Berdyaev 1935).

By January 1984 the negotiations between the State Energy Commission and the Nyungar people associated with the Lockridge land had reached an understanding based on a compromise. Nyungar people acknowledged the need of white people for gas. They therefore agreed to the gas pipe passing through old Aboriginal camping grounds provided that when it came to the Bennett Brook it went above ground. The details of an above-ground crossing were not worked out at that time, although the technical feasibility of an above-ground crossing was not denied.

There was initially a ministerial confirmation of the proposed compromise. Then in May 1984 the tentative agreement that had been reached was set aside when the State Minister for Aboriginal Affairs authorised a below-ground crossing. The change of decision has never been fully explained but the story seems to be as follows. A member of the Aboriginal Planning Authority had, it was said, told the Minister for Aboriginal Affairs that Robert Bropho on the phone from Melbourne had agreed to a below-ground crossing of the brook. Robert Bropho said that his phone call had been witnessed and that he had said no such thing. The fact that one person did not have the authority 'Nyungar way' to alter a consensual judgement of other Nyungar people was ignored. The accusation was, however, a serious one. It placed a strong onus on the extended family grouping, who had up to that point been speaking on behalf of all the kin groups associated with the brook and the land, to try and repair the situation. The months that followed were ones in which these Nyungar people sought to have the ministerial decision reversed. In October 1984 that had not been achieved.

Nyungar people read the configuration of tangible signs to understand the nature of a situation. This way of interpreting the world permits the deliberate use of signs to convey particular meanings. So when Granny Bella Bropho's extended family chose certain kinds of persons (grandparents and grandchildren) to camp on the island in the city, they were expressing something quite specific. The camp on Heirisson Island in the middle of the Swan River in the heart of Perth was an act of signification.

On Monday 6 October 1984 the morning commuters travelling into the centre of Perth by the bridge across the Swan River known as the Eastern Gateway to the City, saw a small group of tents pitched in full view of the road on the downstream side of Heirisson Island. Adjacent to the road were a line of land rights flags and a notice explaining about the threat to Aboriginal 'sacred places'.

The move to Heirisson Island was explained to me by Robert Bropho as resulting from a meeting the previous evening of the extended family living on the Lockridge land. They had decided they should move before dawn. There had been ongoing discussion on how to express their intense concern and consternation about the threats to the Bennett Brook and Lockridge land from the gas pipeline and the proposed road. Various possible expressive acts had been mooted as the decisive act of desecration appeared imminent. The choice of Heirisson Island, however, was probably intimated by the recent ceremonial placement of a sculpture of Yagan there to commemorate National Aborigines Week. Yagan is remembered by name as one of the original Aboriginal residents of the Perth area at the time of the coming of the whites. He was involved in altercations with them and was eventually killed. The sign of his immanent presence was an incipient act of transformation.

The composition of the group gathered on Heirisson Island must be considered to understand the meaning of the act. This was not a camp of young men waiting for a fight. Nor was it a gathering of drinking people who would from the socially invalidated space of time out of mind perform acts of mindless violence. Instead, what had been gathered together was an unguarded company of little children, nursing mothers and grandmothers. It was an extraordinary constellation of persons—a spiritual self-exposure. They had laid aside the defences, for good places for small children are normally well protected by brothers, cousins, youthful uncles and dogs. Instead, the scenario for a massacre of innocents had been assembled. That such an image was on the minds of Nyungar campers was revealed to me when they told me of the newborn baby who might have been drowned when a sprinkler was set up to soak the inside of one of the tents. They had travelled back to Lockridge that day taking the baby with them. Their movements and decisions were thus marked with special meaning for the choice they had made had avoided harm.

The vulnerability of such an exposure of home and hearth could be felt sitting there hearing yells from the highway. Rough tones of insults, some an inaudible shouting, others the frank expressions of brutal stereotypes. The women would quietly ask each time whether I had heard what they had to 'put up with'. 'Ignorant they are', a small grey-haired woman said, 'got no manners'. They spoke quietly of nocturnal threats—a carload of inebriated white youths had driven close to the tents, a man had come and exposed himself and then thrown money down beside the camp fire. The vulnerability was intensified as few people, white or black, prepared to join with them in this expression of their desperation at the threat to their home and heart.

Small gifts of food were in fact brought to the camp, as well as blessings of blankets and other bedding. These tokens of support did not assuage the sense of standing alone but they did seem to counter the cacophony of curses from the highway which began at dawn. The gifts were not the wherewithal of reciprocal obligation. They did not require gratitude as much as excused the failure of others to sit down with them. I asked Granny Bella whether the camp was 'too lonely'. My enquiry was whether they experienced spiritual and physical desertion on this windy stretch of land in the middle of the city. Granny Bella corrected me. It was not 'lonely' but 'quiet'. The familial solitude was being maintained but their spiritual roots had not been damaged by standing alone.

There had, I was told, been a moment when overwhelmed with despair, the group had considered packing up the camp and going back to the Lockridge land. It was in that moment that Edna Bropho, Robert's wife and herself a descendant of one of the other kin groups associated with the land, had said that they should not pull down the tents but put some more up, for at the weekend others would surely come and join them. So for some days the expanded vista of khaki tents was a sign of hope and trust.

The day the health inspector came, the television crew had already been waiting for a couple of hours. Edna Bropho took command of the situation, giving permission for the inspector to walk around the tents, saying that she had told the younger women to clean the portable toilets that morning but had not had time to inspect them herself. The man returned nodding affirmatively and saying that it had been an excellent idea to cover the rubbish with a tarpaulin to keep the seagulls away from it, that the site and the sanitation presented no health risks. Amid the declarations of the care expended on clearing up and the obstacles to rubbish disposal, there was a pause. It was indeed a silencing of talking. Ushered along by a retinue of grandchildren, big and small, Granny Bella Bropho moved slowly past our group and entered the main tent. Within the tent a grandson had placed a chair in a central position facing out to where we stood. The woman, who all regarded as speaking for the land, had made her presence known. Her arrival created a sign of the continuity of life and spirit across the generations, for now four generations were present.

A Trinity of tales

Rumours had reached the campers' ears through hints made by the media presence, that the Perth City Council was planning to forcibly evict them. Edna Bropho declared that they could not and would not move, that she had told her husband she would maintain the camp in his absence and she must do so. An hour before the council officers were expected, she gathered the smaller children into her tent and instructed the mothers to keep their other children close to them. Granny Elizabeth and Edna acknowledged my presence in the shade at the edge of the tent, by recalling stories and sightings of the *Wakal*. Neither of them had previously given me their own experiences of the *Wakal's* presence.

The telling of stories of other times and other places can bring a creative commentary to bear on the unfolding act of signification. There are moments in which volition appears to be rendered impotent by objectifying and alien forces. Stories can bring spiritual insights and inspiration to bear on what individuals feel they are able and want to do. In other words the addition of a story to an inchoate situation (that is, to an unfinished and as yet not fully interpreted moment in which the significance is still being created and worked out), can give courage and strength to those who must determine how to act. The gathering of ominous tangible signs can thus be set in conjunction with the invisible but potent intimations of additional presences.

There was the man from Milgenew, they remembered, who had seen the *Beemara* (water snake) and had died. As harbinger of death, the snake may be both sign and instigator of imminent demise. The man who died had been a northwest Aboriginal man. They did not state explicitly whether the sighting of the snake had in this case been the cause or harbinger of death. The uncertainty is neither philosophical vagary nor theological mystery. The point is that the individual is the ultimate interpreter of their own dying. It is the agony and the triumph of volition that one must embrace one's death to capture meaning, to avoid 'losing one's death'.

The arrival of the youngest child, a baby of only a few weeks, diverted Granny Edna's attention to ensuring the immediate safety of the 'littlies'. Granny Elizabeth continued talking. She said she always remembered the story her mother used to tell them. Elizabeth was the descendant of another family who had lived on the Lockridge land. She had spent most of her life, however, in other parts of the southwest. What she was about to share was her personal knowledge of concerns of the spirit drawn from intimacy with other places. Thus she was to share her understanding of the present moment expressed in stories which had been given to her and were now hers to retell.

She began by naming a small town in the adjacent country some forty kilometres from the city. There had been two wells there, two *Wakals*. When the two Old Boys (snakes) had talked together there was a sound of booming and a rainbow went from one well to the other. One day her father's brother, then a boy, had killed one of the snakes and there had never been a rainbow since then.

Now the rainbow that went from well to well was a special sign, an arc of communion, for usually rainbow-snake emanations are said to be not complete bows but rainbows with tails. The rainbow embodiments of the *Wakal* are understood as benevolent manifestations. In recognising the *Wakal* as a rainbow the Nyungar belief resembles that of other Aboriginal people who know the rainbow serpent under a variety of names. This particular sign, however, was destroyed. To remember the two snakes, the two *Beemaras*, in the two wells, was to recall both the sound and sign of conversation and its cessation.

That destruction lay within the company of close kin. No reason was given for the destruction although it went against the social injunction—which is still observed—against killing both water snakes and carpet snakes. The boy who had killed the snake had got very sick and his face had come out in red pimples. He had been hospitalised. This wanton killing had threatened his own being. Then his mother had taken her *wana* (digging) stick, Granny Elizabeth continued, and tapped the well where the snake was killed. The boy recovered.

The story is extraordinary. In it, the remembered and known ancestors act upon a stage beyond good and evil. This is no morality play where a destructive act brings just deserts. There is also no alien killer. Nor must the familial killer suffer eternal penalty for his act. The *wana* is not a magic wand banishing disease but the wooden and earth digging implement of understanding. Here the older people must incorporate the good and the bad in a non-retributive acceptance. The disbelief and disregard of one's successors must not threaten the generational process, the superordinate value of survival.

The story Granny Elizabeth told presented a correction to the initial recollection which hinted at the *Wakal*'s superlative power of retribution. The implication of the story was indeed a double-edged one. By maintaining that Nyungar people could themselves commit senseless acts of destruction, the imaging of white people as the stereotypical and archetypal destroyers was resisted. For by owning the destructiveness of Nyungar individuals, Nyungar people could maintain that the white forces which threatened to carry out a destructive act were also individuals. It was a way of thinking that led to a refusal to regard laws and departments of administration as 'things' disassociated from the human beings who had created and maintained them. As a consequence Nyungar people insistently asked to speak to individuals and in situations where those persons were not embedded within the settings that maintained them as types and in roles. At the same time the story owned the reality of destruction. It implied that the *Wakal* in the Bennett Brook could also be destroyed but that such a killing would be the work of individuals. The story thus provided a gloss on the situation. It was not social comment but rather a commentary on the true nature of the situation.

Granny Elizabeth then said she would tell me a yarn 'which is still going'. She agreed to tell it slowly so that I could write it down. The story began with the sign of a transformed landscape: 'Lake Grace is the shape of a tree'. The point was that the country bears an abiding evidence to the verity of the story. That this was a story of the Dreaming was signalled indirectly in the remark, 'These little birds were humans'. In the creative era the animal and the human were not separated forms. 'This is a yarn which is still going.' The story that 'is still going' is one which speaks of an immanent reality.

> These little birds were humans and there was a big Eagle and he used to go round killing all these little birds. He used to live on a great big tree. And these little birds sent for the little *Budden*, the Cat Bird, jumps around, and he had to kill this big Eagle. So he went and got his tommyhawk and he climbed the tree and when he got to the Eagle he was asleep and snoring. And he hit him on the head with an axe, stone axe that they have. The Eagle was terrible full of little birds he was killing. And the moment he killed him the big tall tree fell and all the roots were coming out—numble, numble, numble [the sound of the roots coming out]. And the little *Budden* jumped back of the other little birds. And they were all crying. They thought he was dead. '*Congonor, congonor, congonor* [uncle dead].' And the little *Budden* came along swinging his little stone axe. '*Congon ere.*' And all the little birds looked around and they saw the little *Budden* coming. They was all crying and laughing with joy. And the band struck up and I left.

The ending took me completely by surprise. I had never heard a story ended in this way before (although it does resemble the endings of the Zande trickster stories collected by Evans Pritchard). It was only on reflection that I understood this to be a summary and joking assertion of a celebration which should not be interpreted without laughter. The hero had not in fact conquered the gigantic destroyer but rather his act of bravery had created a communion between those willing life. For it was not in the end the small Cat Bird alone but also the tree toppling which ended the massacre of the little birds. Noting my astonishment, Granny Elizabeth also added the usual kind of ending: 'When the tree fell there was a clump of tree growed there and a hole where he jumped. That's why they call it Lake Grace.'

The Nyungar people of the southwest are not oblivious to the suffering and dying of their people in the past, although they prefer to recite the stories of survival. However, it is hard not to interpret this story of a little company trying to overcome a huge and hungry creature as a reflection on the situation in which the campers on the island found themselves. Being a Dreaming story it implied a great deal more than the comfort of situational similitude. The Nyungar people on the island were not simply in the same situation as the beings of the creative era. The recitation of the story was an invocation of the creative will that is. It was an empowering of the company of waiting campers.

Granny Elizabeth's final story again challenged whether the listener could see the nature of reality:

> This old Aboriginal was sitting down in his little old *mia mia* [camp] with his dog and his *keili* [boomerang] and spears. (This is real this one.) And he was sitting down by the campfire with his old legs crossed and his boss came along and said, 'Hey Jack, would you come and look after my place for a week?' And he said, 'Yes master, but what about who's gonna look after my home?' And he said, 'Just for one week wouldn't hurt you, you can stay in my place.' 'Righto, master.' So Jack went to look after the master's place. One night he was sitting down having his tea and he saw something at the window. And he went to the other window and he saw something there. And he was that scared and he couldn't have his tea. And he ran to the door and opened it. And he ran towards his home where some other Aborigines was. And before he got to the home, he had to cross a creek. Instead of jumping over, he jumped up and fell in the water. And he heard the noise fell in the water too and it was his dog. And he got out and run soaking wet and said to the other Aborigines, 'I seen him there, *jinggi, jinggi*' as he thought it was a ghost. He told the blokes his *nganock* [beard] was wipe, wiping. But they told him it was an old billygoat.

The three stories were not told as part of the communal interchange of memories. Rather they were a declared recital, carefully signalled by initial announcement of story telling and concluded with ritualised words of ending. Granny Elizabeth had mediated to us the received words of the ancestors. In the situation of threatening uncertainty, Granny Elizabeth who camped there as a homeless woman but by her own volition, had set us within a landscape of destroyed, mistaken and continuing spiritual truths. She had presented a challenge offered in the form of a blessing (a gift of stories). The small being who dares to stand up to and face the gigantic and potentially dangerous form, not to demonstrate their own *Maban* (spiritual power), but on behalf of their people (the other little birds), may act as catalyst in a re-establishment of the creative ordering of the world. The telling of the three stories was a careful configuration of meaning and metacommentary woven into the waiting moment.

A confrontation and forced removal from the island did not in fact eventuate. Toward evening a letter was delivered to Edna Bropho indicating that prosecutions leading to fines of $100.00 for the infringement of local by-laws could result from continued residence on the island.

The City Council officer to whom I spoke prior to the anticipated two o'clock eviction indicated that the Council had received numerous phone calls criticising the Council for not enforcing the by-laws. On the other hand, the Nyungar people on the island had understood there existed, if not State government support, at least tolerance of their right to signify physically their distress about the Lockridge land. Further, the Nyungar people understood from the Police Department that the police had been advised not to harass them. Police surveillance from the central police station across the park had been discreet and minimal. The Health Department official's acknowledgement of the maintenance of a clean and hygienic camp seemed to further strengthen the case for stopping. The City Council officer pointed out that the State government did not have jurisdiction over the park.

There had been times when it had seemed that there would be a forced termination of their stay on the island, but it had not yet happened. It was when Borelli, the Italian man who had been promoting 'land rights for all' had begun to float the idea of a counter-camp on the other side of the road that the group decided they should go home. Their Nyungar relatives had begun to express consternation to one another at what might happen if a group of drinking white men—this was the presumption—spent the weekend adjacent to the camp of oldies, young women and littlies. They planned to send someone to talk to Robert Bropho. A hand-delivered duplicated letter arrived from the island before they had done so. The letter said that the people on the island had suffered for forty days and forty nights and now 'black ideas' must resolve the situation.

Forty day and forty nights

The refusal of representatives of the State government to engage in a witnessed discussion in the open air with the group camped on the island was grounds for the Nyungar people's expression of frustration and sadness. After all, the campers pointed out, anyone could see that they had no guns. The idea was floated of camping beside the steps of Parliament to make the journey to dialogue that much shorter for the State Premier. The group did not reach a consensus on the suggestion. They remained where they were for forty days and forty nights.

This time period is one of repeated biblical significance. Biblical concordances indicate that it was the common duration of critical situations of punishment, fasting, repentance and vigil. Perhaps even more pertinent were the most well known references to this time period. The Great Flood was caused by forty days and forty nights of rain (the angered *Wakal* is associated with flooding as well as with the rainbow of covenant); Moses stayed on the Mount forty days and forty nights to receive the Ten Commandments; the battle between David and Goliath (comparable with the story of the Cat Bird and the Eagle) was preceded by the latter showing himself to David for forty days; and finally of course it was the period that Jesus was tempted in the wilderness. I do not know which of these particular moments, if any specific one, was in the campers' minds but the point is they were evoking a tradition and setting themselves in conjunction with both the Children of Israel and with Jesus. The final construction given to the days of camping was of a time of suffering.

One of the newspapers referred ironically to Robert Bropho as 'king of an island'— undoubtedly an allusion to the nineteenth century king movement in Western Australia, but also perhaps unwittingly to the mocking of the 'king of the Jews'. Yet the blatant vulnerability of the kind of camp they established was expression and assertion of the dilemma of survival, not of conquest. This was not an aimed and assertive taking of land but the demonstration of a terrible anguish. If the place of home and the spirit of that place is damaged or destroyed then there will be no subsequent generations. To expose the little children to the danger of the city is no more or less irresponsible than to tolerate what is already threatening their existence. To see their mothers and grandmothers arrested by force and perhaps incarcerated is no worse or better than to see the place of home, the bodies and life-giving spirit of their ancestors damaged. That the former is an act of will, a deliberate choice indeed, makes it perhaps a less harmful sight than the murder of a sacred and personified place.

The resistance is above all moral. For the appeal that Nyungar people make is about the value of all life-forms. It is a perception of the world in which each emanation of life is not only inter-related but is the embodiment of spirit and of value. Thus, Nyungar people do not and have not in the past sought to destroy or root out the exotic trees and plants. Despite the recognition of the changes that introduced species bring, they show respect for the forms of life that have taken root.

That the biblical imagery was understood by other Nyungar people became evident from a question put to me: 'What's Bobby achieved? Forty days and forty nights, his Jesus hasn't come. What's going to happen?' Then with a wry laugh the well respected Nyungar grandmother added, 'Burke [the Premier] thinks he's the Christ now then?'

A meeting at the brook

The idea of calling a meeting of all the kin groups associated with the Bennett Brook came from discussions between the State Energy Commission, the office of the State Minister for Aboriginal Affairs, the Sites Department of the Western Australian Museum and the Aboriginal Legal Service. Suggestions had been made that the view that the gas pipeline should go above-ground when it reached the brook was not one held by all the Nyungar people associated with the land. The meeting at the brook was to be a way of reassessing the validity of all the words that had already been uttered. The meeting was set for 1 April, 1985.

It was mid morning on a hot, late summer's day. The screeches of crows and the softer shrieks of a whirling flock of pink galahs were the predominant sounds. The land was bone dry. The heat vibrated off the street of the country town, situated some 200 or so kilometres from Perth. Several extended families who had once lived on the Lockridge land now called this particular town home. They nevertheless retained an active concern for the Bennett Brook and the land around it.

In the distant shade of a small cluster of trees near the railway line a group of Nyungar people were sitting and watching. Old Fred, white-haired and in his mid sixties, who had been brought down to Moore River Native Settlement as a child and had remained in Nyungar country, moved slowly and circumspectly across to a parked car. Standing in the slight shade of smaller trees near the depot for agricultural supplies, he interpreted the scene and the times. He explained the apparent indolence was of people having nothing to do. The shire employed only half a dozen men. The shire men, in their new stationwagons and utes, paused to pass greetings and drove off again.

The children of the Nyungar men who had sheared and cropped for the local farmers had been made redundant by mechanisation. Old Fred paused to ask whether I thought the Seaman Land Inquiry would get anything for the southwest Nyungars. My expressed doubts were met with head nods as he pointed out matter-of-factly that the land of the southwest was the richest farmland. He asked my elderly South African companion about the condition of the Nyungars in Africa. He said he has heard yarns but then he had seen it on television—little children trying to suck milk from shrivelled up titties. 'Terrible thing', he said. The African comparison led from Ethiopia to Soweto and to what he had heard about 'the battle' between Wetjalas and Nyungars. He had heard yarns about it 'down Pinjarra way', he continued. (This was a reference to what white people called the Battle of Pinjarra. Nyungars speak of it as a massacre.)

He asked me whether I had ever seen the photos of Rottnest. I asked him whether he meant the one of Aboriginal prisoners with chains around their necks and ankles. He nodded and explained that of course a lot of them were probably murderers doing their time for having speared white men. He went on to ask whether I had ever heard yarns of Nyungars coming back after ten or fifteen years from doing their time. 'Reckon they never did come back.' Uncle Neddo, another elderly Nyungar man and Granny Bella Bropho's half-brother, who was listening, affirmed Old Fred's conclusion. Old Fred explained that there would have certainly been yarns if any of them had come back after they had done their time. I could only confirm that I, too, had never heard stories of returned prisoners. Old Fred went on to explain that he knew about Rottnest because of the pictures he had seen, not because of what he had been told. He explained that a lot of Nyungar knowledge of the past was like that.

Old Fred and Uncle Neddo continued discussing the things they could no longer remember clearly and the things the younger generation no longer knew or cared about. The issue of not caring had come from my comment that a grandchild of the old people who lived on the Lockridge land had said he did not care whether the gas pipeline went under the brook. Uncle Neddo responded fiercely, 'You know what they say, don't care was made to care.' Uncle Neddo demanded to know who that person was, declaring that one person should not have the whole say. The man was, in fact, his nephew.

We had found a cool place to sit down and, listened to by his nieces, Uncle Neddo had talked at length about his memories of the Lockridge land. He had given us a performance of the evening scenes beside the brook. At the end of the week the men with their pay would stay on the east side of the brook and make a big fire and play two-up. 'Could bet away your next day's pickings', he said laughing. He extemporised the conversation between the men. Then he became the waiting women asking where the men had gone, then seeing the big fire in the darkness and coming to order them home. Later he became the scuttling young boy hurrying from his own family's camp on the way to his aunty's camp so that the white boss would not see him. They were not meant to be on the boss's property. It was a remembrance of everyday jocularity. Then he became Old Granny with her pipe and her bent body and wrinkled face. The 'real old girl's' extraordinary success at two-up had led the others to suspect that she had already become a spirit, he said.

The old grandmother had joined in the joke by asserting that she was indeed a *janak* (a devil/ghost).

Uncle Neddo said that he would certainly be travelling to Perth for the meeting on April Fool's Day. His boss had already given him permission to take the day off. We had been talking about the *Wakal*. In a burst of anticipation Uncle Neddo declared he would try and find a rainbow suit to wear for the meeting. We laughed. The probability of finding such a garment in a small country town was not at issue. Uncle Neddo said he would get his niece who was in charge of the Aboriginal Progress Association to find one. It was the vision of Dreaming association and a glimpse of *Maban*. He would come as a living sign, an iconic presence. The talking went on. A little later Uncle Neddo returned to the image of the rainbow suit. This time, stretching out his arms and bending his body to form an arc, he acted out the scene with white officialdom. 'Go over me please', he said. He had become the *Wakal*. The costume and improvised act was not comedy but metacomedy. Transcending the despair of disbelief and disregard, the old man performed a premonitionary ritual. By revealing essential and secret being in carnival colours, in an explicit exposure of the link between man and land, he hoped to be heard. He would speak as the *Wakal* Man, a manifestation of Nyungar variety in a pragmatic experimental exhibition for the white man. The realities perceived normally with the inner eye of understanding should be shown in their width of explosive laughter.

Cajoled by our soft laughter at his imaginative transformation into mythic being, he declared that the Bennett Brook should be made into a tourist attraction. They could bring them in buses to show them the place of victory where Nyungars made the pipeline go over the brook. Despite the remonstrations of his niece, he went on talking. He was chuckling. They could put a plaque there, telling the story of the *Wakal* and 'since the Americans don't know anything' place a huge plastic snake alongside the brook. The place would become 'famous'. We were all laughing loudly now.

The imagining of a plastic snake was a mockery of both signifier and seer. The vision of rainbow presence was converted into a vulgar constancy, a perversion of place. It was told in the bristling tone of a man who hesitated to separate person and place. The old man, who a few moments before had been the living arc of articulating rainbow, was now parodying his own performance.

The jester who must clown out his social reality knows he risks being taken seriously. The erection of a plaque, of a revelation of the meaning, would be a token of a fake tangibility. Meaning and relationship cannot be separated. The establishment of significance on a grand scale may itself be an act of desecration, for it denies the dialogue and the bond of kinship.

A meeting with remarkable men

On April Fool's Day representatives of the various Nyungar families associated with the area met at the Bennett Brook. 'We could do with a feed. The old people are terribly hungry,' Uncle Neddo whispered in my ear. He had brought a carload of Nyungar people down from the northern wheatbelt. He was wearing his good clothes—a modest country and western style of dress. The company of Nyungars who had been connected with the land were gradually gathering around Uncle George in his wheelchair in preparation for the meeting. Uncle George's half-brothers had lived on the Lockridge land and his mother's sister had lived on Eden Hill. He had come from a hospital bed to be present at the meeting. It was a moment of reunions. Uncle George who was 'crippled up' had, after years, caught up with his old cousin, Willy, who was almost blind. Edna Bropho with a hand resting on each of them testified to those around her that here were her 'two old uncles'. Another middle-aged woman also quietly asserted her kinship with Uncle Willy. The members of families who were not related stood slightly apart as did the handful of Nyungar people who had come to show their support for the families who had lived on the land. The little children ran up and down to the bushes at the edge of the brook, watched over by their mothers and aunties. The company gathered beside the brook was a reunion of four generations.

Granny Bella had not come as she was sick. The two people who had been born on the land, Old Girl Alice and Des Parfitt, were also absent. Nevertheless, the old people had chosen to stand together with the younger ones. Uncle Willy was the first to speak. He declared that the pipeline must go over the brook, not under it, because of the *Wakal*. His rasping, almost hoarse voice was decisive. He had spent his childhood on this land, he went on to explain.

The Nyungar company followed meticulously their own protocol for speaking. The oldies spoke first. Then the generation of active grandparents. When the white spokesperson handed the drawings of an above-ground crossing of the brook to the incorrect person, that man handed it, without even a cursory glance, to the person accorded social recognition as spokesperson for the land. He immediately showed it to the male representatives of two other families who had long associations with the brook. Indeed, although I had noted it at the time, a Nyungar woman present at the meeting later drew my attention to this meticulous observance of familial rights.

I was also told after the meeting that Uncle Neddo had brought a snake down to the meeting in his car. I had asked what sort of snake. 'Oh, just a brown one.' Behind the formal and serious performance of the meeting had been the conceptualisation of another drama. The man in the rainbow suit would get the snake, transformed into the very likeness of the *Wakal*, and throw it at the feet of the spokesperson for the State Energy Commission or, alternatively, he would put the snake in one of the little paperbark trees beside the brook and then lead the white man down to it.

The whispered script which ran alongside the solemn declarations of the sacredness of the place, countered the disregard accorded to the utterances of the oldies. One of the young Nyungar women had wanted to hit one of the white people, more for the tone than the content of the words. The hidden ploy had helped the company to hold her. Nonetheless, there had been a gradual shift from a compromise to a proclamation of protection. Edna Bropho had, in ascending pitch, declared that beautiful lilies grew along the brook. The lilies and the little fish would be destroyed by the proposed edifice of concrete and steel. Another Nyungar man, Richard Wilkes, a descendant of Old Teddy Wilkes, took up the theme of destruction. They did not want a gas pipeline here at all. Uncle Willy, crouching down and fingering the earth, reiterated in a hoarse staccato that this was the *Wakal's* place.

Later, when I told Uncle George what was being said, he had laughed and said it would have been a carpet snake. The carpet snakes, while not synonymous with the *Wakal*, are treated with respect and not killed.

The alternative dialogue intimated the reflexivity of Nyungar thinking about situations in which their way of perceiving is, by their own agreement, compromised. For the negotiation of discursive procedure is a partial relegation of the Nyungar way of understanding the world. The Nyungar reality exists alongside the white world view. The compromise creates moments of humour and moments of anguish. The according of a moment of speech to the oldest person associated with the land, without however treating such a verbal attestation as a visible manifestation of the Dreaming, is interpreted as disrespect. Such lack of respect for the oldies and the Dreaming begins to corroborate an understanding of the situation as a moment of invalidation of what is most precious to the Nyungar people.

In a later reflection spontaneously offered, Uncle George said that Nyungars had agreed to follow a format of discussion which was 'the white way'. He said that if it were 'Nyungar way', they would have acted differently. They would have gone straight to the spring and sprinkled sand in the water. They would have spoken to the Old Boy (the snake) and told him the details of the matter. Then they would have waited and watched for a sign. Uncle stopped to explain that the *Wakal* did not actually speak in words but expressed his meaning in tangible forms. He finally summarised the situation of inequality: 'We've got nothing to stand on...can shoot us down like dogs.'

Conclusion

More than three years have passed since the initial discussions about the gas pipeline. Several more meetings have been called. The matter has not yet been resolved. In the meantime, however, a boat ramp has been put in across the river from Success Hill and a lot of the bush on Success Hill has been cleared. The Nyungar people who care about the land have noted the deaths that have occurred during the time of the negotiations. Two of Granny Bella Bropho's sons have passed away, Harold Gydgup and Old Girl Alice are finished, and a small baby died in tragic circumstances. There is a recognition too of a mounting sense of anger and frustration among the young people associated with the land as the words of their elders seem impotent to protect the place they regard as home.

There is a special pain involved in having your beliefs acknowledged as genuine and still having them effectively denied. The legislation which is meant to guarantee protection to sacred places seems rather to produce a situation of double bind— the validation of Nyungar spirituality is set together with decisions to negate the manifestation of spirit. This, from a Nyungar point of view, is more than a destruction of legal evidence. It is a mutilation of the physical expressions of their oneness with the land and such an act of desecration is a threat to the existence and survival of people.

The humanitarian argument which attempts to understand the violence and debauchery of some Aboriginal individuals as a reaction to stress and loss starts most often from the premise that we are dealing with spiritually and culturally deprived and depleted individuals. The importance of what is being discussed here is that what Nyungar people are experiencing appears as an active attempt to destroy them. They see themselves faced not only with ethnocide but with genocide.

The issue for Nyungar people is above all one of survival. The remaining piece of land adjacent to the brook stands for the lives of the old people who lived there and whose spirit is still present in trees and earth. The springs and watercourse are evidence of the spiritual presence and the generative potential of the place of home. Yet the land means more than this. For the Nyungar landscape is an updating and contemporising of history. To destroy the matrix of inter-relationships and affinities held in the particular constellation of trees and watercourse, camps and tracks, is to destroy not only signs and evidences of past lives, but also to deny a seminal dimension and expression of meaning to present and future ones.

13. Peter Sutton — Myth as history, history as myth

In this chapter[1] I discuss a particular aspect of the role of myth in the older Aboriginal traditions, and the role of history in the construction of cultural identity by present-day Aboriginal people, particularly those in urban and rural centres. This is followed by an analysis of conflict between Aboriginal and non-Aboriginal historians over the domain of Aboriginal history. Finally, the chapter shows in what ways traditional myth and urban Aboriginal history both resemble each other and differ, a theme touched on by Gaynor Macdonald (Chapter 10).

Myth as history

In 1975 Hiatt published a summary of earlier interpretations of the purpose of Australian myths. He suggested that these fell into four main categories, none of them mutually incompatible: myth as history, myth as charter, myth as dream, and myth as ontology.

Under the heading of myth as history he summarised the views of Mathew, Ehrlich, Spencer and Gillen, Roheim, Tindale and others. Their conjectures included the views that myths recorded the migrations of different 'races', ancient customs and forms of social organisation no longer practised, cataclysms of nature and environmental changes, and the previous existence of extinct or absent animal species. Hiatt (1975, 16) felt, however, that for the purpose of categorising the then present and future trends of Australian myth interpretation, 'probably "Myth as history" could be closed down, at least for the time being, and the space used instead for "miscellaneous influences"'. Furthermore, a new box would have to be opened up to accommodate the Dutch and French structuralists, and certain compartments would need to make room for more eclectic approaches (Hiatt 1975, 16–17).

While accepting the usual arguments for abandoning speculative historicist interpretations of traditional myth, the category should be retained. This is not because several scholars have continued to fancy that Aboriginal myths record, for example, a 1793 eclipse (Tindale 1974, 135), the creation of crater lakes 10,000 years ago (Dixon 1972, 29), possible memories of extinct megafauna (Tindale 1974, 119; Flood 1983, 145–47), ice age land bridges (Dixon 1972, 29), and even the arrival of *Homo sapiens* in Sahul (Flood 1983, 29–30). There are other, less ethnographically and logically shaky grounds for seeing myths as transformed history.

Hiatt (1975, 16) takes the general view that Australian myths were best understood as 'proto-analytic insights into the stuff that dreams are made of'. In conjunction with initiation ceremonies they were 'a form of applied psychology in which, to put it perhaps too boldly, principles underlying the nightmare are transposed to a conscious and collective level for the purposes of social integration and adaptation' (Hiatt 1975, 16). The psychological experiences of the growing child are thus a key element in the construction of Aboriginal cosmogony through their projection as myth and their enactment as ceremony. In this work, Hiatt leans heavily toward a psychoanalytic approach to myth and is sceptical about most other approaches. Stanner concentrated on myth as ontology, and RM and CH Berndt are identified by Hiatt as the key proponents of a functionalist view of myth as moral and social charter (see RM Berndt 1970). The last, in particular, was a view he was at some pains to refute (Hiatt 1975, 5–7). It is a view still occasionally espoused by other scholars (eg Yengoyan 1979, 406; see also discussion in Swain 1985, 111–14 of the 'charter hypothesis' of literature).

Hiatt again attacked the charter approach in a paper given at a meeting of consultants to the Australian Law Reform Commission's Aboriginal Customary Law Reference (Hiatt 1983). He said that while certain anthropological authorities backed the view that Aboriginal law and morality had their foundations in religion, and it was a view readily appreciated by what he calls 'the ordinary White Australian', in his opinion it is false. He then gives evidence for his view, mainly citing myths which could hardly be interpreted as moral tales. He adds, 'It seems to me that the really serious content of Aboriginal religion from the point of view of law is the mythological ratification of land ownership' (Hiatt 1983, 10; see further discussion in Jones and Sutton 1986). This last statement can be seen as adding a whole new category of interpretations to those Hiatt had established nearly ten years earlier. I suspect, in passing, that this development is related to the involvement of anthropologists in detailed land ownership studies in Cape York and in land claims research in the Northern Territory since the late 1970s.

This is myth as charter, but as charter for rights and obligations of possession, control and custodianship, not as charter for a moral system. In a sense it is also myth as history, since so many places in the Aboriginal landscape have specific mythic creation or transformation stories characterised as taking place in a distant past, or at least in a logically prior dimension of the timeless. Significantly, the entities which are called Dreamings over so much of north and central Australia are instead called 'Stories' in a large area of northeast Australia, and 'Histories' in northern South Australia. Their sacred sites are called Story Places and History Places respectively (cf von Sturmer 1985, 263).

There is no need to see the narrative details of the myths simply as imagery which is based on the psychology of childhood and dreams, and then applied to landscape in an arbitrary way. There is a strong argument for seeing site-related Aboriginal myths—and most of them are so related—not merely as invented pasts, but as in many cases a combination of invention and memory. This hypothesis is ostensibly easier to sustain, on the basis of my own field experience, in northcentral Australia than it is in Cape York Peninsula.

In one area of northcentral Australia, the paths taken by certain Dreamings in their travels closely match the residential life-histories and ceremonial histories of certain key men associated with those Dreamings. In most of these cases the shifts of the Dreamings from one area to another also parallel very closely the history of their owners' succession to site interests held in the recent past by others who have either failed to produce agnatic descendants or who have been politically eclipsed. These cases recall Howitt's speculation regarding the eastern Lake Eyre Aboriginal traditions, that the *pinnarus*, living leaders, 'bosses', were the *mura-muras*, the patrifiliative ceremonial totemic beings at Dreamings (Howitt and Siebert 1904, 129).

Some of the more modern literature has contained similar suggestions. Strehlow (1970, 95) says that the 400 mile route of certain Honey Ant mythical beings in central Australia could 'surely be explained most readily by assuming an historical basis for events described in the corresponding...myth', although he offers no fine-grained evidence of how such a transformation of event to religious narrative took place. Worsley also indulges in what he calls 'conjectural history' in suggesting that human migration-routes in the Groote Eylandt area have become embodied in certain clan myths, but he also offers some 'probably historical material' as supporting evidence (Worsley 1967, 148).

In one case I have studied in northcentral Australia an individual was marginalised by the movement of others, justified by Dreaming travels. In another case I am certain that the decision to allot a certain set of sites to a group with previous primary land attachments some distance away has amounted to the superimposition of the interests of this group, in a politically and ceremonially dominant position, onto those already held in the area by three other groups. I am sure of this case because two other anthropologists have left evidence of the relevant land tenure situation as it was in the 1930s (Stanner 1934; Strehlow 1938). Moreover, I was present for a critical afternoon on which this case of succession was established by means of a long discussion of mythology. A new, territorially expanded version of the key relevant myth was floated at a meeting of senior men who, after some debate, settled on 'one story' and ratified the correct version. This version had been publicly stated for at least three years before this time. The meeting appeared mainly to function as a ratification, or at least a speeding-up, of a change already well advanced.

A combination of the earlier documentary evidence and my own observations support the view that one of the roles of mythology in that region is to provide an idiom, a legislative code in the third person, in which relationships between known people, their residential histories, their pursued claims to land attachments, and their totemic 'selves', must not only be ratified but negotiated. The individuals concerned seem to be viewed as though they were primary instantiations of the totemic group, somewhat like the 'kinship I' and 'heroic I' reported for some more hierarchical societies (see Sahlins 1983, 523, 536).

Malinowski stressed the *post hoc* ratification of social change by means of myths, although in the Australian case it is necessary to add, I think, that myths go further than enshrining the status quo—they are also, in real speech situations, a code in which changes in the status quo are effected by the interlocutors and their audience. Malinowski (1926, 284) said, for example,

> Whatever the historical reality of their unrecorded past may be, myths serve to cover certain inconsistencies created by historical events, rather than to record these events exactly. The myths associated with the spread of powerful sub-clans show on certain points a fidelity to life in that they record facts inconsistent with one another. The incidents by which this inconsistency is obliterated, if not hidden, are most likely fictitious; we have seen certain myths vary according to the locality in which they are told. In other cases the incidents bolster up non-existent claims and rights.

In the area of north Australia with which I am concerned here, senior men, at least, spend a lot of time not only discussing but debating mythology. One such debate took place, briefly, before the Aboriginal Land Commissioner in the early 1980s, in the middle of evidence during a land claim. This was not a disagreement of innocent and differing memories, nor a case of 'cultural breakdown' or 'decaying traditions'. It was, as such debate often is, systematically normal and, for want of a better word, traditional.

This same region, like others reported in the literature (eg Munn 1964, 92 on the Warlpiri; Munn 1970, 146 on the Pitjantjatjara), is one where men not infrequently refer in ordinary conversation to Dreamings as 'me', 'my father', or 'my father's father'. In the third person they may refer to particular Dreamings by the names of living people (cf similar Maori practice, Sahlins 1983, 523). One of my first gaffes in working in this area was, after being given an account of how various men and their fathers used to meet at a certain site to hold ceremonies, to ask in what season of the year they had done so. The men speaking to me had been referring to mythic rather than personally remembered events, and my question caused some confusion for a moment. On reflection it seems, though, that the question was not as wide of the mark as it may have seemed. Of Dreamings, men in that area often say, 'He was a *man* then, you know.'

Dreamings are people in their other aspect; people are Dreamings in their human aspect. Narratives occasionally blur the person–Dreaming distinction. This approach seems strongest in the wider central Australian region. It is far less pronounced in coastal western Cape York Peninsula, where it is rather easier to maintain an analytical distinction between myth and history. Curiously, though, this is an area where historical narratives are often told, involving remembered human kin, but where the content, form and nature of delivery of the narratives, as well as their political import, are highly similar to those of religious myths.

There are many contrasts between desert culture and Cape York culture in this domain, and I will outline some of them briefly in order to avoid supporting the equation of desert culture with 'Aboriginal culture', an equation still often encountered but one which is erroneous.

In western Cape York Peninsula there is far less identification of site-specific mythic beings with the spirits of the relevant site-owning group members, than one finds in central Australian systems. There simply is no uniform relation between clan sites and clan totems. While a clan's totems are referred to as 'dear father's father' (*puul + waya*) or as 'sibling' (*kooenhiy*), depending on language, the sites containing the essences of a clan's totems may in many instances lie in the estates of distant and different clans or in no known estate at all. Conversely, a large proportion of site totems have no counterpart in the totems which identify their owners' clan. Furthermore, few myths in the region yield 'Dreaming tracks' which pass through long ordered series of sites; of those which take this form, few could be said to effectively define the territorial interests of particular descent groups. Relative human sedentism and the sedentism of mythic characters are rather well matched. In spite of this, mythic events are, as elsewhere in drier Australia, highly site-specific. But rights to publicly recount (perform) myths, at least within one broad regional population of many hundreds, seem relatively unrestricted. People are extremely relaxed about telling stories from neighbours' countries, as a normal after-dinner adult pastime. This is not the same in the areas of desert Australia with which I am familiar. In western Cape York there are song genres (eg *Piithal, Thaatharam*) which have no associated mythology or mythological site reference, and many site-specific myths which have no associated ceremonial songs. Finally, the proportion of totemic sites in Cape York Peninsula which lack any associated narrative mythology seems extremely high by comparison with inland Australia, in spite of their designation in English as Story Places.

History as myth

There is a category of Aboriginal stories which are distinguishable from Dreaming myths, at least in most instances. One of their distinguishing marks is that key figures are identified as particular kin of the living, usually with remembered personal names (including English names), and they are not generalised ancestral beings or uniformly agnatic forebears of clan members, for example. One may call them historical narratives but this has its drawbacks, for some such stories are interwoven with events of the Dreaming (eg Goetz and Sutton 1986). Even living people have associated with them experiences which are merged, in the telling, with Dreaming encounters, at least in inland desert Australia. (In western Cape York Peninsula people frequently encounter ghosts and monsters, but do not as readily interweave mythic identities and remembered actual kin.)

Even where Dreaming events and characters are absent and the narrative may be labelled more historical than mythological, the approach to historical evidence is essentially the same as that in myth. The narrator constructs a version of the facts that may have some relationship, even a recognised one, with events recorded in documentary sources, but it is unconstrained by those sources. This is exemplified well by the Roper River case presented by Morphy and Morphy (1984), and by accounts of a visit to the upper Victoria River system by Captain Cook (P McConvell personal communication; Rose 1984), a well documented historical person, but one whose logs make no mention of inland travel in Australia. Another case is the popular account of Dutch exploration of Cape York Peninsula, documented for the seventeenth or eighteenth centuries, which Aurukun people believe took place in the life-times of ancestors who lived roughly between 1870 and 1950. In this case a mission superintendent is said to have brought to Aurukun a book recounting the Dutch visits, and I have put forward the hypothesis that this written version has been interwoven with selective memory of actual events (Karntin and Sutton 1986). In other cases, Biblical myths have been superimposed on local landscape by Aboriginal story tellers. Noah's Ark is found in part of Western Australia (Kolig 1980) and the death and resurrection of Jesus of Nazareth occurred at Nambucca Heads in New South Wales (Calley 1964; Sutton 1983).

These instances bring to mind relevant generalisations of Malinowski (1926, 284):

> The historical consideration of myth is interesting, therefore, in that it shows that myth, taken as a whole, cannot be sober dispassionate history, since it is always made ad hoc to fulfil a certain sociological function, to glorify a certain group, or to justify an anomalous status. These considerations show us also that to the native immediate history, semi-historic legend, and unmixed myth flow into one another, form a continuous sequence, and fulfil the same sociological function.
>
> And this brings us once more to our original contention that the really important thing about the myth is its character of a retrospective, ever-present, live actuality. It is to a native neither a fictitious story, nor an account of a dead past; it is a statement of a bigger reality still partially alive.

With those comments in mind (but with a critical sense of the limits of dispassionate sobriety!) I want now to move the discussion from traditions that have come down in a long line from the Aboriginal cultural past, to a related set of cultural innovations.

History and the construction of identity

The last two decades of cultural reconstruction in rural and urban Australia have been characterised by a search for roots and history, attempts to revitalise certain elements of what is perceived as traditional culture, efforts by Aborigines to control Aboriginal studies and the teaching of Aboriginal culture as domains of paid work, and the emergence of a new form of Aboriginal intellectuality.

The last of these is perhaps the most complex and elusive; it also pervades the others, as attempts are made to have it serve as their controlling ideology. In its most distinctively evolved form, this new intellectuality is both reflexive and inventive. It requires occasional rituals of public speaking, but it is only identifiable with difficulty as being in a direct line of descent from traditional Aboriginal intellectuality, which is so concerned with formal performance in its public expressions. The practitioners of the new intellectuality are concerned centrally with constructing a metaphysic of identity. They promote a belief in inherited and inherent Aboriginal powers of perception and understanding, and on historically constituted contemporary identity. A number of people engaged in this activity, which is part of a general Aboriginal cultural revitalisation, have spoken of it essentially as a process of self-realisation: 'We didn't know who we were'; or 'I had to find out who I was'. This movement should be placed in historical context.

For some decades before the 1960s there was a long period of real if partial and gradual assimilation to the dominant Anglo-Australian culture, if not everywhere then certainly in much of Australia. By assimilation I mean that many of the cultural changes experienced by Aborigines have been toward, rather than away from, the European Australian lifestyle. Aboriginal culture thus reached a point where many people lived, at least superficially, more like Europeans than like traditional Aborigines (cf Barwick 1964; Beckett 1964). Apart from a resurgence of ceremonial activity in the Great Depression in northern New South Wales for example (see Elkin 1975–76, 147), it was not really until the 1970s that there seems to have been a sudden wave of realisations amounting to the view that assimilation did not necessarily result in absorption, total sameness or disappearance. This view is now dominant, and is facilitating assimilation to the dominant white-collar professional Australian culture more successfully than official assimilationist policies of the past which were based on an expectation of absorption.

Particularly since the 1970s, official sponsorship of Aboriginal culture and the gradual removal of public policies of assimilation have lent support to a development whereby it is no longer exceptional for Aborigines to explicitly proclaim their distinct cultural identity. Much of the ideological push for this development, as well as much of its early rhetoric and techniques of public demonstration, was absorbed from the black rights movements of the USA (Pearson and Cocks 1982), and received added pushes from the general recognition of a Fourth World component in modern states, the multiculturalism phenomenon, and a heightened awareness of minorities generally. These have been international developments. (See Keesing and Tonkinson 1982 on island Melanesia for another example.)

At the same time, the last twenty years has also been a period of unprecedented incorporation of Aboriginal people into pockets of the Australian economy and its administrative structures, mainly in the service sector and associated activities. The terms of this incorporation probably could not have been predicted thirty years ago. To maximise access to this arena of incorporation one must proclaim, not suppress, one's Aboriginal identity. There is, of course, a catch.

In exchange for special recognition, jobs and earmarked funds, many Aboriginal people have been willing to knuckle down to the nine-to-five requirements of the bureaucracy, although somewhat loose approximations to official hours and performance levels are tolerated in many cases. The stock in trade of these Aboriginal employees has had to be not only an 'ability to communicate effectively with Aboriginal people', as the job advertisements put it, but also a committed combination of sameness and difference. To get and hold the job one has had to possess or learn many basic skills and attitudes required of public servants in an industrial state, but at the same time one has had to be self-identified as 'different'.

In a minority of cases this difference-from-others may be largely at the diacritic level—that is, one's distinctive Aboriginality may consist to a large extent of repeatedly asserting it. In such instances a pressure to evolve a distinctive intellectuality can be said to have arisen partly as a result of reflection, as well as of debate, on the problem of justifying demands for special consideration and powers in the absence of conspicuous evidence of individual disadvantage. This pressure also comes from exposure—for some, an exposure intensified and subsidised by special educational programmes—to non-Aboriginal intellectual traditions.

As the 'melting pot' and the colonial 'worker's paradise' have given way to the replacement dreams of perpetual ethnic diversity and culture-as-industry, it has become a matter of shame, rather than pride, to have severed the bonds to one's tradition. If the tradition you had in the past was taken from you, you must reconstruct one. Even in the majority of cases, where Aboriginal identity is much more than merely diacritical, the sense of cultural disinheritance is strong and the move to reconstruction is rapidly growing. Urban conditions, in which Aboriginal contact with non-Aborigines is perhaps at its most intense, are not inhibiting but possibly even enhancing these processes. Gale and Wundersitz (1982) have found, for example, that the importance of kinship in Aboriginal residential arrangements in Adelaide is not decreasing but increasing.

I have already mentioned the role of contact with international political and cultural movements, and of contact with mainstream Australian education, in the rise of the new Aboriginal intellectuality. Non-Aboriginal sponsorship of the relevant ideologies has played an important role in their espousal by Aborigines. Another important role in this process is now also being played by urban Aboriginal contact with the old Aboriginal intellectuality.

Through employment in remote Aboriginal agencies, and in some cases through participation as claimants or witnesses in land claim tribunals, Aborigines from 'settled' Australia have in the last ten years come into intensified relationships with other Aborigines from more traditional Aboriginal cultural backgrounds. Literate Aboriginal people from coastal Queensland cities, for example, have become liaison officers, clerks, researchers and receptionists in land council bureaux, legal aid offices and remote servicing agencies. Adopted and welfare-reared urban people in Darwin, Katherine, Adelaide and elsewhere have traced lost links to parents and other relations in the bush. These developments have required a new form of cultural adaptation, a process of learning to live a lifestyle containing both the new and the old, and to use unfamiliar language, for example. It has required urban Aborigines to deal with their stereotypes of bush Aborigines as wild and dirty. For the more traditional people, simultaneously, these contacts have sometimes required them to take on a radically new conception of urban Aborigines.

This set of changes amounts to an incipient trend toward breakdown of both social closure and cultural distinctions between urban and remote Aboriginal people. The communication networks of the individuals concerned are linking Aborigines to each other on a continental scale to a new degree. It is still not uncommon in a large city, for example, for long term urban people to have a relatively restricted personal acquaintance with other Aborigines. Several such people have told me, 'The Aborigines I know have mostly been just my own [extended] family' (cf Gale and Wundersitz 1982, 83). Occupational and geographical mobility are changing this. Such changes, especially as new kinship links become established through parenthood, are contributing toward a pan-Aboriginal connectedness that has been lacking in at least the recent past, except in the realm of political rhetoric.

It has been the new material conditions of life, underpinning new forms of consciousness and new personal linkages, and many of them won by an originally political activism, that have begun the process of construction of the continent-wide Aboriginal consciousness which political proselytising, alone, has failed to achieve. The failure of attempts to revive traditional practices such as initiations, with perhaps two exceptions (Borsboom and Dagmar 1984, 47 on the Gascoyne District, Western Australia; R Kelly, personal communication 1986, on northern New South Wales) is to be contrasted with the vigorous and widespread Aboriginal interest in discovering and publishing the histories of families and communities from the longer 'settled' parts of Australia. Scores of individuals and groups are now researching their own pasts, both through written and photographic records and the collecting of old people's memories. The desire to unearth or reconstruct genealogies and mission histories is strong. Much of this work is officially encouraged and funded, for example by the Department of Aboriginal Affairs, the Australian Institute of Aboriginal Studies, the National Estate grants programme, and by other bodies such as the State museums. While a proportion of the research or writing involved is carried out by non-Aborigines, and there is a certain amount of concealed ghost-writing, Aboriginal interest is certainly vigorous at a grass-roots level. Usually intensely local in focus, the Aboriginal history movement is nevertheless sweeping the whole of urban and rural Australia, and has even reached southern Cape York and the Kimberley.

As one Aboriginal colleague has emphasised to me, this type of cultural self-realisation has in part been made possible by knowledge of English, by literacy, and by interaction with academically trained non-Aboriginal researchers (R Kelly, personal communication 1983). Yet these have been facilitating factors, not determining ones. A particularly important factor has been an emerging new Aboriginal intellectuality with its own world view.

In traditional Aboriginal culture the historic past, including genealogical memory beyond two or three generations, is usually quickly forgotten and often actually suppressed, except perhaps as it is selectively maintained for a time or transformed into myth (Stanner 1966, 139–40; Sharp 1970, 386; Maddock 1982, 36; Morphy and Morphy 1984, 461). But the new approach to the past is different. Written, photographic and taped records are seen as highly useful in history making, no matter how far back in time they go. Archaeological records are also used, and denied, depending on who is using them. For some, radio-carbon dating has established a powerful political weapon in the fight to have Aboriginal prior occupancy of Australia recognised. I heard 'the Dreamtime' identified as '40,000 years ago' one day near Kempsey, a contrast with more traditional views which combine a view of the Dreaming as the timeless present with a sense of the 'Creative Period' happening about three generations before the present. Urban Aboriginal history construction is a statement, moral and political, about the suffering, resilience and persistence of a colonised and displaced people, but it is also a search for a background and underpinning to what must now be assumed to be an indefinite state of future difference. In this sense it is the creation, as much as the explanation, of a separate identity.

In these terms urban history construction is remarkably similar in function to the Dreaming. The past is also the present, as one of its aspects. The past is not transcendent or remote, but underpins and echoes present and continuing reality. Just as the Dreaming is the person, in one facet of its complex nature, the Aboriginal person is likewise the historical Aborigine—not merely the survivor but the embodiment of the scarifying processes of conquest, dispossession, resettlement, missionisation and welfareism.

Under this view the contemporary white Australian can sometimes also be defined and identified as the historic coloniser, not merely as their descendant or beneficiary. This became particularly clear to me late one night as I walked along Adelaide's

Hindley Street and came upon the following scene. A policeman was kneeling on the back of an Aboriginal man, handcuffing him. An incident of violence had just occurred. Other Aboriginal people were looking on, most of them were vocal. Some were boys in their early teens and younger. My friends and I arrived in time to hear one of the young Aboriginal boys shout at the policeman, 'Captain Cook cunt!'

A clash of views

The emergence of an urban Aboriginal intelligentsia, however, loosely interlinked and internally competitive, at the core of which have been people with an interest in history, has been accompanied by a clash of their views with those of academics. Some Aboriginal people in urban Australia believe that non-Aborigines are inherently incapable of understanding Aboriginal history and, therefore, should leave the field. 'Our heritage, your playground' has become a slogan for this camp (although see Kelly 1982 for a contrary Aboriginal view). Similar attacks have been made on anthropologists—I was told recently by an urban Aboriginal woman, 'You just wouldn't know or understand [traditional culture] because you're not Aboriginal.' These views sometimes rest on an explicitly expounded theory of racially inherited ability which resembles genetic determinism and, therefore, racism.

The inborn-capacity theory, unlike the attack on non-Aboriginal appropriation of Aboriginal cultural property allegedly entailed in Aboriginal studies, is possibly an exception to the generalisation that the source of ideas among the Aboriginal urban intelligentsia has largely been external. It has, though, struck a sympathetic chord among disaffected European Australians, and has given Aboriginal culture, perhaps for the first time, an exportable form. Yet from the defensible (if ex cathedra) 'We Aborigines can get the feel of things [Aboriginal]' (Moriarty 1969, 76) to the hippie paparazzi grooving on Dreamtime vibes (see Simpfendorfer 1980) there seems to be a descent into kitsch. Between some of the urban Aboriginal modern mystics and the counterculture movement, cultural appropriation appears to have been mutual.

Other clashes have been over matters of fact and reflect a conflict of views on the nature of historical or anthropological evidence. On one occasion an anthropologist was publicly attacked by some urban Aboriginal seminar participants for referring to what he regarded as the historical inaccuracy of oral traditions about a voyage of Captain Cook in 1770 (C Anderson, personal communication). As in the Victoria River case cited above, these traditions had Cook visiting places which his log does not say he visited. The exchange became heated when Aboriginal participants defended the truth of the oral traditions against the non-Aboriginal documentary approach to evidence.

On another occasion, an Aboriginal participant in the Australian Law Reform Commission's seminar on customary law in 1983 vigorously opposed the views of the anthropologist Les Hiatt, who had been arguing against the view that Aboriginal law and morality were based on myth and religion. Hiatt's view seems to have been interpreted as an attack on urban Aboriginal views of traditional society. In particular, 'owning' the Aboriginal past seems to have been at issue, at least in the mind of Hiatt's opponent (McBryde 1985; Donaldson and Donaldson 1985, 19–20). Although Aboriginal historians represent a range of attitudes, those at one extreme of the spectrum see research and publication on the Aboriginal past as a claim to a political and occupational owning of that past, something they say is the exclusive property of Aborigines. Hiatt was making universalist observations in what some others would prefer to see as a territorialist context. This was a clash not merely of interpretations of fact, but of cultural standpoints and power groups.

The fact that Aboriginal and non-Aboriginal historians often have different approaches to verification, for example, is sometimes interpreted as arising from different levels of intellectual or scholarly quality. Under the received canons of objectivist method taught at universities, this may be true. In that sense, and where approaches to empirical rigour do differ fundamentally, calling both approaches 'history' may be misleading. It cannot be assumed that this ambiguity is either innocent or unintended. Without this single umbrella label it is difficult to argue that the two approaches compete for a single precious space, that of legitimate authority on the Aboriginal past. Although proponents of both approaches have argued for dominance or exclusive possession of this space, neither have argued for its existence. This is curious, since a moment's reflection shows that it is clearly problematic.

The creation of problematic single spaces is not confined to those concerned with Australia since colonisation. Archaeologists have been somewhat puzzled, even rocked, to find that some urban Aborigines express resentment at the use of the term 'prehistory' to cover Aboriginal archaeology before the time of written records. Although the term was never intended as a put-down, it has been interpreted as such by people who resent the juxtaposition of 200 years of 'history' with 40,000 years of 'prehistory'. And the tactical shock value of defining history as the total past, rather than as a documentary time span, has been great. It is also in the heavily lexicalist tradition or urban Aboriginal rhetoric.[2] Some urban Aborigines now believe that the

Aboriginal people originated in Australia, angrily denying the assertion that they migrated here from Asia in the Pleistocene.[3] These beliefs are not the same as those of the older mythic traditions, especially as they have arisen in opposition to a fundamentally contrary schema rather than simply in juxtaposition to an array of like explanations, as Aboriginal myths did in the past.

It is now time for anthropologists, historians and archaeologists to move more rapidly toward understanding this ideological conflict instead of merely playing their assigned roles in it. In this case, understanding involves more than personal acquaintance with proponents of both sides of any particular argument. It involves delving into the cultural and sociological origins of the debate. We should try to understand it just as we would if we observed it happening between two groups in another culture.

One element of such an understanding must bring to consciousness the philosophical underpinnings of the two contrasting views. There needs, for example, to be an analysis of what constraints are perceived as defining one's ability to understand another culture. The relationship between world view and the tests one applies for assessing the factuality or supportability of assertions need to be compared for both sets of disputants. Another element in such an understanding must be a grasp of the competitive relationship between those scholars, bureaucrats and activists who are Aboriginal and those who are not. This is more than just a question of salaried and grant-funded jobs, although the matter of job competition cannot be ignored. It is importantly a question of competition for control of the construction of information about Aboriginal culture in the public domain in Australian society. In Sansom's (1980) terms, it is competition for ownership of 'the word' on Aboriginal history in books, educational institutions, museums and the media. To represent this totally expectable activity as a simple contest between Aborigines and whites, or between academics and non-academics, or between a right wing and a left, would be to misrepresent it. The alignments are both more numerous and less conveniently pre-fabricated than these.

Because a perception of history is now powerfully constitutive of urban Aboriginal identity, it has on occasion given rise to perhaps unexpectedly high levels of emotion and to practical efforts to exclude non-Aborigines from the field in recent years. The domain being contested is not, for many Aboriginal people, a set of propositions about the world 'out there', it is a dimension of what they increasingly perceive themselves to be. From a bird's-eye view—that privileged position none of us ever really attain—the domain of Aboriginal history will necessarily be seen to include this identity construction, but it must also include the scholarly documentary work, and the clashes—and collaborations—of the various participants in the field.

There is something about bird's-eye views which confers on them a highly persuasive power, even where they may be most closely identified with the ideology of a ruling culture and, for that reason, reviled. Interpretations which account intelligibly for all other interpretations, as well as for the social roles of their purveyors, have a built-in advantage in any debate.

Conclusion

In a number of ways, traditional Aboriginal approaches to myth and remembered events, and the newer Aboriginal understandings of history, resemble each other. Neither is heavily committed to the canons of empiricism. Both are heavily constitutive of identity, and charged with strong feelings. Both are highly local in reference. Both focus on identities and events without giving central importance to generalisations about processes or external forces. Both reflect mixtures of, on the one hand, the social solidarity of the group and, on the other, social conflicts and boundaries. Both are linked to competition for economic and political benefits. Both constitute an interactive code for re-negotiating the status quo. Both emphasise history as the property of particular people rather than as the province of everyone. And they emphasise past (or eternally prior) states of existence which bear tenuous (or only superficial) resemblances to the known and physically observable present.

The two are also different in several ways. They have divergent approaches to both absolute time and relative sequencing. They treat documentary sources with radically different degrees of interest, but with not too dissimilar degrees of scepticism when occasion demands. They differ fundamentally on the acceptability of the specialised occupational role of the historian-of-others, and of the linked cultural domination, political incorporation and economic entrenchment entailed in such a role as a paid professional in modern Australia. They differ radically in the degrees to which they attempt to account for, and therefore to intellectually encapsulate and come to terms with, the existence, arrival and dominance of non-Aborigines in Australia (cf Sharp 1970, 395–96). Doubtless these lists of comparisons can be extended. On balance, I think the similarities outweigh the differences.

Notes

1. This paper was presented at the 1985 Conference of the Australian Anthropological Society in Darwin. I wish to thank the following individuals for personal communications and comments on a written draft of the paper: Christopher Anderson, Philip Jones, Ray Kelly, Gaynor Macdonald and Janice Newton.

2. This method seeks out key words ('Aboriginal', 'prehistory', 'half-caste', 'informant', 'primitive', etc) and attacks their unwanted implications in order to remove or replace them as symbols of oppression and white intellectual hegemony. Deliberate public stumbling over long or erudite English words well known to the speaker is another device of the same rhetorical style.

3. See Brody (1983, 14–16) for a similar account of Canadian Indian resentment of the 'self-styled expertise' of archaeologists on the same subject.

References

Barwick, D.
1964 The Self-conscious People of Melbourne. In M. Reay (ed), *Aborigines Now: New Perspectives in the Study of Aboriginal Communities*, Angus and Robertson, Sydney.

Beckett, J.
1964 Aborigines, Alcohol, and Assimilation. In M. Reay (ed), *Aborigines Now: New Perspectives in the Study of Aboriginal Communities*, Angus and Robertson, Sydney.

Berndt, R.M.
1970 Traditional Morality as Expressed Through the Medium of an Australian Aboriginal Religion. In R.M. Berndt (ed), *Australian Aboriginal Anthropology: Modern Studies in the Social Anthropology of the Australian Aborigines*, University of Western Australia Press, Nedlands.

Borsboom, A.P. and H. Dagmar
1984 Cultural Politics: Two Case Studies of Australian Aboriginal Social Movements, *Bijdragen tot de Taal-, Land- en Volkenkunde* 140, 32–55.

Brody, H.
1983 *Maps and Dreams*, Penguin, New York.

Calley, M.C.
1964 Pentecostalism among the Bandjalang. In M. Reay (ed), *Aborigines Now: New Perspectives in the Study of Aboriginal Communities*, Angus and Robertson, Sydney.

Dixon, R.M.W.
1972 *The Dyirbal Language of North Queensland*, Cambridge University Press, Cambridge.

Donaldson, I. and T. Donaldson
1985 *Seeing the First Australians*, George Allen and Unwin, Sydney.

Elkin, A.P.
1975–76 R.H. Mathews: His Contribution to Aboriginal Studies, *Oceania* 46, 1–24, 126–52, 206–34.

Flood, J.
1983 *Archaeology of the Dreamtime*, Collins, Sydney.

Gale, F. and J. Wundersitz
1982 *Adelaide Aborigines: A Case Study of Urban Life 1966–1981*, Development Studies Centre, Australian National University, Canberra.

Goetz, H. and P. Sutton
1986 Conflicts with Native Police. In L. Hercus and P. Sutton (eds), *This is What Happened: Historical Narratives by Aborigines*, Australian Institute of Aboriginal Studies, Canberra.

Hiatt, L.R.
1975 Introduction. In L.R. Hiatt (ed), *Australian Aboriginal Mythology. Essays in Honour of W.E.H. Stanner*, Australian Institute of Aboriginal Studies, Canberra.
1983 The Relationship Between Aboriginal Religion and Aboriginal Customary Law. In Australian Law Reform Commission and Australian Institute of Aboriginal Studies Report on a Working Seminar on the Aboriginal Customary Law Reference, Sydney 7–8 May 1983, Law School, University of New South Wales, Australian Law Reform Commission, Sydney.

Howitt, A.W. and O. Siebert
1904 Legends of the Dieri and Kindred Tribes of Central Australia, *Journal of the Royal Anthropological Institute* 34, 100–29.

Jones, P. and P. Sutton
1986 *Art and Land: Aboriginal Sculptures from the Lake Eyre Region*, South Australian Museum, Adelaide.

Karntin, J.S. and P. Sutton
1986 Dutchmen at Cape Keerweer. In L. Hercus and P. Sutton (eds), *This is What Happened: Historical Narratives by Aborigines*, Australian Institute of Aboriginal Studies, Canberra.

Keesing, R.M. and R. Tonkinson (eds)
1982 Reinventing Traditional Culture: The Politics of Kastom in Island Melanesia, *Mankind* (Special Issue) 13, 297–399.

Kelly, R.
1982 Aborigines and Academics, *Aboriginal Sites Newsletter* 5(1), National Parks and Wildlife Service, New South Wales.

Kolig, E.
1980 Noah's Ark Revisited: On the Myth/Land Connection in Traditional Aboriginal Thought, *Oceania* 51, 118–32.

Maddock, K.
1982 *The Australian Aborigines. A Portrait of Their Society*, Second Edition, Penguin Books, Ringwood, Victoria.

Malinowski, B.
1926 *Myth in Primitive Psychology*, Kegan Paul, Trench and Trubner, London.

McBryde, I. (ed)
1985 *Who Owns the Past?*, Oxford University Press, Melbourne.

Moriarty, J.
1969 The Situation as I See It. In J. Warburton (ed), *The Aborigines of South Australia. Their Present Condition and Future Development*, Department of Adult Education, University of Adelaide, Adelaide.

Morphy, H. and F. Morphy
1984 The 'Myths' of Ngalakan History: Ideology and Images of the Past in Northern Australia, *Man* 19(3), 459–78.

Munn, N.D.
1964 Totemic Designs and Group Continuity in Walbiri Cosmology. In M. Reay (ed), *Aborigines Now: New Perspectives in the Study of Aboriginal Communities*, Angus and Robertson, Sydney.
1970 The Transformation of Subjects into Objects in Walbiri and Pitjantjatjara Myth. In R.M. Berndt (ed), *Australian Aboriginal Anthropology: Modern Studies in the Social Anthropology of the Australian Aborigines*, University of Western Australia Press, Nedlands.

Pearson, C. and C. Cocks
1982 Black Power, *Labor Forum* 4(2), 15–19.

Rose, D.B.
1984 The Saga of Captain Cook: Morality in Aboriginal and European Law, *Australian Aboriginal Studies* 2, 24–39.

Sahlins, M.
1983 Other Times, Other Customs: The Anthropology of History, *American Anthropologist* 85, 517–44.

Sansom, B.
1980 *The Camp at Wallaby Cross: Aboriginal Fringe Dwellers in Darwin*, Australian Institute of Aboriginal Studies, Canberra.

Sharp, R.L.
1970 Steel Axes for Stone-age Australians, *Human Organization* 11, 17–22, 1953. Reprinted in T.G. Harding and B.J. Wallace (eds), *Cultures of the Pacific: Selected Readings*, Free Press, New York.

Simpfendorfer, P.
1980 Australian Sacred Sites, *Cosmos* 8(3), cover, 3.

Stanner, W.E.H.
1934 Unpublished field notes, Australian Institute of Aboriginal Studies, Canberra.
1966 *On Aboriginal Religion*, Oceania Monographs No 11, Sydney.

Strehlow, T.G.H.
1938 Report on Dunmarra Station and Report on Trip to Daly Waters (NT), Australian Archives, NT CA 1115, Patrol Officer Alice Springs and Jay Creek, CRS F126, Item 59.

1970 Geography and the Totemic Landscape in Central Australia: A Functional Study. In R.M. Berndt (ed), *Australian Aboriginal Anthropology: Modern Studies in the Social Anthropology of the Australian Aborigines*, University of Western Australia Press, Nedlands.

Sutton, P.
1983 Field notes in the author's possession (northern New South Wales).

Swain, T.
1985 *Interpreting Aboriginal Religion: An Historical Account*, Australian Association for the Study of Religions, Adelaide.

Tindale, N.B.
1974 *Aboriginal Tribes of Australia*, University of California Press, Berkeley.

von Sturmer, J.
1985 Reviews of *Gularabulu* by P. Roe, edited by S. Muecke, and *Banggaiyerri* by B. Shaw, *Mankind* 15, 263–66.

Worsley, P.
1967 Groote Eylandt Totemism and *Le Totemisme Aujourd'hui*. In E. Leach (ed), *The Structural Study of Myth and Totemism*, Tavistock, London.

Yengoyan, A.A.
1979 Economy, Society and Myth in Aboriginal Australia, *Annual Review of Anthropology* 8, 393–415.

Index

Aboriginal customary law 201, 221, 223, 252, 263
Aboriginal deaths 19-20, 181
Aboriginal history 1-2, 21-22, 30, 32, 79, 98, 251, 260-65
Aboriginal hostels 6, 9-10, 85-86
Aboriginal identity 3, 7-8, 14, 21-22, 27, 31, 33-34, 47, 53-54, 57-59, 65, 69-79, 82-85, 88-89, 91-94, 97-98, 101, 117, 137, 143-45, 251, 257-59, 261, 264-65
Aboriginal identity categories 3-4, 6, 9
Aboriginal identity formation 2-3, 6, 33-34, 69, 71-72, 76
Aboriginal legal services 10, 17, 223, 243, 259
Aboriginal organisations 17, 32, 35-37
Aboriginal protest 30-31, 35-36, 219
Aboriginal style 77, 82-85, 92, 145, 159, 161
Aboriginal subculture 10-11, 16, 27-29, 31-32, 53
Aboriginality 68, 70, 74-75, 93, 113, 259
Aborigines' Welfare Board 34-35, 37-39, 43-45, 47-52, 123, 126, 134
Adelaide 3, 6, 9-16, 77-96, 259, 261
adoption of European values 8-10, 15
alcohol 2, 4, 9, 11, 19, 27, 29, 42, 50-53, 61, 74, 85-86, 128-30, 132, 147, 151, 153, 167, 201, 211, 222-23
ancestral beings 5, 18, 21, 227, 229, 238, 240, 242, 245, 249, 253-55
assimilation 1, 4, 7, 33, 42, 44, 65, 117, 159, 257-58
assimilation policies 4, 29-30, 33-34, 37-38, 43-44, 50, 52, 55-58, 61, 77, 137, 258
attachment to land 12, 20, 27, 30, 79, 137

Baines, P. 18, 20, 22, 180, 227-50
Barwick, D. 1-5, 7, 10-17, 20-21, 27-32, 98, 133, 258

beats, runs and lines 14, 17, 70-71, 74, 119, 131-34, 141-43, 145-49, 151-53, 156, 191
Beckett, J. 1, 4-5, 11, 13-17, 19-20, 22, 50-52, 117-36, 141, 179, 191, 258
Bell, J.H. 1, 3, 5, 7-9, 11, 15-16, 19-20, 43-44, 61, 122
Bennett Brook 227-28, 231-34, 243, 245-46
Berndt, C.H. 1, 3-4, 9-11, 17, 19, 102-03, 196, 252
Berndt, R.M. 1, 3-4, 9-11, 17-19, 102-03, 196, 252
biblical myths and imagery 242, 256-57
Biddle, E.H. 1, 8, 12-15
Birdsall, C. 8-9, 13-14, 66, 137-58
Bourke 117, 123, 125-26, 131-32
Brisbane 6, 12
Broken Hill 117, 125-26
Bropho, R. 2, 6, 9, 15, 19, 228-31, 234, 241-42
Bryant, J. 4, 7, 9, 15, 17, 20

Calley, M. 1, 4-5, 13-16, 50, 132
Carnarvon 144-46
Carter, J. 2, 6, 14, 22, 65-76
ceremonies 20, 45, 120-21, 167, 203, 207, 251, 254, 260
child rearing 12-13, 17, 98, 102, 147-48, 151-52, 171-72
Christianity 11
Christian concepts 227, 241-42
Christian revivals 134
churches 32
Condobolin 117, 124-26, 131
Crick, M. 1, 3, 17, 22, 78
critique of dominant society 5-6, 54-55
cultural 'revival' or 'revitalisation' 22, 257

Darling River 119-20, 123-26, 129-31
Darwin 1, 16, 159-78, 266
Dhan-gadi 2, 33-64
dispersal policies 30, 119

269

dispute processing 18–19, 202, 208, 211, 214, 218–20, 222
Dixon, R.M.W. 103, 251
Dreaming 77, 164, 175, 227, 239, 245, 247, 252, 261

Eades, D. 7, 11–12, 19, 21–22, 68, 97–116
Eckermann, A.K. 1, 6–7, 9, 13–14, 17, 20, 65
education 17, 31, 35, 42, 61, 69, 81, 87, 97, 100, 122, 126, 153, 155
   pre-schools 17, 67
   primary schools 67
   secondary schools 69–71
eliciting information 2, 11, 68, 104, 106–12
Elkin, A.P. 43, 61, 121, 128, 258
employment 4, 9–10, 15, 21, 29, 61, 67, 70, 81, 86–87, 99, 113, 122–23, 128, 130, 137–38, 147, 149
   pastoral and farm work 2, 15, 29, 66, 122, 126, 128, 142, 243
   employment in cities 15
   migratory workers 2, 29–30
   seasonal work 15, 50, 66, 126, 142, 164
   semi-skilled 10
   skilled 10
   unskilled 15, 126
entertainment 4, 11, 16, 29, 46, 58, 84–85, 87, 99
Evans-Pritchard, E.E. 186, 239
exchange economy 3, 16, 159–61, 163, 166, 169, 173, 176
extended family 80, 99, 102, 104, 137–38, 141, 143, 145, 234, 260
extended households 12, 28

fathering 169–71
fighting 3, 18–19, 85, 169, 179–205, 207–15, 217–18
fighting ring 179, 181
fight story 179–80, 186, 196–97
Fink, R. 1, 4–5, 8–9, 11, 15–16, 19, 50–51, 53, 55, 58, 132

'flash' 9, 57, 129, 135
foster-rearing 12, 14, 28, 171, 173–74
Foucault, M. 22, 35, 38, 43, 61
fringe dwelling 2, 7–10, 16, 35, 50, 122, 159
fundamentalist sects 29, 132

Gale, F. 6, 8, 10, 12–15, 17, 94, 259–60
gambling 2, 16, 50–53, 61, 66–67, 132, 211
Genet, J. 22, 72–73, 75
ghosts and spirits 19–20, 91–92, 244–45, 256
Gilbert, K. 4–5
Goffman, E. 35, 50, 56, 72–73
Goody, E. 14, 170, 172
Gooreng Gooreng 3, 107
government settlements 5, 7–8, 35, 37, 39–42, 44–45, 47–48, 54, 56, 58, 60–61, 118, 122–27, 141, 181, 230–31, 233, 243
grandmothers 12, 148, 154–57, 244–45
Griffith 117, 122, 125, 131

Hamilton, A. 13, 104
harbingers of death 19–20, 29, 237
Harris, S. 13, 20, 105
Hausfield, R.G. 1, 3, 12–13, 61, 135
Haviland, J.B. 103, 206
health 19–20, 28, 35, 100, 169
'helping' 16–17, 159, 167–69, 174–76
herbal curing 19–20, 29
heterogeneity 3, 7, 9–10, 19–20, 78
Hiatt, L.R. 202–03, 208, 224, 251–52, 263
'history-stories' 21, 30–31, 180, 189, 196
housing 9, 12, 61, 67, 153
Howard, M.C. 1, 4, 10, 137–38, 142, 191
Hume, L. 4–5, 12
humour 27, 30, 91

idioms of stigma 2, 6, 65, 72–76
indirectness 104–13
Inglis, J. 4–5, 8–9, 17

institutionalisation 33–38, 40–41, 47–48, 50–51, 54
integration 1, 4
interactional sociolinguistics 22, 97, 104, 113

Jordan, D.F. 3–5
juvenile offences 85–88, 90–91, 201

Kelly, R. 260–62
kinship 14, 68, 77–83, 85, 89, 92–94, 98, 102, 117, 120, 128, 132–34, 137, 141, 151, 170, 172, 204–05, 207–08, 228–30, 245–46, 259–60
  allegiance 27–28, 31, 183–85, 193, 211
  fictive extension 80–82
  networks 3, 7, 9, 12–13, 16, 28, 30, 70, 77, 83, 98, 105, 119, 131–33, 151, 153, 155, 182, 184, 186, 190, 198, 203, 211
  obligations 4, 9, 13, 15–16, 27, 29, 55, 66, 82–83, 97–98, 102, 113, 128–30, 143–44, 148, 151, 170, 192
knowledge 20, 22, 68
Koepping, P. 5, 8, 12
Koori 2, 13, 27, 46, 58, 61, 68, 74, 77, 180–82, 184, 186–88, 191–94, 197–98, 215

Lachlan River 119–20, 195
land rights 30, 85, 171, 234, 252, 254, 259
land tenure 20–21, 252–54
Langton, M. 1, 12, 18–19, 195, 201–26
language 2–3, 5–6, 11–12, 22, 29, 32, 45, 58–59, 68–69, 76, 83–84, 89, 90, 92, 94, 97–98, 100–02, 113, 117, 119, 137, 205
La Perouse 3, 5, 11, 55
levelling devices 5–6, 13, 18, 58
liberalism 34, 43–44, 60
Lickiss, J.N. 8, 12–13, 19

Lyons, G. 10, 15

Macdonald, G. 14, 18, 21–22, 179–200, 202, 209–11, 251
market economy 21, 118, 159–61
marriage 9, 19–20, 128, 130–34, 147, 154, 169, 171–72, 202–05, 211
  endogamous 6, 8, 28, 127
  divorce and 14, 127, 135, 171, 173
  intermarriage with non-Aborigines 5–7, 9–10, 14, 29, 98, 118, 134
  prohibition of close kin marriage 2, 13–14, 29, 128, 130–33
  rules 14, 29, 117
matrifocal household 12–14, 17, 127, 151
medical care 17, 69, 81, 122, 130, 152–53, 167
Melbourne 4, 10–12, 14, 17
Menindee 121–25, 130
Merlan, F. 3
migration to the cities 6–8, 10, 15, 81, 122–23, 137
Mildura 117, 125, 131–32
missionaries 29
mission(s) 5, 7, 49, 82, 141
  values 5
  policy 5, 77
mobility 119, 127, 130–31, 133, 146–50
modes of dress 2, 29, 68, 84, 113
money 41, 53, 159–63, 165–66
  privatised 165–66, 173
  'rectored' cash 16, 165, 176
  transformed 159, 176
Moree 17, 132–33
Morphy, H. 256, 261
Morphy, F. 256, 261
Morris, B. 2, 5, 19, 33–64
Murray River 11, 79, 94
Murri 3, 208
mythology 20–21, 72–73, 120, 137, 180, 196, 251–56, 264–65

Narrinyeri (Ngarrindjeri) 9–10, 84
Nunga 9, 89–91
Nyungar 3, 8, 14, 17, 20–22, 66, 137–38, 141–42, 157, 196, 227–50

pan-Aboriginal consciousness 21, 30–31, 78, 98, 260
'passing' 9, 27, 30–31, 51
paternalism 30–31, 55, 58
Perth 20, 146, 148–49, 152–54, 157, 227, 234–36, 245
philosophy of action 16, 160–61, 164, 176
philosophy of money 159–61
Point McLeay 6–7, 79, 84, 94
Point Pearce 79–80, 84, 94
police 19, 44, 47, 50, 52, 71, 101, 168–69, 192, 202, 210, 212–14, 216–20, 222–23, 241, 262
poverty 15–17, 27–28, 142
prison 19, 43, 52, 60, 201, 212, 220–21, 223
protectionist policies 4, 6, 65, 118
    Aborigines' Protection Act 39, 42, 50
    Aborigines' Protection Board 35–37, 122–23, 126
    Protectors of Aborigines 47

racism 4–6, 28, 31, 34, 42, 50, 58–60, 65, 69, 71–72, 98, 118, 201, 218, 262
rainbow serpent 237, 245, 247
Read, K. 72–73, 75
Read, P. 10
'rearing-up' links 143–45, 147, 151, 169–75
Reay, M. 8–9, 17, 46, 50–53, 59, 132–33
recreation 70, 81, 87, 98, 150
religious beliefs 2–3, 18–20, 29, 32, 137, 227, 248, 252
religious practices 18–20
reserves 7–9, 27, 32, 35, 44, 48, 79–82, 197, 227–28
resistance 2, 33–35, 44, 47–49, 52–53, 60, 137, 159, 219, 242

Robinvale 4–5, 7, 17, 20
Rowley, C.D. 1, 50, 142, 159–60, 224

sacred places 5, 20, 234, 242, 247–48, 252
Sansom, B. 12, 14, 16, 18, 21–22, 79, 151, 159–78, 180, 184, 189, 196, 264
Schwab, J. 3, 6, 10–11, 77–96
segregation 4, 33, 35, 42, 66, 77, 118–19
self-determination 4
service exchange 16, 161, 163, 166–69, 172–76
shaming 4–5, 18, 28, 57–59, 73, 128, 185, 193, 209–10, 259
sharing 15–16, 29, 52, 66–67, 85, 98–99, 103, 159–61, 166, 192, 194, 228
Sharp, L. 208–09, 265
sickness 77, 121, 203
Sider, G. 33, 54, 61, 191
sister-cousins/brother-cousins 102, 141, 144–46, 149–53, 156
Sitlington, G. 8–9, 17, 132–33
skin colour 6, 68, 74, 94–95, 98, 117, 132, 149
Smith, H.M. 1, 8, 12–15
Smith, L.R. 4
sniffing 85, 91
socialisation practices 13, 57–58, 69, 73–74, 143
Social Security payments 9–10, 15, 41–42, 66, 68, 122, 128, 142, 163
sorcery 19–20, 203
Spicer, E.H. 4
sport 4, 11, 16, 29, 151, 194–95, 211
Stanner, W.E.H. 167, 202, 204, 252–53, 261
stereotypes 5, 72–76, 117, 133, 231, 235, 260
surveillance 35–43, 60
Sutton, P. 21, 196, 251–68
Swan River 227–28, 231–32, 234
swearing 3, 17, 68, 74, 201–26
Sydney 12, 125

Taree 212–14
Taylor, J. 203, 208–09
Thompson, D.F. 206–08
Tindale, N.B. 134, 251

unemployment 10, 15, 27–28, 42, 99, 122

violence 17–19, 77, 167, 203–04, 209–10, 212, 216, 218–19, 223
visiting 8, 14, 30, 129–31, 133, 144–45, 189
von Sturmer, J. 105–06, 252

Warner, W.L. 202–04, 208
water snake 227, 229–33, 236–39, 242, 244–48
Wilcannia 118, 123–26, 129–31, 134–35

Wilson, P. 19, 187
Wiradjuri 3, 14, 18, 21, 119, 179–200, 202, 210–11
witnesses 18, 161, 164–65, 168, 175–76, 184, 188–89, 222, 241
women 16–17, 145–46
    senior 148–49, 151–56
    women's authority 17–18, 151–56
    women's domain 18, 40
Wongaibon 119–20, 122, 124
work ethic 10, 159
Wundersitz, J. 6, 8, 10, 12–15, 17, 94, 259–60

Young, E.A. 7–8, 12, 15, 19